2000 TIPS
for Teachers

TES
THE TIMES EDUCATIONAL SUPPLEMENT

2000 TIPS
for Teachers

edited by **NICK PACKARD & PHIL RACE**

**KOGAN
PAGE**

First published in 2000

Kogan Page Limited
120 Pentonville Road
London N1 9JN
UK

Stylus Publishing Inc.
22883 Quicksilver Drive
Sterling VA 20166-2012
USA

© Nick Packard and Phil Race 2000

British Library Cataloguing in Publication Data

A CIP record for this book is available from the British Library.

ISBN 0 7494 3182 2

Typeset by Kogan Page
Printed and bound by

Contents

Part 2   Particularly for primary teachers   89

Foreword

Every teacher knows that surviving teacher training is only the beginning. The classroom itself will come up with more challenges than the toughest exam paper, and experienced teachers build up an invaluable armoury of long-term strategies and quick fixes that every novice would give a right arm for.

At a time when teachers are busier than ever – more marking, more government initiatives, more record keeping, as well as the demand for ever-higher standards – few have time to read research, and many find that even the opportunity to share ideas and advice with colleagues is limited.

This is where *2000 Tips for Teachers* comes in. Well-organized and clearly laid-out, it offers an invaluable collection of ideas and hints that are tried and tested, imaginative and, above all, practical. It's a book to be browsed through and dipped into – and while new teachers will find it a lifeline, experienced practitioners too are bound to find a wealth of new ideas to make their lives easier and their teaching more effective. Whether the issue is introducing yourself to a class for the first time, organizing resources, working with colleagues, coping with stress or using the Internet, this book contains down-to-earth advice.

At the *Times Educational Supplement*, we know from our postbag that teachers are always keen to improve their professional practice, but cannot always get the help they need when they need it. Our new section, 'You and Your Job', which comes complete with handy hints on a variety of subjects, is designed to support our readers, but never could we aspire to the dizzying heights 2000 tips at once, covering virtually every eventuality. I am delighted to be associated with this excellent compendium, which I am sure teachers will enjoy putting into practice in their classrooms.

Caroline St John-Brooks
Editor, Times Educational Supplement

Our aims in this book

This book is designed to be a useful compendium of sound and practical ideas to help classroom teachers in primary and secondary schools to do their jobs to the best of their ability. Many of the suggestions in this book are aimed particularly towards those who are new to the profession, but many other tips should be found useful by even the most experienced of teachers. The book aims to help teachers who are extremely busy simply keeping up with their work, and whose time for reading the literature on teaching and learning is limited, but who may welcome ready-to-use practical suggestions on a wide range of their everyday activities.

ORIGINS OF THIS COMPENDIUM

This edition is based on four of the existing Kogan Page '500 Tips' series. Part 1 contains much of the content of *500 Tips for Teachers* (Sally Brown, Carolyn Earlam and Phil Race), which appeared in its second edition in 1998. Part 2 is derived from the companion volume, *500 Tips for Primary Teachers*, written by Emma and Nick Packard and Sally Brown in 1997. Part 3 continues to address primary school teachers, and is based on *500 ICT Tips for Primary Teachers,* written by Nick Packard, Steve Higgins and Phil Race in 1999. Part 4 is based on *500 Tips for People Working with Children with Special Needs,* written by Betty Vahid, Sally Harwood and Sally Brown in 1999. Although these separate books were originally addressed separately to secondary or primary teachers, we have found that quite a lot of the content transcends the primary–secondary divide, so we invite readers of this book to make use of the Contents pages and Index to find the elements that could be most relevant to them wherever they lie in the present compendium.

We hope you will find the differences in tone between the respective parts refreshing, with the inner parts less formal than the outer ones! We believed it best not to try to interfere with the individual voices of the authors of the original works.

PLEASE DON'T READ THIS BOOK COVER TO COVER!

This book is designed to be dipped into, with readers selecting those areas that are of most interest to them. We have assembled 22 sets of tips, each set intended to be relatively complete in itself. We have grouped the sets into four main parts, although sometimes these divisions have been rather arbitrary, with some sets being perfectly capable of being sited in two or more categories. However, as this is a book for grazing on rather than devouring whole, we don't consider that problematic. We hope, however, that the Contents pages and part titles will help you to find quickly those parts of the book that could be of most immediate value to you.

THIS BOOK DOES NOT AIM TO COVER EVERYTHING!

Obviously even a fairly extensive book of hints and tips is meant to support, and not replace, the broad learning achieved by teachers on properly accredited training programmes. This book is designed to be a handy supplement to such programmes. Furthermore, we know from our own work that many of the most valuable and important lessons are learnt only by practice, having a go at things, and trial and error, rather than reading what has already been written about them, or hearing experienced people tell us about them. Experienced teachers are bound to have learnt innumerable wrinkles of their own from their practice, but we hope that they will find useful food for thought in this book amidst all sorts of ideas that they have already developed for themselves. We hope newly qualified teachers, however, will find that this book is a useful companion to them in their first year or two of practice, helping them to handle each new situation as they meet it.

ACKNOWLEDGEMENTS

The editors of this compendium would like to remind readers of the fact that they are only two of the many sources of experience and advice represented in this book. The experiences of Sally Brown, Steve Higgins, Betty Vahid, Sally Harwood, Emma Packard and Carolyn Earlam pervade the suggestions throughout the book. Added to this are the countless friends and colleagues who helped us to prepare the four volumes on which this book draws, and who have given us feedback on our earlier writing. We hope that this collection of suggestions helps to make the learning experiences of pupils of all ages that little bit richer, and the professional lives of our readers that little more fulfilling.

Nick Packard
Phil Race
July 2000

Part 1

Tips across the curriculum

Techniques for effective teaching and classroom management

Planning and assessment

Using teaching and learning resources well

Supporting pupils' learning

Providing personal and pastoral care

Being an effective colleague

Information and Communications Technologies

TECHNIQUES FOR EFFECTIVE TEACHING AND CLASSROOM MANAGEMENT

This section contains some advice on some basic teaching techniques, particularly interaction with pupils. This is perhaps one of the most difficult areas on which to give advice, because the way we work with children tends to be a very personal thing. Techniques that work with one teacher can sometimes prove to be completely useless to another, and it is really important to develop your own style, with which you feel comfortable. People tend to talk about 'natural authority' as though it were something that one is either born with or not, but in reality everyone has good days and bad

2000 Tips for Teachers

days. One of the principal advantages of being an experienced teacher is that you have learnt not to take unpleasant experience too seriously and you can learn from mistakes. In this section, we aim to share some very practical tips on teaching techniques. If you have already passed the stage of needing such suggestions, please look ahead to later sections of the book.

1. Meeting a class for the first time

There is no second chance to make a good first impression! First impressions are crucial in any work with people and none more so than with new pupils. The old adage, 'Don't smile until Christmas' holds a grain of truth – its always easier to loosen up later than it is to start to lay down the law once your class has decided you're soft!

- **Don't forget to introduce yourself** – and spell your name out on the blackboard if necessary. Pupils in primary school usually know their teachers quite well, and see the same teachers for a greater proportion of the time than in secondary education. It can be quite stressful for pupils to start a new school, or a new year, in which they may encounter 20 new teachers in the space of a week.

- **State clearly what you expect of your pupils** – what they can and cannot do in the classroom. Establish a few simple rules of behaviour and always stick to them. You may also wish to invite pupils to put forward their own suggestions for additional ground rules.

- **Learn your pupils' names as quickly as you can** – any instruction is much more effective if directed to an individual. Your work will also be more effective if you never forget that your class is made up of individuals, and know them as such.

- **Help pupils to learn each others' names** if they don't know them already. One way of doing this is to form them into a large circle, and ask each pupil to say, for example, 'My name is Cheryl, and this is my friend Mark, and this is Clive, and…', seeing who can say the most names. This helps you learn their names too!

- **Help pupils to get to know each other** (at the same time helping you to get to know them). For example, conduct a class round along the lines of, 'My name is Jean, my favourite thing in the world is pizza, and my pet hate is spiders.'

- **Show your pupils where they're heading.** Give your pupils a clear idea of what they will be doing in the next few weeks and why they are doing it. Help them to see how your work with them fits in with the syllabus, National Curriculum programmes of study and so on.

- **Make sure your pupils know how they will be assessed.** Which pieces of work are more important for assessment? Which areas are revision of material they have already covered?

Emphasize the need for them to look after their own work and take responsibility for their own progress, especially where there is continuous assessment.

- Use the first lessons to **find out what pupils already know** about the subject and build on this in your planning. You could make this into a quiz or get them to write something that is personal to them, which will help you get to know them.

- **Explain which resources are available for pupils to use,** which they can access themselves and which resources are to be obtained from the teacher, or in the library or resource centre. Encourage pupils to take responsibility for the resources in their classroom, for example keeping an eye on the number of rulers, rubbers and so on, ensuring that the stock lasts all year.

- **React firmly if any of your rules of behaviour are transgressed.** This is especially important in the first few weeks. Show the class that you notice everything that is going on and are not willing to ignore anything. Name the pupil who has done something you don't like, but be aware of individual personalities and notice if what you say is having an extreme effect on anyone. You may need to tread carefully with pupils who feel insecure or nervous. Don't be drawn into arguments; when you know pupils better you can be more flexible.

2. Gaining attention and settling a class down

Nice as it would be if all pupils were sitting quietly, ready to learn, and attentive at all times, this is not the nature of the young of the human species! Here are some tips to overcome human nature – but remember that different things work for different people, so find your own styles:

- **Try doing nothing first.** Stand there, very still, absolutely quiet. The pupils closest will notice, and the word will gradually spread. Give it a moment or two before you decide that another tactic is needed!

- **Don't shout (yet)!** If all is not quiet, avoid the instinct to shout, 'Be quiet' at the top of your voice! Start a quiet conversation with two or three pupils who already look ready to listen to you.

- **Take advantage of human curiosity.** It sometimes pays to whisper! Human nature includes not wishing to miss anything. Whisper to those closest to you, and many of the rest will stop talking and listen.

- **Drop a non-attender in it!** Ask a question to those who are already listening, but end with the name of someone you know has not been paying attention. Watch as all eyes turn to this pupil: the effect of someone being found out by their peers not to have been listening.

■ **Have ways of making pupils listen.** Start with something that needs careful listening – for example a tape-recording or video played back quite quietly.

■ **People love praise.** Praise those who are paying attention, particularly if they don't normally, rather than grumbling at those pupils who are not yet paying attention.

■ **Begin with a task.** Start a session with something for pupils to do. Have printed instructions on handout materials, or write them on the blackboard in advance.

■ **Select some targets.** Pick on some 'known' live-wires in the class by name, giving them particular tasks to do at the start of a lesson, as leaders of groups of pupils.

■ **Don't take chaos as a personal affront.** Don't regard initial chaos as disrespect to you. Regard it as human nature and natural until something interesting comes up.

■ **Few want to be left out of some fun!** If you can do this (we're not good at it!) start a lesson by very quietly saying something really amusing to those who have already 'settled down'. The rest will soon become eager to be included in this.

3. Coping with interruptions

'If only I could just get on with my teaching!' How often have we thought this. When we're interrupted, it's natural to feel emotions including anger and frustration. However, at these times, all eyes tend to be on us – not least to see how we react. The following suggestions may help you deal with interruptions with dignity:

■ **Accept that you are in fact being interrupted.** Trying to carry on as though the source of the interruption was unnoticed tends to do more harm than good, as most pupils will probably be concentrating on the interruption, and how you react, rather than on what you had been saying or doing just before the event.

■ **Keep track of where you were.** Make a mental note of exactly what you were doing just before an interruption, so that when you have dealt with it, you can pick up the threads without having to say, 'Now, where was I?' Also, check whether there are connections between things you do and the probability of interruptions.

■ **Accept that some interruptions will be important and necessary.** When this is so, make sure that anyone responsible for the interruption is not criticized or made to feel embarrassed.

■ **Be patient with colleagues.** Be particularly careful when interrupted by a colleague or other member of staff. Even if the interruption is unwelcome and unnecessary, it is best to have a quiet word with the person concerned later, rather than let any frustration be noticed by your pupils.

■ **Turn interruptions into positive learning experiences.** When possible, draw useful learning points from interruptions by pupils. The more they feel that their interruptions are taken notice of, the more likely they are to avoid making unnecessary ones.

■ **Keep individual feelings for individuals.** When a particular pupil is making too many interruptions, try to have a private word later, rather than a public show of annoyance. Tackling issues in the full glare of the whole class can be useful, but should be used with caution.

■ **Have something to do ready for anyone who interrupts.** Have a list of relevant questions about the topic of the day, so that anyone who interrupts can be put on the spot if necessary with a question to answer. This can work well at discouraging interruptions!

■ **Watch your distance.** Move up close to anyone who has made an unwelcome interruption. Pupils are much less brave when you're standing over them than when you're at the other end of the room.

■ **Look for the causes of interruptions.** If there are frequent interruptions, it could be that pupils are tired of listening and need to be given something definite to get on with. Avoid the 'I've started, so I'll finish' approach.

■ **Learn from colleagues.** When you have the chance, observe how colleagues cope with interruptions. The more techniques you have at your disposal, the more versatile your approach becomes.

4. Learning names

You will know yourself how irritating it is when people forget your name. Calling someone by name makes any message you wish to communicate all the stronger and more personal. However, we often seem to have a whole bunch of new names to tackle at once: the following suggestions may help you with this task. There will always be some names that are very hard to remember, but it's worth making the effort – you may be the only person who does learn such names:

■ **Let pupils decide their names!** Ask your pupils to tell you the version of their name they wish to be known by and attempt to call them by it unless it is too daft for you to cope with. Michael might hate being called Mick, but Salim might prefer Sal.

■ **Be careful with nicknames.** Be cautious about using nicknames that seem innocuous enough to us, but cause the class to fall about hysterically every time you use them. It may well be that you are unwittingly being drawn into using an unknown (to you) vulgar expression or promoting an 'in joke' to which you are not party!

■ **Address questions to named pupils.** To help you to get to know some names, choose people from the class list to answer (easy) questions and bit by bit memorize the respondents' names.

- **Make a map of the names.** Use a seating plan to note names of pupils next to where they are sitting and try to encourage them to sit there for the first few lessons until you are more familiar with the class.

- **Once you've got them, use them.** Once you know some names, use them every time you speak to those pupils (without making them feel they're being picked on!).

- **Make names visual.** Some pupils will be happy to wear name labels for the first few days of a session, or you could use folded cardboard name labels on the desk: remember to get them to write their names in really large letters.

- **One step at a time!** Concentrate on first names for the first part of the school year, and pick up the surnames as you go on.

- **Take care with the repetitions.** Find out any pupils who share a first name and learn these first. Once you have learnt the three Matthews, two Traceys and four Alis you have made a good start!

- **Make sure you have their names right.** Check you are using the right names for pupils and encourage them to correct you if you get them wrong. Also check out how to pronounce unfamiliar names. It's dreadful to find out at the end of the year that you have been getting one wrong from the beginning.

- **Be persistent.** Don't expect to learn all the names all at once: build up gradually over the weeks. Don't be too hard on yourself if you never master all of the names, especially if you teach lots of different groups. But do your best: pupils do tend to be critical of teachers who don't make an effort to learn names.

5. Avoiding disruption in your class

This is an area a great deal easier to write about than to follow through – but we all keep battling against the unpredictability of the human factor!

- **Establish a few, clear rules for behaviour in your class.** If possible, involve the pupils in the development of these rules. The more ownership you can allow them to feel regarding the rules, the more likely they are to at least try to follow them.

- **Reward good behaviour immediately with positive feedback** – a smile or a few words of praise or encouragement. Try also to ensure that you are quick to reward the good behaviour of any pupils who are often guilty of bad behaviour – they may really respond to some positive feedback.

■ **Deal with any misdemeanours before they become major incidents.** Often, it is best to deal with minor incidents as privately as you can. Public confrontations arouse too much interest!

■ **Establish what the sanctions will be for transgressing the rules.** Ensure that such sanctions are reasonable, practicable and consistent.

■ **Avoid unreasonable expectations of pupils – but don't demean them either.** Ensure that the level of the work you set is suitable for all the individuals within the group, and that pupils experiencing difficulties have manageable targets. Direct the emphasis of your comments towards the work or lack of it. This involves getting to know what each pupil is capable of, and setting realistic targets.

■ **Look for signals.** Be adaptable – change the pace or content of a lesson as soon as you realize it's not working well. Changing your approach on the basis of feedback you receive is a strength, not a weakness!

■ **If a particular pupil is causing problems,** immediately remove this pupil to another part of the room. This is a way of demonstrating that you have observed the problem, and also provides such a pupil with the opportunity to start afresh.

■ **Provide 'cooling-off' time.** If you, or a pupil, lose your tempers, try to allow a few minutes for you both to calm down – take the pupil involved out from the room for a short while. It can pave the way towards progress to say something along the lines of, 'I'm sorry this happened. How can we make sure that this sort of thing doesn't happen again?'

■ **Investigate the causes of bad behaviour.** Talk to a pupil who has caused problems away from the class, on a one-to-one basis, and try to find out the reasons for misbehaviour. Sometimes the reasons (once known) will be very understandable and forgivable.

■ **Have ready something interesting to give the class to do.** This can be invaluable when you need time to calm down yourself, or when you need to have those few quiet words outside the door with an individual pupil who has been causing problems. Prepare a verbal quiz or game for the last 10 minutes, either as a reward for work well done, or because you have finished a useful activity and need a change.

6. Using blackboards

There's a blackboard or whiteboard in most teaching rooms. We sometimes feel so close to this in our professional lives that the term 'life at the chalkface' is in common use! How we use the most straightforward of our visual aids can make a big difference to how much our pupils learn:

■ **How visible are your etchings?** Check that the size of your writing is such that the pupils who are furthest away from the board can read what you put on it.

■ **Aim for the top!** Ensure that you make good use of the upper half of the board, and only use the rest of the board if you know that pupils at the back aren't screened from viewing by those closer to the board.

■ **Show your agenda.** Use the board to write questions that you will be discussing, so pupils can continue to see the questions as you develop with them the answers.

■ **If you are left-handed, you may find writing on the blackboard difficult.** This is not your ineptitude, but because you are pushing the chalk. It has taken some teachers years of distress to discover this! Left-handed chalk-users (eg me, Phil Race) sometimes find that standing a little more to the right than usual, and pulling the chalk that bit more, helps improve the situation.

■ **Be heard as well as seen.** Don't talk to the class while you're writing on the board with your back to your pupils. When possible, arrange the room so that you can maintain eye-contact with most of your pupils even while you're writing on the board.

■ **Be prepared!** Whenever you have the chance, prepare a blackboard in advance for a class, so that pupils can see straightaway an outline of the things you're going to talk about in the forthcoming lesson.

■ **Get your pupils' words on the blackboard.** Whenever you can, use the blackboard to write up things that pupils tell you in answer to your questions, so that they can see their thinking being valued and acknowledged by you. When pupils see you write up *their* words, their ownership of what is going on is increased, and their attention may improve.

■ **Let pupils have a turn with the chalk.** Make the blackboard 'everyone's' territory. Ask pupils to write things on it; for example, questions they want to ask, ideas they want to discuss, and interesting things they want to talk about.

■ **Use the blackboard as a classroom resource.** Give groups of pupils 'blackboard tasks'; for example when starting a new topic, ask groups to compose and write up '10 questions we want to know about it'.

■ **Be careful with the rubber!** Before you erase comments suggested or written by pupils, give a further acknowledgement of the value of these comments.

7. Organizing practical lessons

Practical lessons can so easily turn into chaos if not well organized, however well planned the content is. Don't try anything new with a class unless you have done it yourself in advance and know it works – and save time in demonstrating by showing 'the one you made earlier':

- **Put safety first.** There is a wide range of safety legislation, particularly covering equipment and materials that are potentially hazardous. If your work involves dangerous things, take every opportunity to get yourself some relevant safety training. If something were to go wrong, the buck could rest with you.

- **Check through the materials you require before the lesson starts.** Ensure they are prepared for use. You can waste many minutes (seems like hours) trying to unscrew a jar while the class gets bored and runs riot.

- **Assemble your materials in labelled boxes or trays.** This is well worth doing when it is a lesson you will repeat, and can save you much time organizing the same materials in future.

- **Engage the help of the class.** Let pupils help to distribute materials and equipment, and with clearing up at the end of the session. It will save you time and help pupils learn how to look after resources. Allow plenty of time for clearing up; it may take much longer than you think in the early stages.

- **Make sure you have enough materials for everyone.** Or at least have enough for pupils to work in pairs. When pupils are not fully involved themselves, they tend to experiment in ways of which you would not approve!

- **Give short, clear instructions about the task required.** Ask questions of those pupils who seem not to be concentrating to ensure that they have understood. Their repetition of the requirements of the task will reinforce the instructions to the others.

- **Make demonstrations snappy.** When you are demonstrating an activity or an experiment it's easy to take so long explaining the 'right' way of doing something that pupils who are itching to try it themselves at first become turned off.

- **Establish firm rules of behaviour.** Disruption or silliness may prove not only counter-productive to learning, but can turn out to be very dangerous, for example if your class is working with chemicals or electrical equipment.

- **Avoid the necessity for pupils to queue for your advice or opinion.** Teach pupils to be self-reliant and resourceful, and to help each other if they can't do something or find something. You could discuss sources and strategies for support before beginning a task that should be completed independently, such as, 'Ask three before me'.

- **Bring the class back together at intervals.** Talk to the whole class during activities. Everyone may be working at a different rate, and some pupils will need this structure to avoid being left behind.

- **Evaluate the activity.** Make time towards the end of a practical lesson for some kind of evaluation. You may not have had time to get round to every individual, and in this way you can ensure that all pupils receive some feedback.

8. Doing yard/bus/break duties painlessly

'Oh no, not all this as well?' you may have exclaimed, when first you discovered that you were expected to do such duties! Sadly, being a teacher is not just about teaching. We also need to help keep the school going during the times when we're not teaching. The following suggestions may help you tackle this with equanimity!

- **Get a whistle!** Don't worry that they're a bit old fashioned. They can help you gain attention in noisy circumstances – as long as you don't overuse them.

- **Make sure you know the rules.** Know what is allowed and what is not. Try to get a thorough briefing from an experienced colleague who can show you the ropes.

- **Be seen, and heard!** Should you need to enter the toilets or go behind the bike shed, announce your presence loudly. You are less likely to have unpleasant surprises that way!

- **Wrap up warm on cold days – and be prepared for rain!** Such duties are made more miserable than ever if you are unsuitably dressed. If you can get a hot drink as well, so much the better.

- **Try pairing up with a colleague.** If your duties turn out to be a hard chore for you, you can either keep each other company or cover each other for short periods so that you each get some sort of break. A 20-minute yard-duty can feel a lot longer than two 10-minute half-duties. If possible, shadow a colleague on the relevant duty before your actual turn comes up, so that you know what may be expected of you before you tackle it on your own.

- **Pave the way.** Try to be especially well prepared in advance if you know you will be teaching immediately after a duty. This can ensure that you are not too flustered at the start of the ensuing lesson. Give the class something to do that really keeps them busy while you get your breath back!

- **Have contingency plans for what to do if things go wrong.** Check out what the school policy is on minor accidents or incidents. With younger pupils, it may be useful to have readily available supplies of antiseptic wipes and plasters.

■ **Keep your eyes peeled!** It isn't possible to have your eyes everywhere, but you can often prevent trouble by stepping in before it happens. The price of peace is eternal vigilance!

■ **If fights break out, think carefully about your interventions.** You can restrain pupils using 'reasonable force' where the safety of a pupil or a colleague is threatened, but these conditions may not be easy to interpret. Under no circumstances should you ever strike a pupil.

■ **Use such duties as occasions when you can build up good relations with pupils outside the classroom.** Be careful, however, not to put yourself at risk of seeming to have favourites, or of giving excessively exceptional attention to particular individual pupils.

9. Ensuring equality of opportunity within your teaching

The suggestions in this section relate to anti-oppressive practice in all areas, including race, gender, sexuality, age and disability. It is increasingly necessary in our society to tackle inequality head-on, and the sooner the better. The following suggestions should help you treat all pupils (and colleagues) equally, and help them to value equality:

■ **Check that you are behaving in the same way towards all pupils.** Check that you are not treating pupils, whatever their background, differently in lessons, when you ask questions or let pupils give comments.

■ **Arrange that group work is done in mixed-gender groups.** At certain ages pupils' natural tendency is to sit in same-gender groupings, and you may have to intervene in natural seating arrangements. Don't work from gender lists when arranging groups; use a more random characteristic such as birth dates or hair colour.

■ **Get your tongue round *all* your pupils' names!** Make an effort to be able to pronounce the names of pupils with names unfamiliar to you, without any hesitation or insecurity. Allow them to keep telling you whether you've got their names right or not yet.

■ **Avoid discriminatory typecasting.** In designing class exercises, case-studies or scenarios, ensure that you are not typecasting roles according to race, gender, sexuality, age or disability. Also, avoid the tendency to ask only boys to help to move furniture, lift boxes, open jars and bottles, or to ask only girls to tidy up or clean benches.

■ **Help colleagues to avoid discrimination.** Be sensitive to instances where colleagues violate equal-opportunities principles, and bring such occasions to their notice. Don't expect an easy ride when chastening some colleagues on their practice in this respect, but continue to give them the chance to be reminded that it is an important issue.

■ | **Watch your sense of humour!** It is dangerously easy to attempt to say something amusing, when in fact the fun is at someone's expense. Do not use jokes or anecdotes that could be interpreted as oppressive to any group.

■ | **Raise pupils' awareness of equality issues.** Encourage pupils to confront issues of inequality objectively, and help them to work out practical and viable solutions to problems involving equal opportunity.

■ | **Be on the lookout for pupils who may be affected by inequality.** Seek feedback from all pupils to probe any feelings they may have regarding being treated unequally in any respect.

■ | **Reflect equality in your own work.** Proactively seek to work collaboratively with colleagues of different race, gender, sexuality, age and ability, whenever the opportunity arises.

■ | **Don't let pupils get away with bias.** Censure any pupils who display inappropriate bias in things they say or write, and help them towards attitudes which enable them to demonstrate equality values.

■ | **Try to take note of gender responses.** Teachers, and the education system in general, are often accused of gender bias because boys appear to be doing less well than girls. Watching how boys respond to different tasks and activities may help you to plan for and use activities that help redress the balance once in a while.

10. Strategies for raising achievement

The focus of teaching and learning is centrally concerned with adding value to student achievement through a variety of techniques that enhance pupils' performance across the curriculum. The following suggestions are designed to help you to do so strategically:

■ | **Plan and prepare for a clearly structured lesson.** Make sure that you have clearly defined learning objectives for each session, which identify the goals towards which you are striving. These should be monitored and reviewed regularly, for example in the UK against National Curriculum programmes of study.

■ | **Clarify for pupils your expectations for each session.** Tell them what you expect them to be learning or practising within that period of study, and ensure this links with your overall plan. This need not be a rigid template for activity, but should provide a framework with which you can vary activities to fit the occasion.

■ | **Remember to set differential goals for pupils, according to their ability or prior experience.** Pupils all need to be extended and challenged: if you set identical work for all, this will satisfy few.

- **Ensure that the pace and timing of the lessons are appropriate.** It helps if you vary activities within a session, so that interest and motivation are maintained and so that pupils experience a variety of activities. A series of well-paced, brisk activities, with clearly defined deadlines for the class, help pupils to achieve more fully.

- **Aim to involve pupils in their own learning.** This can be achieved by asking pupils to consciously think about their own learning processes, and to become involved in setting personal targets. In this way, pupils develop autonomy and lifelong learning skills that enable them to move on to further study or employment more confidently.

- **Provide for pupils a visible means of demonstrating their own progress.** This could take the form of a chart or planner which pupils can mark in when particular milestones have been achieved. These are also effective means of helping pupils to develop their time-management skills.

- **Set targets against previous achievements.** If possible, ensure that each pupil is able to maximize potential by reviewing previous performance, setting interim goals, monitoring outcomes, and offering feedback. Use this information to set future targets.

- **Remember that pupils of different gender may need different styles of management.** In the UK, there are noticeable trends whereby boys tend to under-perform, producing less well-presented work, having poorer self-organization skills, and taking work less seriously. To raise achievement, you may need to set for boys shorter, more specific goals, with closer monitoring and stronger structuring of tasks.

- **Integrate the setting of homework into curriculum planning.** Ensure that homework relates to classroom tasks, has specific measurable outcomes, and generally challenges pupils. Encourage pupils to make use of a personal planner as a means to ensure that they take responsibility for their own workloads and achievements.

- **Make sure that literacy skills are reinforced across the curriculum.** All teachers should take responsibility for assuring high standards of presentation, spelling, punctuation and grammar. In addition, an awareness of subject-specific vocabulary needs to be inculcated in all classes.

- **Integrate assessment into learning.** Make sure that assessment tasks link fully with stated learning goals, and ensure that performance criteria are specific, achievable, transparent and available. Assessment tasks will help students to achieve fully when they are pitched at the right level – neither too undemanding, nor too difficult to mitigate against a reasonable chance of success.

- **Aim to promote an ethos of achievement in the classroom.** Aim to ensure that high standards are not just an aspiration, but are an expectation. Pupils with high ambitions to reach their own full potential are most likely to be successful when teachers continuously set high standards as a norm.

PLANNING AND ASSESSMENT

Assessment is a really crucial area of any teacher's work and one that can have a key influence over the ways in which pupils develop and improve. We too are subject to assessment ourselves from time to time, formally through inspection and less formally, but equally importantly, when we get feedback on our work from our pupils, their parents and our colleagues.

Assessment is one of the most powerful driving forces for learning. It is often the case that pupils (and students in general) don't get down to serious learning unless some form of assessment is coming up. A danger is that in our efforts to help pupils to learn everything that is important, we assess too much, giving both our pupils, and ourselves, an intolerable burden of work. Much has been written on assessment in schools that we do not intend to replicate here: instead we offer a few suggestions on how to cope with what many teachers see as the most arduous chore of our professional lives!

Among the issues we mention in this section is that of implementing new structures in our educational provision. While such innovations are taking place (sometimes painfully) in many parts of the world, the particular structure we have selected to form the basis of some specific suggestions is the implementation of GNVQs (General National Vocational Qualifications) in England and Wales.

11. Assessing pupils' work

It often feels that we spend more time marking pupils' work than teaching them. This is probably no bad thing, provided pupils are gaining much from the feedback we give them. The following suggestions may help you enhance this feedback, and at the same time ease your marking load:

■ **Work out exactly what you are intending to measure.** Sometimes there will be a less time-consuming way to go about assessing pupils' work. For example, you don't need a full essay to measure their ideas about a topic; an essay plan or list of bullet points may show their ideas just as well, yet be far quicker for them to do, and for you to mark.

■ **Prepare, and share, marking schemes.** When designing assessed tasks for pupils, work out in advance the marking scheme you will use to assess their work, and give them clear pointers about what will gain them marks. There is clear evidence that the more pupils know about how assessment works, the better is the standard of work they produce.

■ **Let pupils contribute to the assessment criteria.** From time to time, involve pupils themselves in the task of working out marking schemes for their work, and use their suggestions in your assessment of their work.

■ **Design tasks that are straightforward to assess.** Save yourself time and energy by making it easier to mark pupils' work. For example, it is much quicker to mark their answers to printed short-answer or completion questions, or multiple-choice tests, than to work through a pile of essays.

■ **Explore the possibilities of computer-marked tests or exercises.** The use of computer-delivered assessment has grown rapidly in the last few years, and you can save yourself a lot of boring, routine marking by using it. The computer can also be used to give feedback responses to your pupils, either during or at the end of the test, and can work out for you the class scores lists.

■ **Keep clear records.** Design your own grids so you can see at a glance the performance of all the pupils in a class. These can alert you to those pupils falling behind in their work, and can be very useful at parent–teacher interviews.

■ **Make room for your own feedback.** For example, get pupils to pencil in a fairly substantial margin at one side of the paper, or even to pencil off a 'feedback comments' box at the foot of each page.

■ **Be aware of pupils' feelings when receiving assessed work back.** Remember that the moment that pupils get back some marked work is a time of heightened emotion for them. This means that they can be particularly sensitive to any comments you have written on their work, especially the first comments they read.

■ **Remember the importance of scores or grades.** When you give pupils a score or a grade, this is the first thing they look for and will dominate their reactions to your comments on their work. If the score is high, they may ignore most of your feedback comments. If the score is low they may be so dispirited that they don't read any feedback comments at all. Decide whether giving a score is important, or whether it may be worth giving feedback comments only at first, and working out the scores later.

■ **Be careful with the crosses.** Remember how demotivating crosses beside mistakes or wrong answers can be. Similarly crossed-out words (for example where spelt wrongly) can be discouraging. Explore other ways of showing pupils their mistakes, such as using a fluorescent highlighter pen to pick out words and phrases, with margin notes giving explanations.

■ **Look for better things than ticks.** Ticks are good news for pupils, but it's often worth adding some positive feedback comments, such as 'good point', 'nicely put', 'well done', which are even more encouraging.

■ **Give pupils the chance to redeem a poor assessment.** For example, use schemes where the best five out of eight assessments make up the coursework grade.

12. Giving pupils face-to-face feedback

Face-to-face feedback to pupils can be very powerful and productive, but it can also be traumatic both for them and for us. The following suggestions may help you to maximize the benefits of such feedback, while minimizing the dangers:

■ **Remember pupils' feelings.** Remember that pupils can feel quite tense when getting face-to-face feedback from a teacher. They may see us both as experts and authority figures. The tension can cause them to receive our feedback in a distorted way, where they take our words beyond the actual messages we wish to convey.

■ **Use the benefits of face-to-face feedback.** Face-to-face feedback can give pupils much more information than written feedback, through facial expression, tone of voice and body language.

■ **Beware of the lost impact.** The main problem with face-to-face feedback is that it is transient. This means that pupils can't reflect objectively on this sort of feedback, as human nature means that they will remember particular parts of the feedback and forget other parts.

■ **Don't forget the dangers of subjective reactions.** Pupils' states of mind can affect their receptiveness to face-to-face feedback. If they happen to be feeling positive and optimistic at the time, they may remember the positive parts of your feedback, while if they are feeling tense or negative at the time, the parts they will remember most will be the critical things you tell them.

■ **Check that your messages are getting across.** An advantage of face-to-face feedback is that you can observe at once the effect that your words are having on pupils. When you can tell that your message is not getting across, you can go into more detail.

■ **Decide what to tell individuals, and what to share with groups.** It's worth deciding when best to give face-to-face feedback to individual pupils, and when to give feedback to pupils in groups. Highly specific feedback is best saved for one-to-one interviews, but it can be worth giving general feedback about common mistakes to groups rather than individuals.

■ **Prepare a written summary.** When you have a lot of feedback to give pupils (particularly to a whole class rather than individuals), it's useful to prepare summary notes of the main points you wish to convey. You may even be able to duplicate these notes, and give them out as permanent reminders of your main points.

■ **Always start and end on a high note.** Sometimes, face-to-face feedback will necessarily be hard to take by your pupils. On such occasions, try to make sure that you have some positive things to say about their work, and start and end with such points.

- **Watch for the effects on pupils.** A strong advantage of face-to-face feedback is that you can judge the effect it is having on pupils, from their facial expressions and body language. If they appear to be particularly sensitive to your comments, you can soften your approach accordingly.

- **Face-to-face feedback is always two-way.** Exploit the opportunity of using face-to-face feedback occasions to find out more from your pupils about how they feel their learning is going. Asking questions such as, 'Why do you think you're finding this difficult?' can be useful. How, and indeed if, you intend to record the outcomes of this work will need some consideration.

13. Getting feedback from pupils

Your teaching will be more effective if you are aware of what the pupils' responses and future needs are. It's easy to go through the day without being self-reflective about your work – most of the time you're too busy! But try to make some time to reflect on how your pupils are responding to the work and whether you are having any success:

- **Look everywhere for feedback.** The expressions on pupils' faces are an immediate source of feedback. The way they respond to you, your tasks and instructions is feedback. You can quickly tell whether they are enthusiastic about something, or bored by it.

- **Ask pupils for general feedback.** Ask open-ended questions. Allow pupils time to work out exactly what the questions mean, and to respond without feeling embarrassed or intimidated. For example, ask them which part of a topic they like most, and why, and which part they find hardest, and why.

- **Help pupils give you specific feedback.** Discuss their work with them on a one-to-one basis with the work in front of you. When they have a problem with part of their work, give them the chance to explain why they think the problem is there.

- **Collect evidence of pupils' views and opinions.** Occasionally give out evaluation sheets or questionnaires designed to seek their feedback on specific issues.

- **Don't make a big thing of 'silly' feedback.** There will always be someone who can't resist giving non-serious answers to evaluation questions. Concentrate on the feedback that is useful.

- **Accept positive feedback.** Resist the urge to shrug off compliments. Give pupils who have positive things to tell you the satisfaction of knowing that their feedback is being received, not stifled.

■ **Accept negative feedback too!** Cultivate the attitude that there is no such thing as criticism, just feedback. Be willing to listen, and to help to draw out any negative feedback from pupils. Better still, thank them for their comments, for example saying, 'I'm glad I now know about this. I'll give it further thought, thanks'.

■ **Help pupils to feel that their comments and ideas are valuable.** Ask for positive and constructive criticism on a particular aspect of the course – explain that you might be redesigning it for future classes.

■ **Collect feedback from groups as well as individuals.** You are less likely to get unconsidered feedback from a group than from an individual. Ask pupils to discuss their work in small groups and ask each group to report back to the rest of the class about how they think their work is progressing.

■ **Get further feedback from your colleagues.** When asked, colleagues are often able to give us further feedback about what they've gathered from pupils about our teaching.

14. Using self- and peer-assessment

The main advantages of using self-assessment and peer-assessment are that pupils find out more about how the assessment system works, and become better able to adjust their approaches to gain credit for their learning. The following suggestions may help you take advantage of these benefits.

■ **Help pupils to see the benefits of measuring their own work,** as a means of looking more deeply at what they have done.

■ **Equip pupils with a set of assessment criteria that they understand** and can apply to their work. Where possible, involve pupils in working out the best way of wording the criteria, to give them a sense of ownership of the assessment agenda.

■ **Never mind the score, feel the learning!** Advise pupils self-assessing their work that the most important outcome is not the score or mark they award themselves, but the decisions they make as they apply assessment criteria to their work.

■ **Trust pupils' judgement.** Avoid the reaction that pupils engaged in self-assessment will be far too kind to themselves. While *some* pupils may do this, most are rather harder on their own work than we ourselves may have been.

■ **Don't interfere lightly.** Rather than re-mark pupils' self-assessed work and give them 'our' scores as a comparison, it is better to give them feedback on the quality of their own self-assessment, and ask them to adjust their assessments on the basis of this feedback.

■ | **Use peer-assessment for increased feedback.** Engaging pupils in peer-assessment (where they mark each others' work) can be even more beneficial than self-assessment at times, because of the thinking that pupils do as they apply assessment criteria to their classmates' work, and then check that the criteria have been applied correctly to their own work.

■ | **Select appropriate tasks for peer-assessment.** Choose with care the nature of the tasks where pupils peer-assess each others' work. The most suitable tasks are those where pupils can benefit a lot from the informal feedback they can give each other about the work.

■ | **Be available as an expert witness.** When pupils are in the process of peer-assessing, offer to give 'judgements' on particular issues, making sure that all pupils are aware of these finer points regarding the interpretation of the assessment criteria.

■ | **Allow for renegotiating of peer-assessed scores.** Act as adjudicator when pupils feel that their scores have been rated too low (though don't expect them to complain if they have been rated too high!).

■ | **Don't be thought to be abdicating your responsibilities.** Be careful not to impose self-assessment or peer-assessment against pupils' will. They need to be convinced of the benefits for them in terms of deeper learning, otherwise they may feel that you are ducking out of something that they feel is your job.

15. Making sense of new structures

Introducing new course structures can seem a nightmare. For example, in the UK, moving into GNVQ programmes is an uphill struggle if you have not previously taught in vocational education, so we will take GNVQs as our example in the suggestions we make in this section. A different philosophy prevails – and as in most teaching, if you can understand the methods of assessment you will soon be able to cope with ways to present the content. In particular, the key to GNVQs lies in pupils accumulating appropriate *evidence* of their achievements as matched against the performance criteria outlined in the specifications:

■ | **Ensure that the performance criteria to be met are clearly identified to the pupils.** Make these clear to pupils, when you set them tasks and assignments. Where necessary, translate the 'official' performance criteria into words which pupils can understand easily.

■ | **Ensure that the tasks set will generate the evidence needed** if carried out properly. Give a range of examples to pupils, to help them see the sorts of evidence they should aim to accumulate as they work through GNVQ programmes.

■ **Plan to cover optional units at the same time as mandatory units where this is possible.** In particular, help to reinforce the connections between things pupils do for optional units and mandatory units.

■ **Help pupils see how a particular task can relate to several parts of their GNVQ programme.** Spend time mapping out where more than one performance criterion, aspect of the range, or unit can be covered simultaneously.

■ **Encourage pupils to cross-reference their own work on a GNVQ programme.** Give them help in identifying performance criteria and achievements as they do them rather than retro-spectively. Make sure that pupils have their own copies of the GNVQ documentation, and help them make sense of the terminology where necessary!

■ **Record examples of pupils' attainment in Core Skills as they happen.** Make a note explaining the skill displayed and the date. This can act as hard evidence of attainment. Encourage pupils to offer spontaneous alternative examples of work they have done that dem-onstrate their Core Skills achievements.

■ **Set short deadlines for the completion of units.** It is always easier to progress if you can establish early on what has already been covered, and have plenty of time left for things that are still outstanding.

■ **Encourage peer-assessment and group discussion.** Try to do this when pupils attain the per-formance criteria across the range required. Get pupils to help each other in tracking their cov-erage of the range and performance criteria, and in keeping their logbooks up to date.

■ **Pay particular attention to the nature of 'good' evidence.** When pupils know 'what it looks like to have been shown to have succeeded', they can focus their efforts accordingly.

■ **Avoid feeling alienated by the GNVQ specifications!** We can all think of other things that we feel should have been included in such specifications, and things that are included that we think are irrelevant. We can indeed adjust our teaching to cover the things we believe should be there, but at the end of the day, we need our pupils to be able to present evidence which matches the specifications as they are.

16. Planning schemes of work

As you know, thorough planning is essential in the modern classroom if you are to succeed in cov-ering all aspects of the National Curriculum. It will be second nature to you to spend a great deal of time on this aspect of your work. But make sure you leave some room for manoeuvre – teachers perform best when they are really interested in the topic, or when they digress to cover something that is particularly relevant on that day. Give yourself leeway to adapt your schemes of work to react to topical issues and enjoy fitting what the pupils need to know to what you care about!

Very recently, the QCA has begun to release exemplar schemes of work for secondary education. The implications of this move are clear: if you don't follow these schemes you need to be very clear about why not, and how you cover the issues exemplified in these publications in your own way:

- **Don't make unrealistic plans.** Although an overall plan for the whole school year is necessary, it isn't wise to plan in detail for more than a few weeks ahead. If you do this, the chances are that circumstances may change and your planning may be inappropriate. One of the features of a good scheme of work is adaptability.

- **Ask yourself what skills are to be learnt and what knowledge is to be gained by the pupils.** Think about this before starting to formulate detailed plans. It is after all their learning outcomes that are the basis of any effective plan.

- **Ensure that your teaching aims and objectives are clearly stated.** You may find it useful to re-compose these aims and objectives following the phrase: 'What this really means for my pupils is…'.

- **Think in advance of the ability range you expect.** Make sure that your plans allow highly able pupils to flourish, but also accommodate the needs and competencies of less able pupils.

- **Plan your assessments as early as possible.** Indicate the types of assessment you intend to use. Make sure that the things that are to be assessed link demonstrably to the aims and objectives you intend your pupils to achieve. Bring variety into your assessment processes, so that pupils with different abilities have their own chance to show themselves at their best in one or other form of assessment.

- **Specify what the expected outcomes will be.** This is best done in terms of the evidence that pupils will be expected to provide to demonstrate their achievement of the objectives. Work out which of the outcomes will be assessable, and how you will approach assessing them.

- **Include coverage of cross-curricular themes and dimensions where appropriate.** Incorporate issues such as equal opportunities, economics, business awareness and citizenship where appropriate, and highlight the coverage in your planning and schemes of work.

- **Identify what resources will be needed and when.** This is best done at the planning stage, to allow time to obtain particular resources relating to individual objectives and learning outcomes.

- **Plan the timescale for covering the objectives.** It is often best to cover as much as possible during the first half of a teaching year, to allow ample time for revision and consolidation of pupils' achievements well before final assessments are made.

■ **Acknowledge your own professional instincts and experience.** When teaching to 'a formula', it is all too easy to feel devalued and disenfranchised. However, with a bit of planning, it's often possible to mould your own knowledge of how you would like to teach a subject, and match it into even the most rigid-looking framework.

17. Invigilating internal exams

Sitting written exams is one of the most stressful parts of life for many pupils. Because of the need to prevent cheating and ensure a quiet environment, exam rooms are all the more hostile! Invigilating exams can be very tedious, but it is a highly responsible part of your work. If candidates get away with cheating, it will be regarded as your fault. The following suggestions may help you to invigilate fairly and kindly. (Remember that there will be specific regulations for external exams.)

■ **Minimize the possibilities of pupils cheating.** Tell them to leave bags in a pile at the front of the room, and before starting the exam remind them to double-check that they have nothing on their person that could be interpreted as a crib. Remind them to check pockets and pencil cases.

■ **Get your timing right.** Ensure that examinations start and finish promptly, and keep pupils informed verbally about the progress of time. Occasional comments such as, 'One hour left to go', '30 minutes left', and so on can help pupils who have lost track of the time.

■ **Try not to intimidate nervous pupils.** Be as unobtrusive as you can, while maintaining your vigilance. You will often see more by positioning yourself behind the candidates, in an aisle.

■ **Keep pupils well supplied with paper.** Walk round occasionally, carrying extra paper, and when you can see that a pupil is about to need more, provide some without the pupil having to ask.

■ **Keep records of the seating arrangement.** If, when marking scripts, the suspicion arises that some pupils have succeeded in collaborating, the seating records can often disprove or point further towards the suspicion.

■ **Act quickly but quietly if you find pupils cheating.** Write on the front of their scripts an appropriate note (for example: 'Incident at 09.42, involving also Janet Davies') and make your own notes about exactly what you saw and what you may suspect.

■ **Have arrangements in place for pupils who need the toilet.** If you're invigilating alone you can't leave the classroom or exam hall personally to escort such pupils there, but you can have a system where there is someone you can call in to see to such events.

■ **With externally set papers, follow the Exam Board regulations to the letter.** In particular, ensure that candidates' scripts bear their names or candidate numbers as required, and that any loose sheets or graphs are fully identifiable.

■ **Be kind and supportive to pupils suffering from exam stress.** Even a smile from you can help relieve their stress. Sometimes you may need to enable a very tense pupil to leave the room for an escorted breath of fresh air. Highly tense or faint-feeling pupils may feel less stressed if they take their exam right at the back of the room, where they feel fewer eyes are on them.

■ **Be ready to solve problems arising from the question paper.** With internal papers, if pupils bring to your attention a mistake or omission in a question, alert the whole group to leave this question alone for the time being, and send for the teacher who wrote the question to adjudicate. With external papers, it may be possible to arrange for someone to telephone the Exam Board.

18. Writing reports

This is always a tedious business, coming as it often does at the end of a busy term. You may have hundreds of reports to write about pupils you may only see once a week and you may be short of time to do it in. However, to each parent theirs is the only one that matters. To do each pupil justice, you need to prepare continuously for report writing, rather than leave it till the last minute. It's a good idea if you are new to the job to check out the school policy on reports:

■ **Keep careful notes about each pupil's achievements throughout the year.** This will save you time later. File and record all of their marked work so you can base your report on clear evidence rather than estimation.

■ **When you are inexperienced, write your reports out in rough first.** Then transfer them onto the requisite sheets when you are satisfied with them. This will slow you down initially, but will help you to avoid errors and problems, especially when you are writing composite reports with other teachers.

■ **Make sure when you refer to a pupil by name, that you get it right!** If a pupil is generally known by a shortened version of the name, using this can make the report less formal.

■ **Make reports constructive.** Try to use each report as an opportunity to give advice on how the pupil can improve, rather than just a means of passing judgement.

■ **Be sensitive regarding whom the report is going to.** Don't assume that everyone lives in a nuclear family. If parents live apart, it's helpful to let both have copies of the report.

■ **Make sure that what you write is readable and accurate.** If the report is hand-written, make sure that your writing is up to it. If you use a typewriter or word processor, make sure that the print quality is acceptable, not too feint, and contains no typographical errors. Check and double-check your spelling: nothing gives parents a worse impression than a teacher who cannot spell! (One of us always remembers an entry on his own report: 'spelling dissappointing!')

■ **Don't use a 'statement bank' clumsily.** Many teachers have a range of comments and sentence elements that they use over and over again for different reports. This can be usefully formalized into a statement bank on a computer or in the mind, so that elements can be called up and combined in different ways to suit each pupil and each report. If this is sensitively done, it can save you time, but beware of writing reports that look as if they have been assembled by a robot. You will need to customize them for each individual pupil if they are not to be meaningless.

■ **Don't try to do too many reports at a time.** Do them in batches so they don't all end up being made of the sorts of banal clichés or unexceptional comments which can stem from our brains when they're tired! Do try not to leave writing reports till the last minute.

■ **Respect pupils' rights to privacy.** Don't leave reports lying around in places where they can be read by anyone.

■ **Try to avoid surprises.** It may be helpful to let pupils know what you have written about them before their reports go home, especially if the news is bad. Security of transmission of the report to parents or guardians will need to be assured.

19. Preparing for an inspection

The thought of an imminent inspection can be intimidating and stressful to the classroom teacher, and often the feeling within the school as the date nears can approach panic. However, an inspection can be a valuable experience in helping you to set priorities and identify your own areas of concern. If you are well prepared and have a clear idea of your objectives as a teacher there should be no worries! These suggestions, however, cannot possibly cover everything that the OFSTED handbook can – we simply give a few hints on how to approach the ordeal!

■ **Ensure that all the necessary policies and documentation are in place** as part of the pre-inspection evidence. If you are aware of areas of concern, make sure that you have identified them as a department and have some strategy in place to begin to tackle them. Ensure that any departmental policies are in line with whole-school policies, for example on assessment, equal opportunities, or discipline.

- **Ensure that all the written policies are actually being implemented** and that all colleagues are aware of their practical application. Try to gather evidence of the implementation of each policy, so you can add detail to the rhetoric when necessary. Of course, this can be tricky in the three months or so between notification and inspection, so implementing policies as you go is essential.

- **Make sure that you have a clear idea of what you are doing and why** – both on a long-term and short-term basis! Make links between the way you go about your day-to-day work with pupils, and the whole-school policies and aims.

- **Have clear written schemes of work and individual lesson plans** which show how what you are teaching fits into the National Curriculum programmes of study or external examination syllabuses.

- **Make it clear how what you do can be measured.** Ensure that what you are teaching – and what pupils are learning – can be assessed, and make it clear how and when this will happen.

- **Be ready to show how you approach mixed-ability groups.** Ensure that your lessons are differentiated to meet the needs of pupils of all abilities.

- **Be prepared to demonstrate variety.** Get in the habit of teaching structured lessons that allow for a range of activities and learning experiences.

- **Be ready to show that you are well prepared and resourced.** Ensure that adequate resources are available and accessible by pupils – label your drawers, stores, bookshelves and so on. Demonstrate that pupils have access to facilities for independent learning.

- **Be prepared to demonstrate the breadth as well as the depth!** Try to identify where you can cover cross-curricular themes and dimensions within your subject teaching and build this into your planning.

USING TEACHING AND LEARNING RESOURCES WELL

The resources we use for our teaching are a crucial element in influencing the quality of our teaching. Outstandingly good teaching materials are not a copper-bottom guarantee of good teaching, but they do tend to improve the teacher's confidence and they tend to be an area of work that pupils comment on, whether adversely or with praise. Most teachers recognize too that the ways in which resources are used makes all the difference, and that planning of activities is crucial to their success. However well designed learning resource materials may be, the learning payoff which pupils derive is only as good as the briefings that we give pupils about how best to get what they need from the materials. Here we provide some guidance on the preparation and use of teaching and learning materials to support effective teaching. We have covered computer-based and electronic resources separately, and in more detail, later in this book.

20. Preparing interesting handout materials

With the availability of photocopiers and offset litho printing, it is increasingly preferable to use handout materials rather than relying on class-issued textbooks. The following suggestions may help you create handouts that are used actively by pupils, rather than simply filed away with their notes. Of course, you may need to collect in and re-use handouts where resources are limited. In such cases it may pay you to laminate the handouts:

- **Try to make handouts look attractive and interesting.** Where possible include pictures and illustrations, so that the materials are attractive for pupils to use. A box or edging makes all the difference.

- **Make it clear what each handout is about.** Use clear headings so that pupils can quickly identify each handout. It can be worth having a numbered set of handouts and a separate index page so that pupils can file them in the correct order when the set is complete.

- **Present the objectives.** Start each handout with a clear statement of what the handout is for in terms of the things pupils will be able to do once they have worked through the handout. Such statements can convey the intended objectives of the handout, or the expected learning outcomes.

- **Use handouts in an interactive way.** Include tasks and activities for pupils to do as they work through the handouts. These can include things to be done in class, and also things to be done as homework tasks.

- **Provide white space for pupils to write on.** Include boxes for pupils to write in their answers to questions in the handouts. When pupils have their own writing on handouts, it adds to their sense of ownership of them.

- **Organize your collection of handouts.** Keep a separate file containing the master copy of each handout, and separate files or boxes containing copies of each handout for issue to pupils.

- **Share your resources.** Make an additional set of copies of your handouts available to other colleagues, in a central location such as a staff-room filing cabinet. Encourage colleagues to share their own handouts in a similar way.

■ **Make handouts that help pupils who are absent.** Create special handouts covering the most important topics in your subject, suitable for pupils who miss important lessons. These handouts may also be useful as revision aids for all pupils nearer their exams.

■ **Build assessment into handouts.** Include self-tests towards the end of each handout, so that pupils can check for themselves how much they already understand, and how much further work they may need to do on the materials.

■ **Make it easy to update handouts.** If possible, have your handout materials stored on computer disk or desktop publishing system, so that you can continuously make minor adjustments and improvements to the handouts, without having to re-compose them from scratch.

21. Preparing learning packages

Open or flexible learning packages have many advantages, including that they can allow pupils to work though selected parts of the curriculum at their own pace, in their own way, and where and when they want to work on them. The following suggestions may help you to design packages of your own, or make good use of existing ones with your pupils:

■ **Work out what pupils can do by themselves.** Identify the parts of the curriculum that may lend themselves best to pupils learning them using learning packages rather than taught lessons.

■ **Make the objectives clear.** Work out clear statements of the intended learning outcomes of learning packages you design or use. Make sure that pupils understand exactly what they are aiming to become able to do as a result of working through each learning package.

■ **Design packages around things for pupils to do – not just to read.** Ensure that learning packages contain plenty of activity for pupils. Make sure that the tasks and activities in the packages are clearly phrased, and that pupils understand exactly what they are supposed to do.

■ **Package up your feedback as well as the activity.** Make sure that each time pupils have a go at a task or activity, there is readily available feedback, so that they can self-assess their work. The feedback may be provided in print in the packages (out of sight of the task questions), or could be delivered personally by you.

■ **'Why did I get this wrong?'** Remember that pupils don't only need to know whether or not they approached a task correctly – if they got it wrong, they need guidance as to what went wrong. Check that the feedback they receive covers this.

■ **Learning packages aren't textbooks.** Make it clear to pupils how learning packages are not like textbooks. Learning packages are things for them to do, not just to read. They will learn much more from having a go at the tasks and activities, than from just reading the information in the packages.

■ **Test out the bits of your package.** Experiment with components of learning packages in class, where you can monitor how pupils handle them. Take particular note of problems pupils have, and add extra guidance to the packages on the basis of this.

■ **Measure what is happening.** Include or add an end-test of one kind or another, which pupils will hand in for marking when they finish working through a package. Use this not only to check their achievements, but also to identify any trouble-spots in the learning package.

■ **Give pupils guidance.** When using an existing learning package, it can be well worth adding a brief set of guidance notes on 'How to approach using this package', highlighting the most important parts of the package, and the best ways of tackling it.

■ **Show pupils where the package fits into their overall course.** Remember to make sure pupils know how much the things they learn using learning packages count for in their overall course.

22. Getting the most from the library

School libraries and learning resources rooms may contain large amounts of useful information; the problem is helping pupils to make the most of them. Don't assume that pupils know how to use libraries or have often visited them. The following suggestions may help them make good use of such resources:

■ **Spell out the benefits to pupils.** Explain to pupils how useful it is to become good at tracking down relevant information in libraries (public libraries as well as at school). Explain how much time it can save them, when finding information to use in writing essays or reports.

■ **Give pupils useful practice.** Set tasks or projects that require pupils to track down particular reference materials you know are in the library or resource centre. Plan the tasks so that pupils become familiar with the ways the materials are catalogued or indexed.

■ **Help pupils develop their searching skills.** Help pupils to develop their skills at focusing on the most relevant materials. Give them clear guidelines to help them know exactly what they are looking for in the materials they consult.

■ **Help pupils to get their references right.** Train pupils in the correct way to refer to the sources of information they quote. Make sure that in your own lessons and handouts you refer to materials precisely (for example: Saunders, D (ed.) (1994) 'The Complete Student Handbook', Blackwell, Oxford).

■ **Encourage groups of pupils to use the library.** Give pupils group exercises to do, using materials in the library, helping them to pick up from each other valuable tracking and retrieval skills.

■ **Value the expertise of library staff where you have them.** Remind pupils how useful the help they can receive from librarians can be. Many public or college libraries have subject librarians, who have a good understanding of their own subjects as well as excellent knowledge of the available books in the field.

■ **Encourage pupils to use their eyes in a library!** For example, when there are several copies of a book, or when particular books are well thumbed, it is probable that these are more useful sources of information than an 'unused-looking' book.

■ **Remind pupils that modern libraries don't just contain books.** They also contain audio-visual materials, CD-ROM databases, and computer-assisted learning packages.

■ **Encourage pupils to make useful notes** when using materials in a library or resource centre. Remind them to make careful notes of which sources they extract information from, so they can locate particular sources again quickly when they may need to.

■ **Alert pupils to the usefulness of contents pages and indexes** when working out whether a particular book is relevant to what they want to find out from it. This can be far quicker than simply scanning through the book itself.

23. Organizing resources

If your room is well organized and ordered, pupils are more likely to respond by tidying up themselves. Giving pupils access to resources also helps them to begin to take responsibility for their own learning and progress. Both yourself and your pupils will have a clearer idea of what is available by keeping stock labelled and sorted:

■ **Arrange well-used resources in easily accessible and labelled storage** so that pupils can help themselves, saving time for more important tasks.

■ **Keep small items such as pencils, rulers, and so on in multiples of 10** so that you can easily check on numbers returned. Give responsibility for looking after certain items to a monitor who will give out and collect in books and other items – this saves traffic jams and needless wandering about.

■ **Ensure that there are plentiful supplies of scrap paper,** available for rough work and drafting. Cultivate local supplies of one-sided scrap paper, such as reprographics departments at local colleges or firms.

■ **Keep valuable or destructible resources locked away.** However, don't make it appear that these resources are unavailable to pupils; instead help them to see for themselves that they need to handle these resources with care.

■ **Use boxes, jars and trays to keep small items together.** A clear system of labels can turn a collection of boxes, jars and trays into an accessible resource collection.

■ **Emphasize the need to respect tools, materials and equipment** and the need to use them carefully and safely. It is easy for pupils to abuse resources simply because they do not feel any ownership or realize the value of such resources, or the difficulty in replacing certain items.

■ **Assemble collections of stimulus or source material in labelled boxes** so that pupils can track them down easily and use them independently.

■ **Collect together worksheets and other task-briefings** and keep them in accessible storage for pupils who happen to finish work early, or to give them out as 'extension tasks' for more able pupils who may benefit from additional challenges.

■ **Try to make regular times when you sort out your materials and resources.** Weekly is ideal, but half-termly will do. The longer you leave it, the longer it will ultimately take you to sort them out.

■ **Require pupils to take responsibility for the resources they use.** Don't let them get away with sloppy return of materials or incorrect placing of resources. Getting them to take this responsibility necessarily means that you have to ensure that they are allowed sufficient time at the end of class to put things away properly before they rush off to their next session.

24. Making do with limited resources

Unfortunately this is an ever more important aspect of the job in these times of Formula Funding and restricted budgets. Teachers have become adept at managing with very little in many areas of the curriculum. So it pays to be aware right from the start that resources are not infinite. When it's gone it's gone!

■ **Keep a strict eye on stock.** Always count in and out small items that are easily taken away (often without thinking). Get one of the more conscientious pupils to take responsibility for certain resources.

- **Save expensive consumable items for special lessons or the culmination of a project.** Explain to pupils that such items are difficult or impossible to replace, and solicit their help in conserving and protecting them.

- **Use scrap or recycled materials** – encourage the imaginative and creative use of such resources. Link this to lessons to be learnt about environmental issues and conservation.

- **Prepare your own worksheets and handouts.** This can be much less expensive than giving out published materials.

- **Help pupils to value resources.** Try to ensure that pupils are taught the correct way to use materials and equipment and that they understand their cost.

- **Invite pupils to contribute resources.** Rather than asking for donations, you can ask the class to bring along for the day specific things that may help in the particular lessons to be conducted. Make a 'shopping list' of resources that would be useful, and ask pupils to put their names besides any items they could bring along. (Make sure, however, that disadvantaged pupils are able to contribute something useful and don't feel excluded.)

- **Beg, borrow and steal!** Much as it goes against the grain for people who believe that their profession should be adequately resourced, when times are hard, any solution is better than none! When you know exactly what you need, it's well worth asking local businesses or organizations if they can help provide some things on your 'wanted' list.

- **Use outside sources.** For example, the British Association for the Advancement of Science provides a service of free talks to pupils by practising scientists, who will often bring along a range of expensive equipment to use in demonstrations.

- **Maintain good contacts with local colleges.** It's often possible to arrange for a school party to visit a college at no charge, for a day which includes opportunities for pupils to use equipment that would not be available at school.

- **Find out what is available from large companies.** Several large organizations provide a range of education booklets and videos, as part of their promotion policies. These materials are usually available on request, at no charge, and can provide the basis of useful class activities.

25. Making your classroom into an attractive learning environment

Secondary schools can often seem alien, impersonal environments where only serious business goes on. Take some tips from primary teachers and put some effort into making your room your own space – after all, you will be spending a good chunk of your life there!

■ **Choose strong, bright and warm colours** if you are given any chance to have your say about the decor. Pupils appreciate such colours much more than the neutrals, and they really do notice! If the room is in need of decoration and funds are not available, use posters, coloured paper and remnants of fabrics to cover the messy bits. The use of different textures and materials can make a cold room much more welcoming.

■ **Display pupils' work to improve the surroundings.** Displays can be attractive and interesting, and visually stimulating, and are good educational practice anyway.

■ **Encourage pupils to bring in interesting pictures to add to displays.** They will feel a sense of ownership, and in this way will feel it's also their responsibility to look after their environment.

■ **Use plants to make the room look more attractive and personal.** If you have tutor groups in your room, involve them in taking responsibility for the care and watering of the plants.

■ **Books do furnish a room** – as well as being useful to read. They can make a classroom look more interesting. Use colourful designs on book jackets as part of your display – make the layout of the bookshelves accessible and welcoming by providing headings and illustrations.

■ **Carpets are (nearly) magic!** It's increasingly common now for classrooms to be carpeted, as it is often cheaper than vinyl; choose the option of carpets whenever you have the choice. It not only makes a classroom feel warmer and more pleasant, but it cuts down considerably on noise.

■ **Assemble interesting objects** as well as pictures in your room. You might choose these to relate to what you are teaching, or just because you like them. Unusual items can stimulate creative work in many areas.

■ **Do your own minor maintenance.** For example, if the door is squeaky, oil it. If the door shuts noisily, you may consider sticking the odd piece of draught-proofing strip strategically, to muffle the sound of the door closing.

■ **Rearrange the furniture.** With pupils' help, you can make major transformations in the layout of a classroom quite quickly. They too will usually enjoy the change. It can also be a useful move when you feel that the class geography needs to be adjusted to disperse cliques.

■ **Keep an eye on your access.** Ideally, you need to be able to go right up to any pupils as they are working, to give them individual advice or feedback. Pupils who feel they are safely isolated from you may not do much work!

26. Making effective displays

Classrooms can be made visually interesting with displays of pupils' work and other materials that can stimulate and inform. Don't worry if you feel you have little artistic skill – if you follow a few guidelines you can make anything look attractive:

- **Pupils' own work will usually be the focal point of a display.** Choose examples from across the ability range – one of the reasons for displaying work is to show that it is valued. If they have produced good work which is not well presented you can often get them to re-present it more clearly for a special display. Make sure you include pupils' names on their work.

- **Include photographs, newspaper cuttings, artefacts, fabric, found objects** – anything to add colour, texture and interest. Pictures and other relevant information can make the display informative as well as visually stimulating. Examples of the work of others – writers, poets, scientists, illustrators and artists – will also act as stimulus.

- **Use the display to inform others of the work of your class** – add a few sentences of explanation about your aims and methods in producing the work.

- **Involve your class in displaying their own work** – they will enjoy this and feel more ownership of the room. But don't forget to teach them what to do! However, often they will come up with original and exciting ways of doing it which should be encouraged and facilitated. Get them to wordprocess some of their work for display, and involve them in producing headings and illustrations.

- **Strong, clear lettering is essential** – if you find lettering difficult (who doesn't!) try using a stencil or use computer-generated type. If you use a computer, beware of using too many different fonts in one display – two is generally plenty – and vary the effect by changing the size and style. Sometimes hand-written capitals (not bubble writing!) or italics can liven up a dull display. Use simple headings in bold lettering – underlining can look tacky.

- **The choice of background is important** – if in doubt choose a strong dark colour (you can't go wrong with black sugar paper). If you want a coloured background, pick out a predominant colour in the work to use. Mount light pieces of work on a dark ground and vice versa. If your paper is white and the background is light or medium in tone, it may help to draw a thick black line around the edge of the paper with a marker – this makes the work stand out and is cheaper and less time-consuming than double mounting.

- If you are double mounting the work, **use a fairly thin border in a contrasting tone.** The size of the borders should be equal on the top and sides but slightly wider at the bottom – this avoids the illusion of the picture appearing to slide off the mount.

■ **It's best to have plenty of visual information on the display** – avoid vast areas of background scattered with small pieces of work. Line up the edges of the work to give an ordered look, or display work diagonally and sometimes overlap to give a more lively effect. Use different shapes – circles, ovals – to mount work on and vary the size of the work displayed.

■ **Change displays regularly.** They can rapidly become part of the scenery. Keep up running repairs to edges and eradicate graffiti – nothing looks worse than a scruffy display.

■ **Consider the use of borders to enhance the display** – choose an appropriate motif and repeat by stencilling or photocopying.

27. Taking pupils on a trip

School trips can be great fun and highly memorable, but they are a terrific responsibility and need meticulous planning. Make sure you are aware of the school or LEA guidelines for taking pupils out of school, and always follow these guidelines to the letter!

■ **Make sure that the parental permission forms go out well in advance.** File all their responses carefully.

■ **Give pupils (and parents) a detailed printed briefing for the trip.** Include full information about the itinerary, with times and places in case anyone should get separated from the group, and a telephone contact number for emergencies.

■ **Plan the visit thoroughly, with sufficient structured activities to keep the pupils occupied productively.** Boredom breeds disruptive behaviour. Use checklists, questionnaires and task sheets (not just written tasks) to help to focus pupils' activities.

■ **Make sure you don't lose pupils!** Count them in and out at all times, and delegate individual colleagues and any parent helpers to be responsible for small groups. Never let pupils wander off unsupervised.

■ **Ensure that pupils know the standards of behaviour expected of them before they set off.**

■ **Have with you an emergency kit.** Include first-aid equipment, disposable wipes, tissues, sick bucket or bags and so on, as well as spare pens, paper, and anything else you think appropriate.

■ **Let pupils know what they are expected to bring with them.** This includes the sort of clothing that will be suitable and any equipment they may need. Also set clear guidelines about what refreshments may be brought, and how much spending money is permitted.

- **Be where you can see pupils.** When travelling on coaches, you will have better oversight of what pupils are up to if you travel towards the back of the coach, rather than at the front with the driver.

- **Make productive use of travelling time.** Give pupils observation or discussion tasks, especially on the outward journey when excitement levels may be high.

- **Follow-up the trip.** Use activities back in the classroom that make best use of the on-site learning pupils may have done. Use assignments in the classroom which allow pupils to draw together what they have learnt in the field. Display photos, maps and pupils' work when appropriate to keep up the momentum well after the trip is over.

28. Visiting museums and art galleries

Visits to galleries and museums can be a very effective learning experience for pupils but they only work really well when adequately prepared. The visit should be the focal point of a topic of work, rather than an additional extra, because so much can result from the opportunity to see at first hand examples of what pupils are studying. The additional stimulus of new surroundings and being out of school can have tremendous benefits.

- **Visit the museum or gallery beforehand.** Decide what you want the pupils to get out of the visit. Any such visit will usually cover many aspects of the curriculum and might be developed into a fully cross-curricular project. Set a few clear objectives for the visit which are integrated into the course of study being followed in school. If appropriate, prepare worksheets, quiz sheets or handouts using what you have learnt from the preliminary visit.

- **Book your party into the museum well in advance.** Talk to the Education Officer there about what facilities are on offer. Discuss the best time to visit, and how you will take advantage of any specialist help that may be available.

- **Prepare your pupils well for what they will see and be doing.** Do this before the visit if possible, or even on the way to the venue. If possible show some slides or pictures of exhibits – stimulate their interest beforehand. Sometimes the way a museum or gallery presents itself can seem intimidating or boring to young visitors and they need to understand the reasons for and relevance of their visit.

- **Plan the work you will do so that it can be developed further back at school.** Visits often take the form of research, stimulus or fact-finding, and more detailed finished work can be produced later.

■ **Allow enough time in the museum or gallery for some practical work.** This may include investigation, recording and drawing. If left to their own devices, pupils may go through the museum very quickly with an unfocussed eye. On the other hand sometimes an over-reliance on worksheet or quizzes can mean that they look only for the right answers and ignore any possibilities for individual exploration. Many museums have an Education Room where pupils can have a packed lunch or break, or do follow-up work, or listen to a talk.

■ **Ask museums and galleries whether they have learning resources prepared already.** They often put together packs of information, resources and activities relating to their exhibits for schools to use.

■ **Split your class into small groups.** Where there is a lot to see, divide pupils into manageable groups to research certain aspects in detail and report back in school.

■ **Get the pupils to look critically at *how* the work or exhibits are displayed.** Also ask them to look critically at *what* is on display. Is there enough explanation offered to the public? Are the displays clearly ordered and attractively presented? You could get pupils subsequently to produce their own mini-gallery or museum in school for other pupils to visit.

■ **Try to arrange a short talk about the exhibits.** If possible arrange for an expert or member of the museum staff to give such a talk. A new speaker or acknowledged expert in a subject will often have more impact than their familiar class teacher.

■ **Arrange for the pupils to be allowed to handle or more closely examine some of the less valuable exhibits.** This can help to make pupils feel 'more special' than casual visitors to the gallery or museum. They could sketch or make notes of these exhibits in closer detail.

■ **Involve the pupils in displaying what they have done.** When the follow-up work is completed back at school, ask pupils to prepare their own display, bearing in mind the type of display techniques they saw in the museum and how the objects were presented.

SUPPORTING PUPILS' LEARNING

Helping pupils to learn is what our job is all about. All too often the emphasis is on what is taught rather than what is learnt, and this is exacerbated by an excessive emphasis on syllabuses and curriculum matters. Our experiences have led us to believe that study skills are less effective when they are provided as an additional 'bolt on' element of class work. Instead we would argue that it is the job of teachers at all levels to think as much about how pupils are learning as about the content delivered. For this reason, the next section concentrates on how the teacher can help pupils to become more effective learners.

Further advantages of spending time on developing pupils' study-skills can be linked to the increasing recognition of the value of transferable skills (Key Skills) which are highly sought after by employers, and which will also help pupils to reach their full potential when they continue into further or higher education.

29. Supporting pupils who don't read well

Not being able to read as well as those around one can seem to pupils like a major catastrophe – particularly in an education system that bases much of its assessment on pupils' skills in reading and writing. The following tips may help redress the balance a little. These tips are aimed less at helping pupils improve their literacy skills and more at helping them 'access' the rest of the curriculum and cope with the issues they are encountering:

- **Say things as well as writing them.** When setting tasks, provide your briefing orally as well as in writing or print. Make it clear you don't mind repeating the task briefing again for anyone who wishes to hear it once more.

- **Find out who needs help.** Try to identify pupils who have genuine problems with reading, and ensure that they get specialist help from those trained to diagnose and assist pupils with reading problems.

- **Mind your language!** Use short sentences whenever possible in written tasks and instructions. Reading difficulties are often simply problems in the interpretation of long, complex instructions. Consider how the subject-specific vocabulary you use may cause problems for those not familiar with it.

- **Make assessment less dependent on reading skills.** Vary the forms and processes of assessment you employ, so that success does not depend inordinately on pupils' ability to read and interpret written or printed questions. Use spoken questions and instructions as well.

- **Use some tasks where reading is not too important.** Incorporate tasks and exercises that do not depend on reading skills. Where appropriate, single out pupils for praise, when you know of their problems with tasks which would have involved reading skills.

- **Help pupils preserve their self-esteem.** Don't allow pupils with reading difficulties to think that they are 'mentally subnormal' or 'strange'. Keep in mind that it is probably just one small area of intelligence that they have problems with, and that they may be highly gifted in other areas.

- **Help with spelling as well.** Pupils with reading problems often have difficulty with spelling. Identify new vocabulary and help pupils learn to spell new words. 'LCWC' (Look, Cover,

Write and Check) is a useful technique for self-help. Spelling ability is not magic: it is essentially a visual skill.

■ **Help pupils to gain confidence and motivation.** Spend additional time with pupils who seem to have difficulties interpreting written or printed words. It can sometimes be the case that they just need reassurance and confidence building.

■ **Never stop explaining.** Use 'WIRMI' – 'What it really means is…' – as a way of helping pupils put into their own words the meanings of longer sentences or instructions, and encourage pupils to compare interpretations with each other.

30. Helping pupils who don't do maths well

Many people (not least we teachers!) remember their time learning maths at school with little affection. Indeed, this can lead to feelings of mental block against anything numerical or algebraic. Probably, maths is the hardest subject of all to teach really well. The following suggestions focus on how maths is learnt best. Try to make maths fun and accessible sometimes. With some imagination (and useful source books) everyday problems – Saturday wages, League Tables, timetables and darts scores – can provide useful practice:

■ **Accept that numbers *are* a foreign language!** They can't be read in the same way as sentences, or heard in long sequences. When pupils have difficulties, try to find out if they understand the stages leading up to the points where their problems are. Maths is about building bricks and if a key brick is missing, the whole process is blocked.

■ **Celebrate mistakes!** Remind pupils that getting something wrong is as useful as getting it right, if the cause of the mistake can be tracked down and isolated. Give praise for each and every stage that is understood and done correctly.

■ **Help pupils detect mistakes for themselves.** From time to time, use a 'spot my mistakes' exercise on the blackboard (or in handout materials). Plan to show pupils the most likely sorts of mistakes they may make, giving them the opportunity to identify the mistakes without the embarrassment of having made them themselves. Develop pupils' feel for the right sort of answer (estimates) so that they become better at recognizing answers which are silly.

■ **Remind pupils of the importance of practice.** Maths is learnt by doing maths – not watching someone else do it. Include plenty of practice to help pupils consolidate things they have just learnt.

■ **Never mind the speed, is the answer right?** Be careful not to place too much value on speed. Pupils who can do something successfully but slowly, are in a position to speed up in due course, but may become entirely demotivated if they feel under immediate pressure to get things right quickly.

- **Give pupils the chance to learn by explaining.** Let pupils who have got something right explain to others exactly how they did it. They can remember how they learnt it themselves, and can often communicate this better than someone who has known it for a long time.

- **Let pupils see how others tried it.** It is useful to get pupils to mark each other's work in informal tests and exercises. This can alert them to the sorts of mistakes to avoid, as well as to the correct way to approach problems or tasks.

- **Arrange competition between groups rather than between individuals.** Try getting pupils to work in threes, in a problem-solving game, where each trio is given a different problem (of a similar standard), and the trios compete as to which can solve the most problems in half an hour. There is often no 'right' means to getting the correct answer. Different pupils will understand and use different methods. Try to encourage this in your explanations and praise.

- **Have practice material at hand.** Have available a bank of handout sheets of problems to practise with, and encourage pupils who need such practice to do them. Give different pupils different sheets, to avoid the wrong sort of collaboration.

- **Work out your priorities.** For the majority of the class, it is probably more important to cover the basics soundly, rather than to digress into advanced maths. That said, have some difficult problems available to give to those pupils who will respond positively to the challenge.

31. Helping pupils to learn together

Pupils learn a great deal from each other. They can often understand something more easily when someone who has only just understood it is explaining it to them. Most pupils enjoy working in groups for at least some of the time. The following suggestions may help you get the most from group work:

- **Be up front with pupils about your reasons for using group activities:** talk to them about the benefits of cooperative learning.

- **Plan for collaboration rather than competition.** Devise group activities in which tasks can be shared out between group members and expertise can be shared.

- **Help pupils help each other to learn.** Encourage pupils to quiz each other, giving them practice both in working out sensible questions to ask, and in answering questions informally.

- **Involve pupils in each other's assessment.** At its simplest level, this could mean checking each other's answers against a model answer given by you. More sophisticated forms of peer-assessment can be encouraged subsequently, with pupils giving each other feedback against given or negotiated criteria as their evaluative skills develop.

- **Give pupils opportunities to teach one another:** teaching someone else something is an excellent way for them to consolidate their own learning (as we teachers know!).

- **Use different kinds of groups.** When putting pupils into groups for collaborative activity, think about group formation. On different occasions you might like to put them into friendship groups, ability-based groups or learning teams, where you try to balance the range of skills and abilities in each group. Mixed-gender groups, if used sensitively, can bring benefits for learning as well as behaviour.

- **Remain aware of feelings.** Be sensitive about coping with inter-personal problems within groups. There is no point forcing pupils to work together if they can't stand each other. It may be necessary to have contingency plans to change group formations if problems occur.

- **Avoid passengers.** Monitor group activity to ensure that groups do not carry passengers, prepared to piggy-back on the efforts of others. One strategy to help with this is to make the group responsible for making sure that everyone in that group knows what the answer is and how they got to it. Letting the class know that someone from the group will need to report back to the rest of the class, but adding that you will choose who the reporter will be at the end of the task, applies a certain pressure!

- **Distribute any burdens.** Change the composition of working groups at intervals so that any unpopular or difficult pupils are not always working in the same groups.

- **Let groups share their products.** Let groups have opportunities to benefit from the learning of other groups through the use of display materials, presentations and so on.

32. Helping pupils to revise effectively

Exams measure the quality of pupils' revision more than how long they spent revising. The following suggestions may help your pupils adopt effective and productive approaches to revision:

- **Prepare revision aids.** All the way through a course, prepare summaries of main points (or get pupils themselves to do this), explaining that these will be useful for later revision, and that it is never too early to start learning from them.

■ **Help pupils know the agenda.** Prepare lists of short questions covering everything important about individual topics and give these to pupils, inviting them to become well practised at answering the questions.

■ **Get pupils practising.** Use class games where pupils in groups quiz each other using lists of short questions, and keep scores. Suggest ground rules, such as that if the person who is asked a question cannot answer it, the person who asked it can gain the score for that question by answering it instead.

■ **Show the standards and structures.** Where pupils are heading towards exams, give out copies of old exam papers early in the course, so that they can see the structure of the exams and the depth of typical questions.

■ **Let pupils in on how the typical examiner's mind may work.** From time to time, set a class exercise around an old exam question, then get pupils to mark each others' answers using the sort of assessment criteria which would have been used in the real exam.

■ **Help pupils adopt active strategies.** Remind pupils that simply reading something over and over again is a very slow and passive way of trying to learn it. Revision is only active when pupils are applying what they know, and using it to answer questions either in writing or orally.

■ **Help pupils see how they learn best.** Ask pupils how they learnt things (anything at all) that they are already good at. Then remind them that the same processes (learning by practising, and learning from mistakes) can be deliberately applied to things they need to learn for exams.

■ **Encourage pupils to make and use summaries.** Help pupils to make their own concise summaries of the things they need to know. Help them decide what is important and what is just background detail.

■ **Help pupils plan their revision tactics.** Suggest that it is better to do revision in frequent, short spells rather than long, continuous ones. Help pupils to make revision timetables when they are entered for public examinations or end-of-year exams. Remind pupils that everyone's concentration span is quite short, and it is how often they revise something that counts, rather than how long they spend on it in total.

■ **Variety is the spice of revision!** Encourage pupils not to spend too long trying to learn one topic, but to switch topics about every half-hour or so. A change is as good as a rest as far as our brains are concerned – and much more productive than letting boredom set in.

33. Helping pupils to pass exams

Success in exams depends as much upon sensible exam techniques as upon subject knowledge. It is sometimes difficult to give pupils sound advice when the system keeps changing, but the following suggestions are intended to help you assist your pupils in developing their exam techniques:

- **Familiarity breeds confidence.** Especially when heading towards public exams, help pupils to become familiar with the layout and structure of real exam papers, by giving them class and homework opportunities to practise on questions from old papers.

- **What is the nature of the game?** Remind pupils that exams essentially measure their skills at answering exam questions in writing, and that anyone can improve these skills simply by practising writing such answers.

- **Stress the importance of good time-management during exams.** Remind pupils that if they spend too long writing too much for Question 1, and have no time left for the last two questions, they will have lost far more marks than if they'd done a short answer for Question 1 and answered all the other questions.

- **Help pupils to *analyse* old exam questions.** Ask them to work out what the questions really mean. Help them identify the key words in questions, including 'why?', 'what?', 'how?', 'when?', 'compare', 'explain', 'describe' and 'discuss'.

- **Stress the importance of wise decisions.** When pupils have a choice of questions to make, remind them how important it is to make wise choices concerning which questions they will attempt. The only way of doing this is to read each question slowly, carefully and more than once.

- **'Keep checking the questions.'** Suggest to pupils that they should re-read the question they're answering several times while writing their answers. This reminds them exactly what the question is asking, and helps them to avoid going off on tangents.

- **'Show what you're trying to do.'** Emphasize that in numerical or problem-type questions it is important for examiners to be able to see exactly what pupils are trying to do in their answers. If examiners can see the point at which a mistake occurs, they can award marks for the other parts which are correct. If they can't see what went wrong, they can't give any marks at all.

- **'Don't get stuck and have a mental blank!'** When pupils get stuck on a question because they have forgotten something, encourage them to move on to another question they can answer well, rather than becoming panic-stricken or tense. What matters most is scoring points across the whole paper, rather than getting a particular question entirely right.

- **Remind pupils that examiners are human** – just like teachers – and like giving marks for correct answers. Examiners are not simply searching for mistakes. Examiners respond best to clear, well set out answers, well-reasoned arguments, and definite conclusions.

- **'Save time for checking.'** Explain to pupils how useful it is to save several minutes towards the end of each exam, to re-read through everything they have written, correcting obvious mistakes, and adding important points that may have come to mind since writing the answers.

34. Helping pupils to be creative

It is all too easy when teaching to a syllabus or programmes of study to forget that the development of creative or imaginative qualities can be enhanced by your own behaviour in the classroom. You may have a firm idea in your own mind of what you want to teach and may fall into the trap of leaving no leeway for new or unconventional thoughts. Sometimes when work is technically poor or badly presented we may miss its originality or unusual characteristics:

- In setting a task or project **use a broad task briefing or a 'neutral stimulus'** so that pupils have plenty of scope for approaching the task in their own ways, and ensuring that there is differentiation in the outcome of the activity.

- **Accept innovation and individuality,** even if the solutions pupils deliver from your task briefings are not what you had in (your) mind.

- If work is technically poor or if the presentation is weak, **react positively to the ideas and thoughts behind it** and help pupils to develop skills in self-expression.

- **Ask open-ended questions and accept a range of answers.** Try to avoid asking questions to which you anticipate only one 'right' answer (unless you are dealing with matters of fact).

- **Allow time for pupils to experiment, make mistakes and explore ideas.** When presenting pupils with a new area of work, new techniques or materials, give them a chance to explore possibilities and try things out before you launch into a major piece of work.

- **Encourage the use of rough work books.** Pupils may often feel it is easier to be creative in rough books, and you can then help them redraft their original ideas in work where presentation is given their attention.

- **Use brainstorming** with individuals, in small groups or as a whole class. Remind pupils that in brainstorming sessions, all ideas are valued and none criticized.

- **Try to set open-ended tasks that encourage divergent rather than convergent outcomes.** This will not only be more interesting for your pupils, but also for you.

■ **Get pupils to work in groups on a range of ideas.** Don't ask them to pick the best of these, but ask them to find ways to incorporate the best elements of all of the contributions produced in the groups.

■ **Ask pupils to think about 'dream' and 'nightmare' solutions to problems.** 'What would this be like if everything went in the best possible way?', 'Now what would it be like if everything went wrong?'. Help pupils to distil learning points from these activities and the scenarios they think of.

35. Helping pupils to write essays

In many formal examinations, pupils are required to put what they know into the form of written essays. In coursework too, pupils' skills at writing essays may count a lot. The following suggestions may help you to help them to approach this task successfully and effectively:

■ **Help pupils to plan essays.** Show them ways of mapping out the ideas they may subsequently turn into paragraphs in their final versions of an essay.

■ **Remind pupils to look carefully at the title or briefing.** We all know how easy it is to stray away from the main topic, and to end up writing things which (however interesting) are irrelevant to the task in progress.

■ **Help pupils to analyse what is required.** Remind them of the significance of such key words as 'how', 'why', 'when', 'where' and so on in essay briefings. In particular, alert pupils to what they should try to do when asked to 'compare' or 'contrast' or both.

■ **Remind pupils that it takes several drafts to write a good essay.** Encourage them to get their ideas down on paper, and then spend some time rearranging them before they come up with their 'final essay'.

■ **Help pupils to see the importance of firm conclusions.** Any essay usually requires the writer to come to some sort of conclusion – or at least to sum up what has been said. It's important that essays don't just stop in full flow, but arrive at a decisive ending.

■ **Help pupils make good introductions.** There is no better time to compose the introduction than when we know exactly what we're introducing! Suggest to pupils that they should write the introductions to their essays quite late, when they know exactly what their essays will have covered.

■ **Remind pupils of the usefulness of practice.** The best way to become better at writing essays is to write lots of them. Or better still, to plan lots of them – it's possible to plan several essays in the time it takes to put one together.

- **Quantity is not the same as quality.** Remind pupils that it's not a matter of writing a lot, rather a matter of good-quality writing that counts.

- **Get pupils to mark essays for themselves.** Sometimes, the best way to alert pupils to strengths and weaknesses in essay writing is to help them to allocate marks to examples of essays.

- **Give pupils the chance to compose an essay as a group.** This can help individual pupils to learn from each other. It can also allow any criticisms to be shared by the group, rather than received by individual pupils.

PROVIDING PERSONAL AND PASTORAL CARE

The teacher's job does not finish when the bell rings. For many, the pastoral elements of our work tend to be some of the most satisfying and rewarding aspects of our jobs. At the same time, however, this part of our work can be problematic, demanding and exhausting. Sometimes we don't know where to start with pastoral matters and often we don't know where to finish. This section aims to give some guidance on some of the most common issues teachers have to deal with when working on a personal level with children, not only concerned with traumas, but also with the more satisfying task of helping students with preparations for the next phase of their lives.

36. Being an effective form tutor

This can be one of the most rewarding of all the aspects of the work of a secondary school teacher. You can really get to know your pupils as individuals and they will relate to you on a much more human level than they may do to their subject teachers. Schools vary in the amount of emphasis given to the pastoral role of the form tutor, but in most cases you will be expected to get to know your group very well and follow their progress on every level:

- **Get to know your form as individuals.** Learn their names as quickly as you can. Talk to some pupils each day about some aspect of their school or home life. Try not to always talk to the approachable members of the class. Make an effort to involve all the group in activities.

- **Build a collection of 'portraits' of the pupils in your form.** This can be done with the pupils themselves, for example containing details of their hobbies, favourite foods, best-liked music, sports achievements and so on. Try to build up a way of finding out what makes each individual 'tick'.

■ **Be an ally, as well as a teacher.** Make it clear to pupils in your form that you are there to help them. This in turn means that you expect them to tell you when they need your help. Be ready to be their principal contact if they need to share personal or family problems that could be affecting their lives.

■ **Praise good social behaviour.** While such behaviour affects all teachers and pupils, it is often left to the form tutor to be the monitor of general attitudes and demeanour. Invoke 'team spirit' and a feel of belonging – a 'we are the best class' feeling.

■ **Be approachable.** Leave time to talk to your class – don't always be preoccupied with administrative tasks or preparing the next lesson.

■ **Be a trouble-shooter!** Offer to help to 'smooth the waves' when pupils in your form get into difficulties with your colleagues. You will often be able to explain to your colleagues difficulties that the particular pupils are going through, that they would not otherwise have known about.

■ **In form base time, set small tasks that will get pupils working together in different configurations.** This helps to avoid the class becoming polarized into cliques that always work together. You can make a number of different sorts of groupings, including alphabetical ones, astrological ones (birthday month), last-letter-of-first-name groups and so on.

■ **Encourage pride in the form base classroom where feasible.** Providing (or encouraging pupils to provide) posters and plants can help make a form classroom special to the form.

■ **Pay attention to small details.** Some pupils like it when you remember their birthdays or if you comment on their contributions to school exhibitions, performances or sports event achievements.

■ **Recognize individual differences:** you can treat pupils equally without treating them identically. Try to ensure that both genders get equal amounts of time and attention, but don't ignore quiet pupils just because they are no bother.

37. Getting pupils to talk to you

When pupils are talking to you, you have their undivided attention. The more you can get them to do the talking, the more learning they will achieve:

■ **Invite questions from individual pupils by name.** Give them the chance to explain more about their questions, so that everyone becomes interested in the answers.

■ **Make full use of questions pupils ask.** Ask the class if anyone is willing or able to answer a question that a pupil has asked. Give volunteers every encouragement to answer.

■ **Don't 'put down' incorrect answers from pupils.** Gently confirm that the answers are not yet quite correct, and invite further replies from any pupils who have further ideas.

■ **Ask questions in an interesting way.** Make it appear that you really don't yet know what the answers may be. Draw the answers out of pupils by asking them leading questions, which help them to arrive at sensible answers, or by playing devil's advocate against their ideas to help them justify their arguments.

■ **Encourage pupils to contribute their own questions.** Help pupils themselves to think of the questions that the class needs to address. If the class 'owns' the questions, more pupils will be interested in the answers to them.

■ **Be available as an expert witness.** Arrange one-to-one times, where any pupil can come to you and ask you anything or tell you anything. Use what they ask or tell you as an agenda for future class discussions or activities.

■ **Be someone who can find someone who knows.** Make it clear to pupils that they can ask you (or tell you) about anything at all, but that you can't be expected to know all the answers – but can find someone who does.

■ **Let pupils in to selected parts of your world.** Talk to classes about 'share-able' things in your own life from time to time, to help the pupils appreciate that you too have feelings and emotions. But handle personal anecdotes with care; it's easy to become boring.

■ **Accept silly questions.** When pupils ask 'silly' questions, or say 'silly' things, treat them as perfectly reasonable questions or comments, encouraging other pupils to ask questions or make comments.

■ **Bring everyone in.** Identify those pupils who don't ask questions or give comments, and try to draw them in to discussions, for example by giving them the responsibility for taking charge of a group discussion of a matter arising from a question that has already been asked.

38. Helping pupils who don't believe in themselves

Personal self-esteem is important for everyone (including ourselves). Human nature being what it is, there will always be a proportion of pupils who (sometimes for very complex reasons) underestimate themselves. Don't think that you can solve the world's problems by yourself! You'll have too many of your own at first. You may wish to concentrate on teaching and surviving in the early stages! However, some suggestions on how to help pupils with low self-esteem are given below:

- **Capitalize on their successes.** Remind yourself how self-belief usually comes through success. Try to ensure that pupils who have a self-esteem problem are given things to do in which they will demonstrably succeed. It can help to break something up into short, manageable tasks where such pupils can succeed, before going on to the next stage.

- **Be aware of sensitivity when giving feedback.** Take particular care when giving feedback to pupils who may be sensitive because of a self-esteem problem. Avoid the use of any negative 'final language' including such words as 'not satisfactory' or 'wrong'.

- **Help pupils identify their strengths.** Help pupils who are feeling low on self-esteem by reminding them about things that you already know they are good at, and where you can point to evidence that convinces them of their achievements.

- **Help pupils accept their weaknesses.** Encourage pupils to regard weaknesses as not-yet-developed strengths. Help them to believe that the fact that they can't *yet* do a thing doesn't mean they can never do it.

- **Show that weaknesses are really opportunities to grow.** Suggest that pupils regard weaknesses as opportunities rather than threats. Show them that being aware of a weakness is in itself a strength, and a cause for positive self-esteem.

- **Suggest that low self-esteem is part of life at some time.** Remind pupils that most people go through periods of low self-esteem as a perfectly normal and natural part of growing up and developing. Where possible, give illustrations of your own feelings and approaches during such times.

- **Help pupils find out what makes them tick.** Do a group exercise with pupils asking, 'What sorts of things make you feel good about yourself?' Several pupils may discover positive factors about themselves that they had not consciously thought about before.

- **Help pupils to share feelings.** Encourage pupils to go public with (at least some of) their feelings. This will need handling with sensitivity and tact. For example, have a 'feelings washing line' at the side of a classroom, where pupils can peg a piece of paper saying how they feel today and why.

- **Devise tasks where pupils will succeed.** Have a stock of small useful tasks you can give out to pupils who need a boost in their self-esteem – tasks which you know they can succeed at, and which will be seen by others to have been useful and successful.

- **Don't forget your own feelings.** Monitor your own self-esteem, and the contributing factors and circumstances. We never stop learning about how our own minds and emotions function.

39. Coping with emotional pupils

Human beings are an emotional species. By the time we become teachers, we've had a fair amount of experience at handling our own emotions. Pupils, however, will continue to meet emotions quite new to them. The following are some of the ways we can help them:

■ **Accept the emotion** – don't try to persuade pupils to 'pull yourself together now!' There may be times when pupils have so much on their minds because of outside circumstances that they are not able to learn. Be sensitive to this and reduce the pressure or discover if they can be helped through it.

■ **Find out what's behind the emotion.** Gently and carefully gather information on the cause of strong emotions. The first explanations of the cause are often far from the real cause. Yawning and lack of concentration may sometimes be outward signs of inward confusion and distress, not boredom with what you are teaching.

■ **Help pupils put it in their own words.** Encourage pupils to explain how they feel, and why they feel that way. Use questions that help to draw out their feelings, without making judgmental replies at any early stage.

■ **Avoid alienating pupils affected by emotion.** Try to avoid the isolation of any pupil experiencing a strong emotion. Help them to feel that emotions are a perfectly normal part of life, and that there is no shame or weakness involved in having emotions.

■ **Help pupils identify the source of their emotions.** When the emotion concerned is anger, help pupils to clarify the exact causes of such feelings. Often, once the causes have been expressed to someone else, the feelings are considerably relieved.

■ **Help pupils see that emotions are natural.** Openly discuss at 'normal' times the human nature of having emotions and feelings. Explain to pupils how the first time they experience particular emotions and feelings, they can feel quite out of their depth, but that subsequent experience helps them develop their own coping strategies.

■ **Don't go it alone.** Don't expect to be able to deal with all emotional situations on your own. Find out which colleagues are particularly good at dealing with such situations, and bring them in when possible to help you.

■ **Bring in the experts when necessary.** Be on the lookout for emotional problems that would benefit from expert help. When following up such expertise, be careful that no feelings of stigma arise. It is often the sensitive and intelligent mind that ties itself in knots temporarily due to overemotion.

■ **Minimize feelings of weakness.** Do anything you can to minimize overemotional pupils feeling that they are 'different'. Feelings of alienation are often the most distressing part of an emotional episode.

■ **Show that you too are human.** When it is useful, share your own emotions and feelings, and your own ways of coping with swings of mood. Use your judgement to decide which parts of your own experience can be useful for your pupils to learn from.

40. Breaking bad news

Sadly, bad news has to be broken by someone, and that sometimes means us! There is no substitute for a course in counselling, but the following suggestions may provide some ideas about how to break bad news to pupils:

■ **Be sure of your facts.** Make sure you know exactly what the bad news is, and where the information came from. Have contact telephone numbers written down.

■ **Don't do it alone.** If possible, enlist the help of a colleague before you start the difficult task of breaking bad news to a pupil – preferably a colleague of the opposite sex to yourself.

■ **Prepare the way** – find a suitable location that is private but informal (breaking some bad news in front of a whole class could be very traumatic for the recipient of the news).

■ **Be ready for the next steps.** Plan in advance what will be done after breaking the news (for example who will take the pupil to the hospital, or home).

■ **Avoid highlighting bad news.** Call the pupil concerned out of the class as innocently as possible (for example, 'Sorry, but could we go along to Mrs Roger's room where I believe she has a message for you?').

■ **Proceed gently.** If possible, invite the pupil to sit down first. Only then say something along the lines, 'I'm sorry, but I've got some rather bad news for you' then deliver the news as gently as possible, giving what comfort you can as needed.

■ **Accept emotional reactions.** If the news results in tears, it is usually best to encourage by saying, 'That's all right now, let it all out' rather than saying, 'Pull yourself together.' Particularly when you've a colleague present, one or other of you can hold a hand or give a hug as appropriate.

■ **Inform other people with due care.** It may be necessary to tell the rest of the class about the bad news. However, it's important not to break confidences at this stage. For example, it's better to tell them, 'Sheila has had some sad news which will have given her a bit of a shock' rather than to say, 'Sheila's mother has been injured in an accident.'

- **Decide who needs to know what.** Depending on the nature of the news, decide whether all of your colleagues need to be alerted to the details, or just the fact that the pupil concerned needs to be treated with particular sensitivity during the time to come.

- **Keep track of events.** It can make a big difference if you can continue to monitor the situation. This may mean maintaining contact with the pupil or the family, in which case it is important that one person does this rather than too many callers or enquirers.

41. Helping pupils to recover from setbacks

Sometimes circumstances overtake all of us. Pupils may lose a fortnight due to illness, or have setbacks in their family lives that knock them off their stride. Also, pupils often need help in recovering from failure. The following suggestions may help you to help them to regain their momentum:

- **Assemble your first-aid kit.** Build up your own collection of handouts and resources covering key topics in your teaching which you can issue to pupils. This can help you to help pupils make up for lost time when necessary.

- **Encourage pupils to ask.** Encourage pupils who have missed key lessons on important topics to make lists of questions about things they can't understand as they work on catching up. Make time to be available to respond to these questions.

- **Encourage peer-group support.** Help pupils who have missed something to use their classmates as a resource to help them catch up. Explain to the whole class how useful it is to explain a topic to someone.

- **Don't look back yet!** Suggest to pupils who have fallen behind that it is more important to keep up with what is going on at present than to try and do all the catching up overnight. Encourage them to catch up a bit at a time, while keeping up with the rest of the class on current topics as well.

- **Have other ways of catching up ready.** For particularly crucial parts of your course, have alternative learning pathways readily available for any pupils who miss key lessons. For example, turn these parts into small learning packages or interactive handouts, which pupils can work through in their own time. Also, run 'repeat' (rather than 'remedial') sessions on these key topics, for anyone who did not 'get it' first time round.

- **Help pupils not to panic.** Help pupils who have missed something important to keep it in perspective. It may seem like a mountain at the time, but once understood, the problem will be forgotten quickly.

■ **Encourage pupils to regard 'failure' as a useful stage towards success.** Remind them that they themselves are not failures; it's simply that they have not yet succeeded at the particular task involved.

■ **Acknowledge the value of making mistakes.** Give pupils examples of how 'getting it wrong at first' is one of the most natural ways to learn things successfully.

■ **Help pupils look at their tactics.** Where pupils are preparing for a re-sit exam, encourage them not only to explore the parts that caused them problems before, but also to analyse they ways they went about preparing for the exam and sitting it. Indeed, advise pupils that a past failure can be a distinct advantage when it comes to the next occasion.

■ **Tell them about Edison,** whose 100th attempt to make an electric light bulb was successful. He dismissed the rest as '99 ways *not* to try to make a light bulb'.

42. Helping pupils towards university or employment

Sometimes the Careers Advisor is thought to be the one who bears all the responsibility for the future progress of pupils. However, pupils need all the guidance and support we can all give them, in addition to specialist advice. The following suggestions may help you to support your own pupils:

■ **Help pupils make their own resources.** Ask pupils to prepare a Curriculum Vitae as an assessed task. Give them feedback on the ways that their CVs may be viewed by Admission Tutors in universities, or by prospective employers.

■ **Help pupils fly their own kites.** Help pupils to identify strengths in their own experience, which are worth showing clearly when they apply for employment or further education.

■ **Show pupils what counts.** Alert pupils to the things that look 'good' on applications. In particular, extol the virtues of things that show pupils' responsibility, cooperativeness and initiative.

■ **Coach pupils in the art of 'interview technique'.** Use class role-play exercises to help pupils familiarize themselves with the processes of interviews.

■ **Give pupils safe 'dry-runs'.** If possible, engage pupils in making videos of simulated interviews. Remember that the act of capturing an interview on video automatically develops quite acute observation of the processes involved.

■ **Help pupils see what's being sought.** Use case studies to alert pupils to what prospective interviewers may be looking for. For example, show pupils a video of three different interviews for a job, and ask them to list the respective merits and weaknesses of the candidates, and to select the best candidate.

- **Let pupils taste further opportunities.** Take advantage of open days at local colleges or universities to give pupils a taste of what it would be like to continue their education there.

- **Help pupils see what has already succeeded.** Invite past pupils who gained employment or went on to college back to the school to share their experience with pupils.

- **Help pupils find out what they need to be able to do**. Set groups of pupils the task of drawing up an advertisement for a job, spelling out the duties involved in the job, and identifying the experience that is being sought in candidates.

- **Practice makes perfect.** Remind pupils that becoming good at interviews is best achieved by practice, and that one 'bad' interview should not put them off. Encourage them to learn even more from unsuccessful interviews than from successful ones.

43. Coping with parents' evenings

These occasions can prove quite an ordeal at the end of a busy day – especially if you're not well prepared. In some subject areas you could come into contact with 250 different pupils each week, so if you can get into the habit of writing brief notes about pupils' progress as it happens you will find interviews with parents much less worrying. Parents' evenings are not the place to discuss major issues, and if possible you should let parents know in advance if there are serious matters which may need lengthier or more private discussions. As a general rule, there should be no major surprises in store for parents:

- **Establish which parents will be attending.** Talk to your pupils in advance, and tune in to how they feel about parental visits to the school. Discuss with the pupils what they feel their successes and failures have been so far in the course.

- **Make it clear to parents who you are.** This is particularly important when parents' evenings are held in a large space such as the school hall. Have a large card on your table, with your name on it and the subject you teach, or the form you are responsible for.

- **Make sure you know who the pupils are!** If it's too early in the term to have learnt all their names, ensure that you check your notes and marks when the class is present during lessons beforehand. Make very brief notes about any individual achievements or characteristics in your mark book as you become aware of them. This will be an invaluable aid to writing reports later in the term.

- **Take along some examples of the pupils' work where appropriate.** Parents are very interested not only in their own child's progress but also in the type of work done in lessons.

- **Make brief notes of which parents talk to you, and the main points of discussion.** You will often want to follow up particular things arising from the discussion later.

- **Avoid odious comparisons.** Talk about the pupil under consideration, rather than their class-mates or siblings. When such comparisons are indulged in, it can be surprising how far the teacher's words will be reported, and how long the memory can be retained.

- **Look after yourself.** Try to arrange for a hot drink to be brought to you, or at least have in reserve mineral water and mints. These evenings can be very long.

- **Concentrate on pupils' behaviour and achievements rather than personality issues.** Parents may be more amenable to criticisms of what their children are actually doing rather than their children's personality traits (which may be inherited!).

- **Avoid the temptation to get drawn into discussions of the shortcomings of other members of staff.** However justified and satisfying this may sometimes be, it's not very professional!

- **Try not to speed up towards the end!** You may be tired, but the last parents to see you may well have been waiting a long time, and they deserve just as much of your attention as those you saw at the beginning of the evening.

44. Dealing with difficult parents

'Difficult' parents usually are ones who come to complain! The best advice to offer is not to deal directly with difficult parents – but get someone who is paid to do that sort of job to handle it. This does not always work out so easily in practice. The following suggestions may help you when it falls to you to sort out a difficult situation. The first two suggestions are evasion tactics – but you'll need the rest sooner or later too!

- **Refer the complaint to your head of department.** Alternatively refer it to a more senior member of staff and if possible get them to deal with it without involving you in face-to-face contact with the parents. (Perhaps you should also pass on to your senior colleague a copy of this list!)

- **If you have made a mistake, admit it.** Report it factually to your head of department or headteacher and let them sort it out on your behalf.

- **Develop your listening skills!** The cause of many difficult encounters is that parents don't feel that we are letting them tell us what is concerning them. It's all too easy to jump in far too early to try to defend ourselves. Let them have their full say – indeed draw their concerns from them. Then prepare to reply.

- **Think of difficulties in terms of situations and actions, rather than people.** Explain to parents (and pupils) that it has nothing to do with particular personalities, but is a matter of events, consequences and effects.

- **Avoid difficulties 'spilling over'.** When you have had a difficulty with a pupil (or a parent) over one matter, make it clear that this does not cause you to bear a grudge, and that you are treating every new situation as a fresh start.

- **Rehearse the rationale of your own position.** Before you discuss any matters concerning their child with parents, make sure that you are clear in your own mind of the reasons for your actions and behaviour. If they can see your point of view, they are likely to become less difficult.

- **Stay calm, don't get drawn into arguments.** Repeat your own version of events and justify it in a professional manner. Avoid confrontation – know when you can back down discreetly and when it is important not to. When you suspect that there could be major difficulties, ensure that you don't see parents completely on your own.

- **Be prepared to understand, even when you don't agree.** Often, difficulties can be caused when parents can't see that you understand their point of view. If you can convince them that you do indeed understand, but in your professional capacity can't agree with them, they may become more ready to listen to your point of view.

- **Be the first to re-build bridges.** This sometimes goes against human nature, but we teachers as professional people are often better able to re-open channels of communication after a difficulty.

- **Use encounters with difficult parents as a learning opportunity.** Painful as it may be at the time, we can build up a lot of experience by learning from each encounter and asking ourselves, 'What would I do differently if a similar situation arises tomorrow?'

45. Coping with emergencies

We can forgive ourselves for having nightmares about emergencies and how we might cope with them! However, an important part of the learning experience of our pupils is seeing how we cope with the unexpected. The following suggestions may help you rise to the occasion when necessary:

- **Look positively at emergencies.** Remind yourself that each emergency you are faced with is a productive learning experience, and that next time a similar situation arises, you will have your additional experience to help you out.

- ■ **Be prepared.** Anticipate as many emergencies as is reasonable to expect. For example, get some training in first-aid. Being that bit more confident can make a lot of difference to how you feel when coping with a crisis.

- ■ **Expect the unexpected!** 'Emergencies' are by definition 'the unexpected'. Take positive steps to be alert to early-warning signals, so that nothing is really unexpected.

- ■ **Know someone who's good at dealing with the unexpected.** Build your own support network of people who are good at handling difficult or stressful situations. Learn from them, observing their coping strategies.

- ■ **Don't try to do all the coping on your own.** Other pupils may be able to do useful things to help you to focus your own efforts on the most critical parts of the actions needed to handle an emergency.

- ■ **Move the emergency.** When possible, take the emergency to a less public place. A quiet corner of an empty classroom may be better territory to sort out an emergency than in front of a whole class.

- ■ **No one can handle all emergencies first time.** Don't expect that you are required to cope with distinction with each and every emergency you ever meet. When things don't work out, don't dwell on feelings of failure, but rather extract what you can learn from the situation, then let it go.

- ■ **Collect case lore.** With colleagues, build up a collection of case study notes on emergencies and how they were handled. Learn from things that succeeded in the past, and also from things that could have been handled more successfully with hindsight.

- ■ **Be ready to act.** Be as prepared as you can. For example, have quick access to pupils' home addresses and telephone numbers, and ensure that you keep your personal data file updated and close to hand.

- ■ **Don't panic!** Being seen to panic helps no one. Try to appear calm and collected even when your mind is in a whirl! Remind yourself that emergencies are usually over in a very short time – it only *seems* like a century.

BEING AN EFFECTIVE COLLEAGUE

A commonly overheard remark in the staff room is, 'I can cope with the kids, it's the other teachers that are driving me up the wall!' This short section offers some advice on how to work effectively with fellow professionals within the school, how to take care of yourself, and some thoughts on looking to your own future:

46. Working with colleagues

It can be lonely at the chalkface. Yet it does often carry the comfort of privacy. However, with cross-curriculum developments and initiatives, it is becoming increasingly important for teachers to be able to work together effectively and constructively. There are many benefits to be realized from collaborative working, not least the fact that colleagues can take over from us at short notice when necessary. It also helps to feel you have friends and allies when the going gets tough. The following suggestions may help you to take advantage of such benefits.

- **Collaborate with colleagues.** Co-produce with colleagues teaching and learning materials as much as possible so you have co-ownership of resources. The quality and effectiveness of resources produced by more than one teacher is much higher than we could have achieved on our own (your two co-authors have found this in writing this book together!).

- **Keep colleagues well informed.** Carefully brief colleagues working with you, especially any part-time colleagues or temporary teachers who could not be with you during planning discussions for the courses you're teaching. Keep colleagues informed about how your own work is going too.

- **Plan how you will work jointly.** Plan and organize your collaborative work well in advance, for example by using flowcharts to show how your roles will integrate.

- **Plan to be able to cover for each other.** Develop your ability to provide emergency backup for other colleagues to cope with contingencies. Help colleagues become able to take over from you at short notice when necessary too.

- **All work and no play?** Take full advantage of social opportunities to get to know colleagues informally, so you can enjoy each other's company out of the context of your work as well as in school.

- **Don't be seen to disagree!** Ensure that when your views or opinions differ with those of colleagues, you avoid arguing in the presence of pupils! And if you are new to teaching, don't forget you may have a lot to learn from older hands.

- **Keep to deadlines.** Meet deadlines for collaborative tasks when colleagues are relying on you keeping to schedules. Attend meetings promptly and properly prepared.

- **Share your own resources and skills.** Make available to colleagues your teaching materials, including overheads, handouts and exercises. Invite colleagues to observe or participate in some of your lessons, and ask for their comments on how the sessions went. Similarly, respond to colleagues' invitations or requests to sit in on their lessons, and give them feedback kindly and supportively when they request it.

- **Be willing to ask for help.** Seek advice and suggestions from colleagues (even when you don't need it) and make your colleagues feel valued and respected for their help.

- **Monitor collaborative working.** Promote the benefits of team teaching to colleagues, and help them start to work in teams. Take time to review openly the processes by which you work together, and improve and develop these processes whenever you can.

47. Coping with difficult heads of department or senior staff

If you are finding one of your superiors difficult to deal with, the chances are you are not the only one. Find an ally and discuss the problem in confidence – it will give you the strength to carry on!

- **Be careful to distinguish between conflicts of ideas and conflicts of personality.** It's possible to work with people in either situation, but easier to manage when you know exactly what sorts of conflict are involved.

- **Refrain from inappropriately aggressive behaviour in conflict situations.** This includes consciously refraining from sarcasm, cynical remarks and bursts of temper.

- **Find out what other colleagues think too.** Get other colleagues to witness your achievements, as well as your boss. Enlist the support of others in your department and work together as a team.

- **Avoid letting previous differences of opinion colour current interactions.** It's possible to agree on present issues even when you've already disagreed on past matters.

- **Value other people's opinions, even when they're the opposite of your own.** You can disagree completely with what someone thinks about an issue, without taking away their right to have their own views.

- **Avoid the temptation to undermine the professional dignity or self-esteem of 'difficult' senior colleagues.** They will usually be in a position to return such actions doubly!

- **Check that you are indeed trying to do what senior colleagues ask you to do.** Make a note of what you have been asked to do and check this with a senior teacher before and after completion.

- **Identify the exact nature of a difficulty.** Talk about it to senior members of staff on a professional level, ensuring that others understand your situation. Try to develop a simple action plan to help you overcome the difficulty.

- **Cover your tracks.** Ensure that difficulties are placed on the agenda for department meetings, and that decisions are minuted – offer to take the minutes yourself if necessary.

- **Accept that it's not easy being the boss!** There may be all kinds of pressures, of which you are quite unaware, on your head of department.

48. Managing a department

Although you may not yet be in the position of head of department, it's useful to be aware of the issues involved in such responsibilities and the difficulties that might arise. Of course, if you're brave enough, you may decide to copy the suggestions below to your head of department (anonymously?).

- **Hold regular meetings with staff, which are timetabled in advance.** This ensures that everyone is ready to attend, even if there is little on the agenda. You can always cancel a meeting if there is nothing to discuss, but it's sometimes difficult to get colleagues together at short notice when there is something important to decide. Regular meetings, even if only brief, ease communication and foster a sense of belonging to a team.

- **Meetings should always have an agenda and be minuted.** Don't prolong meetings unnecessarily – prioritize items of business and set time limits for discussion if there is a lot on the agenda. Adopt the philosophy that a well-chaired one-hour meeting can always cover as much ground as a half-day meeting!

- **Get members of the department to take the minutes in rotation.** The act of minuting a meeting helps people to distance themselves at least temporarily from their own personal points of view, and overall helps to keep things in perspective.

- **Make the outcomes of meetings definite and accessible.** Ensure that things which must be done are put in writing and accompanied by a completion date, and that all colleagues receive them.

- **Delegate areas of responsibility fairly within the department.** Ensure that new or inexperienced colleagues also take some area of responsibility, however small.

- **Ensure that all staff feel valued and involved.** Involve all colleagues in discussions of the allocation of capitation, and in budgeting and ordering of stock.

- **Adopt a team approach to planning.** Get colleagues to work together to develop policies so that all are involved at every stage. When everyone in the department has a sense of ownership of plans and policies, there is much more certainty that the plans will come to fruition smoothly and quickly.

- **Keep everyone fully informed, but minimize paperwork.** Avoid excessive use of circulated papers and memoranda. These may move swiftly from pigeonhole to wastepaper basket! Use a notice board which all can access to aid communication. Have space on the board for individual colleagues to post replies or reactions to decisions, so that all views can be shared.

- **Plan social as well as business meetings for the department.** When people are friends as well as colleagues, a department runs happily.

- **Acknowledge difficult decisions.** When a decision needs to be taken on a matter where there are different opinions, facilitate a group session where staff can express the strengths and weaknesses they see in various alternative approaches to the decision. If there is no clear outcome, agree on a trial approach, with a review date when the matter will be discussed on the basis of experience of the trial.

49. Covering for absent colleagues

'Oh, but I'm indispensable!' Wouldn't we all like to think so? That fact is that now and again someone is going to have to take over for us, and sometimes at very short notice indeed. Similarly, we need to be able to cover for absent colleagues. The following suggestions may help you make your 'guest appearances' successful – and less stressful for you:

- **If possible get an oral briefing in advance.** When colleagues are taking planned absence, this helps you clarify exactly what you are required to do.

- **Try to have available an assortment of activities for all ages and abilities.** This can prove invaluable when you are left in the lurch without work set for pupils to do. Such activities might include crosswords, word-searches, reading tasks, puzzles and discussion topics.

- **Take with you an emergency pack of paper, ball-point pens and so on, for pupils to use.** Absent teachers often have the set of exercise books at home with them, especially if it is an unexpected absence.

- **Don't allow yourself to get drawn into discussions about how much better you are than their normal teacher!** This may be flattering, but doesn't engender a professional and collegial approach.

- **Don't be overambitious about what you can achieve.** Especially with a one-off substitution, be realistic about what you are likely to be able to do as a relative stranger to the pupils.

- **Don't stand for any nonsense.** Use all the techniques in your repertoire to settle pupils down and maintain order. Remember that pupils will often try to give cover teachers a hard time!

- **Don't be surprised if pupils are angry or resentful about you covering their class.** Some pupils hate change, and you may be replacing their favourite teacher.

- **Keep your sense of humour.** This may be difficult in trying circumstances, but do your best!

- **Be considerate to the absent teacher.** Ensure that pupils leave the room tidy, and count in all materials used. Coming back to depleted stock after an illness or emergency is not encouraging!

50. Coping with stress

Our job can be a stressful one. In addition, there are episodes of stress in most people's lives at one time or another. The following suggestions may help you to handle stressful times:

- **Accept that stress is a natural part of human life.** Accept also that it does not help at all simply to allocate blame for our feelings of stress, or to rail against the situation. It is more useful to find ways of coping with stress than to expend energy on wishing that it wasn't there.

- **Regard stress as useful!** Try to develop the attitude that every stressful situation can be viewed as a useful developmental experience. Learning to cope with stress, or even 'going under' temporarily, can both be used to build up coping strategies.

- **Monitor your stress levels.** Keep track of whether you are stressed or not – you may not realize it when you are in fact stressed. Other people can often tell us about our stress levels – provided we give them the chance and don't shout them down!

- **Decide when stress needs some action.** Accept that a certain amount of stress is actually healthy, raising our adrenaline levels and creative-thinking capacities. The time to worry about stress is when it gets in the way of a balanced, enjoyable life, or affects people around us.

- **Be aware of the symptoms of stress.** Remember that when we are stressed, we can easily magnify small irritations out of all proportion. If you find yourself overreacting to everyday things pupils do, don't blame them, it may be *you* getting things out of proportion.

- **Build up your own support network.** Include family, friends, colleagues and even relative strangers. Getting away from a stressful situation for a while can help us to recharge our batteries and return better able to handle it.

- **Exchange with colleagues and friends strategies for coping with stress.** It's most productive to do this at a time when you feel quite unstressed, as you can then look at the various coping strategies calmly and objectively.

- **It's up to us how we react to stress.** Common as it is for other people to get the blame for our stress, there's little anyone can do to alter how other people are, or how they behave. It is our task to readjust our reactions to stressful situations.

- **Many kinds of stress are completely avoidable.** These include the stress we may feel when we're late, or unprepared. But remember, it's sometimes possible simply to say 'No!'

- **Don't cross too many bridges!** One of the biggest stress factors we have to cope with is the possibility of failure or rejection. It is human nature to worry about many things that simply don't ever happen. Save your mental energies for handling the few things that need your coping strategies.

51. Planning your career progression

When you start out in teaching it may seem a miracle to you that you've managed to survive your first year without having a nervous breakdown or getting the sack! It can, however, be surprising how soon the opportunity may come up to develop your skills and further your career. INSET (In-service Education and Training) opportunities can play a vital part in extending the range of teaching that you can handle well:

- **Attend INSET wherever possible,** if at all relevant to your work. You could end up as the only person around with some specialist knowledge. The more things you know at least a bit about, the greater your employability. Keep an up-to-date record of the training you attend for your CV.

- **The best way to learn is to try to teach!** Make the most of every opportunity to run INSET workshops or discussions within your department or school in your own specialist area. However, if you are new to teaching, don't try to teach any grandparent to suck eggs!

- **Keep yourself informed.** Take an interest in wider educational issues; read the educational press and attend professional association meetings.

- **Set yourself clear goals** – even if they seem unrealistic to start with. Where do you want to be in five years' time and what would it take to get you there? Use the appraisal process to help you clarify and plan your personal and professional development.

- **Cultivate your profile.** Make sure that people know what you are doing in the classroom, and if you are involved in any initiatives, pilot schemes and developments.

- **Involve yourself in extracurricular activities.** Use your outside interests and hobbies to extend your contribution to the full range of things that the school offers pupils and staff.

■ **Take opportunities to work-shadow other colleagues.** One of the most productive ways of improving one's own teaching is to see how other people do it well – and better still, how they do it badly!

■ **Build up your own network.** Take every opportunity to make contacts with teachers involved in your subject in other schools. Exchange ideas and teaching and learning resources with them.

■ **Keep on studying.** Always be on the lookout for ways you can extend the subject range, which one day you may wish to teach.

■ **Build up your own teaching portfolio.** Keep a collection of things you have designed, reflections on new ideas you have tried out. Such a portfolio can be very valuable when it comes to appraisal interviews, or interviews for promotion or new posts elsewhere. It's often a good idea to keep a collection of photographs of activities and events you've organized or planned which might otherwise be difficult to document.

52. Applying for jobs

In most professions, including teaching, advancement nowadays more often seems to come through moving on than by staying put. The following suggestions may help you move on when you want to:

■ **Keep up your CV as an on-going task** – preferably on computer disk. It's extremely useful to be able to print off an updated copy at short notice, when an interesting opportunity seems worth applying for.

■ **Make your CV an interesting read** – not just a catalogue of all the things you've done in your career. If people find your CV interesting to read, they're likely to be keener to find out more about you, and your chance of being shortlisted for a job is increased.

■ **Get your wording right.** Take care in working out the wording you will use in a convincing letter of application for a post. Make such letters specific to the school and the post that you are applying for, and include indications of how you personally would approach taking on the post.

■ **Keep up appearances.** Remember how important the appearance of a completed application form can be. It's often difficult to type information into boxes on printed forms, so decide whether to engage a skilled typist, or to practise yourself on photocopies of the form until you can get it just right.

- **Know what you said to whom.** Especially when you may have several applications in progress at one time, it's essential to keep photocopies of exactly what you said in each particular instance. The exact words you used make ideal reading while preparing for any interview you're called to – it is the selfsame words that are being read by the interview panel.

- **Remember the importance of face-to-face communication skills**. If you are to convince other people at interviews, these skills will be valuable to you. Face-to-face skills at an interview are of course taken as an indicator of how you can work with pupils too.

- **Be prepared for open-ended questions.** Often, at an interview you will be asked to 'tell us a bit about yourself'. Such questions can be harder to handle than direct questions about your experience. Practise giving (say) a three-minute summary of your career to date, focusing on your successes rather than any difficulties you've met.

- **All interviews are useful experiences – even the painful ones.** Regard each interview not as the one-and-only opportunity to achieve the job of your dreams, but as a useful chance to develop and improve your approach in the future. It's often when you don't particularly want the job in question that you're offered the most interesting options!

- **Practice helps a lot!** If you have the chance, practise your interview technique with friends or colleagues. It's good for any of us to become used to the sound of our own voices answering questions and talking about our aims and ambitions.

- **Don't let your technique go rusty!** Apply for new jobs regularly anyway, even when you're perfectly satisfied with your present post. It's always useful experience to take stock of your career to date, and it's often valuable to show your colleagues that you're not necessarily content with your present status. 'Nothing ventured, nothing gained' is a useful motto!

INFORMATION AND COMMUNICATIONS TECHNOLOGIES

In the last 10 years, the use of Information and Communication Technologies (ICT) in schools (and throughout society in the developed world) has expanded faster than most people would have imagined possible.

We continue this part of the book with a selection of suggestions about using various computer-based and electronic means to help your pupils learn effectively and enjoyably. We have also included in this section some suggestions relating to simpler media such as video and audiotape since, when using these, as much care needs to be taken as when using the most sophisticated ICT – in particular, keeping the intended learning outcomes firmly in view, and making sure that pupils learn actively from each medium.

We hope that the suggestions in this section will help you to bring your pupils and your teaching into the modern world of IT. We also hope that these suggestions will help *you* to find out more about any of these technology dimensions with which you're not already familiar.

53. Choosing computer-aided learning packages

Computer-based packages are widely used in schools, and also play a valuable part in open learning programmes, and indeed have largely been developed for the open learning market. As open or flexible learning pathways are used more widely within school provision, the range of computer-based learning resources continues to grow rapidly. There may well exist computer-based packages that will be helpful to your own pupils. The following suggestions may provide you with help in selecting computer-aided learning packages for your pupils:

■ **Remember that it's harder to get a good idea of the effectiveness of computer-based materials than for paper-based ones.** This is not least because it's not possible to flick through the whole of a computer-based package in the way you can with a printed package. It can be quite hard to get a feel for the overall shape of the learning that is intended to accompany a computer-based package.

■ **Choose your packages carefully.** The best computer-based learning packages are not always those that look most attractive, nor are they necessarily the most expensive ones. The best indicator of good packages is evidence that they cause learning to be successful. Where possible, try them out on pupils before committing your school to purchasing them. Alternatively, ask the supplier or manufacturer for details of clients who have already used the packages, and check that the packages really deliver what you need.

■ **Prepare your own checklist to interrogate computer-based materials**. Decide the questions that you need to ask about each possible package. Questions could include:

– Are the materials supplied with workbook elements?
– Do pupils themselves *need* these elements?
– Can support materials be freely photocopied?
– What is the standard of the equipment needed to run the packages effectively?
– What level of technical support and backup will be required?
– Is this available within your school?
– Does the software include individual pupil-progress monitoring and tracking?
– Do the materials make good use of pre-test and post-test features?
– Can the materials run effectively on a network?
– Are there licensing implications if you wish to run the package on more than one machine?
– Can you afford multiple copies if the materials are multimedia, single-access packages?

■ **Try to establish the pedigree of the software.** Some computer-based packages have been thoroughly tested and developed, and have been updated and revised several times since their launch. Such packages normally give some details of the history of their development. Beware of packages, however well presented, that have been published or disseminated without real trialling.

■ **Find out about packages from colleagues in other schools.** Use your contacts. Ask them what packages they know of, which ones work well and really help pupils to learn. Also ask them about packages that they don't rate highly, and about the factors that led them to this conclusion.

■ **Try before you buy.** Computer-aided learning packages can be quite expensive, especially if you need to purchase a site licence to use them on a series of networked computer terminals, or to issue pupils with their own copies on floppy disk. If you're considering buying a particular package, try to get a sample of your pupils to evaluate it for you. Their experience of using it is even more valuable than your own, as only they can tell whether they are learning effectively from it.

■ **Look at how the medium is used to enhance learning.** If the material does no more than present on screen something that could have been presented equally well on paper, it's probably not worth investigating further. The medium should do something that helps learning, such as causing pupils to engage in interaction that they may have skipped if the same tasks or questions were set in print.

■ **Get familiar with the package before letting your pupils loose on it.** There is a learning curve to be ascended with most computer-based packages, and it is best if you go up ahead of your pupils. They will need help on how to make best use of the package, as well as on what they are supposed to be learning from it. Find out what it feels like to use the package. By far the best way to do this is to work through the package yourself, even if you already know the subject that it covers. Find out what pupils will *do* as they use the package, and check whether the tasks and activities are really relevant to your pupils, and pitched at an appropriate level for them.

■ **Check the intended learning outcomes of the computer-based package.** The best packages state the intended learning outcomes clearly within the first few screens of information. Alternatively, the intended outcomes may be spelt out in supporting documentation that comes with the package itself. The main danger is that such packages address a wider range of intended outcomes than are needed by your pupils, and that they may become distracted and end up learning things that they don't need to, possibly interfering with their assessment performance.

■ **If necessary, rephrase the learning outcomes associated with the package.** It may be useful to tell your pupils exactly what the learning outcomes mean in the context of their particular studies. This will help them to concentrate on the most important things in the package.

- **Think about access to equipment and software.** It can be prohibitively expensive to give each pupil access to the software and hardware needed. However, if the package is an important part of their overall programme, ways need to be found to maximize their opportunity to work with it. Some packages come with licence arrangements to use the package with a given number of pupils, or on a whole-school basis, either allowing multiple copies to be made, or the package to be used over a network. Ensure that the software is protected in order to prevent unauthorized copying or unlicensed use.

- **Think how pupils will retain important ideas from the package, after they have used it.** Make sure that there is supporting documentation or workbook materials, as these will help pupils to summarize and remember the important things they gain while using computer-based packages. Where such resources don't already exist, you should consider the benefits of making a workbook or an interactive handout, so that pupils working through the package write down things (or record them) at important stages in their learning.

- **Ensure that learning-by-doing is appropriate and relevant.** Most computer-based packages contain a considerable amount of learning-by-doing, particularly decision-making, choosing options and entering responses to structured questions. Some of the tasks may not be entirely relevant to the intended learning outcomes of your course, and you may need to devise briefing details to help pupils to see exactly what they should be taking seriously as they work through the package.

- **Check that pupils will get adequate feedback on their work with the package.** Much of this feedback may be already built in to the package as it stands. However, you may need to think about further ways of keeping track of whether your pupils are getting what they should from their use of the package. It can be worth adding appropriate, short elements to teacher-marked assignments, so that there is a way of finding out whether particular pupils are missing vital things they should have picked up from the package. One of the main strengths of computer-based learning packages is that pupils can be given instant feedback every time they select an option in a multiple-choice question, or key-in a word or phrase, and so on. The feedback should be much more than just the correct answer to the question or task. Pupils who get it wrong need to find out from the programme *why* their answer or response was wrong, and exactly *what* was wrong about it.

- **Check how long the package should take.** The time spent by pupils should be reflected in the learning payoff they derive from their studies with the package, and this in turn should relate to the proportion of the overall assessment framework that is linked to the topics covered by the package. Many computer-based learning packages come with indications of the expected timescales that are involved in using them, but it's well worth finding out how long typical pupils actually take. Some computer-based packages can make this easier for you by logging the amount of time individuals spend working through them.

- **Think ahead to assessment.** Work out what will be assessed, relating directly to the learning that is to be done using the computer-based materials. Make sure that pupils, before working through the computer-based materials, know *what* will be assessed, *when* it will be assessed, and *how* it will be assessed.

■ **Explore software that keeps tracks of pupils' progress.** Many computer-based materials can be used to track individual pupils' progress through them. This can involve pre-testing and post-testing, and storing the data on the computer system, as well as monitoring and recording the time taken by each pupil to work through each part of the package. Such data can be invaluable for discovering the main problems that pupils may be experiencing with the topic and with the package itself.

■ **Seek feedback from your pupils.** Ask them what aspects of the package they found most valuable, and most important. Ask them also what, if anything, went wrong in their own work with the package. Look in the feedback you obtain for anything that throws light on particular categories of pupils finding difficulties with learning from the package (for example, speakers of other languages, or pupils who are not confident with new technologies). Where possible, find alternative ways of addressing important learning outcomes for those pupils who have particular problems with the computer-delivered materials.

54. Getting pupils used to the idea of learning from a machine

Even though many of your pupils will have a lot of experience of playing with computer-based games, some are likely to believe that they need a human being to teach them, and that they can't learn from mere machines. The following suggestions may help you to win them over, so that they are more receptive to letting computers teach them too (if, indeed, computers can be considered to 'teach' at all):

■ **Remind them that there's always a human brain behind the machine.** When necessary, explain to pupils that the computer is merely a vehicle for storing human expertise, and that it's not actually the computer that will be planning what they should learn.

■ **Perhaps tell them that the computer may be better than you are!** In other words, the expertise that will have gone into the computer-designed learning packages is likely to be broader than that of any one person. The people who put together good-quality learning packages are normally very experienced in their field, and are likely to be expert teachers in their own right.

■ **Explain that working (as opposed to just playing) with computers is an important life skill.** Gaining confidence and competence with computers is likely to spill over into your pupils' future careers and lives, and will make them more easily updated and re-trained as further advances are made in their fields.

■ **Convince your pupils that learning from computers can be great fun.** Once they are over any fear that they will break the equipment, or that the computer will 'think' that they are silly, most people actually take pleasure in getting a computer to work for them. (Only try this one if you are already convinced yourself!)

■ **Remind your pupils of the comfort of making mistakes in privacy.** When pupils get tasks or exercises wrong, in computer-based learning only the computer knows – and computers don't mind! Therefore, it's much better to learn from their mistakes using a computer than when human teachers can see each and every slip.

■ **Point out that when using computers, your pupils don't have to waste time on things they already know.** In class, the whole group is often held up until someone catches up. With computers, anyone who already knows something can press on to something more demanding, without having to wait for anyone to catch up. Computer-aided learning can accommodate pupils' own pace of learning.

■ **Computers don't mind the plea: 'run that by me again'.** Some things are not learnt properly first time round. It's not always convenient (or possible) to ask a teacher to go once more through something that a pupil might find difficult, but a computer will go through it as many times as it takes to get the message firmly home.

■ **Remind your pupils that they learn most things by having a go at them.** When they learn-by-doing using a machine, they're being supported every step of the way, and most computer-based packages are highly interactive, and force pupils into making decisions, working things out, selecting the best answers to questions from a range of alternatives and so on. This means that these aspects of their learning can be much more focused and efficient than in a group-learning situation.

■ **Suggest that teachers are there for more important roles.** While pupils can learn things from machines, human beings are better at helping to measure and evaluate their learning, and explaining in other ways any parts that the computer was unable to teach them.

■ **Remind them that they don't have to work alone with computers.** While it may be intended that the computer-based learning materials are for individual use and independent learning, it can be very useful for clusters of pupils to explore together a learning package. This allows them to compare notes on what they find out, and to learn from each other and explain things to each other. This can be a useful first step before setting out to work through a package in depth, independently.

55. Getting pupils used to mouses and keyboards

It is increasingly recognized that pupils need to be equipped to function in the world of computers, electronic communication and the Internet. Most pupils are highly developed in their use of computers from their experience in primary schools. The skills involved all start with them being able to use the basics of all computer-based systems: keyboards and mouses. Becoming good at using computers, like most other things, is best learnt by doing it. The following suggestions may help you to make the processes of gaining skills in using keyboards and mouses more enjoyable and efficient for any of your pupils who have not already picked up skills and speed in primary schools:

- **Remind your pupils that in most computer operations, not all of the keys need to be used.** The most important keys tend to be the 'enter' key (for commands), the letter keys for text entry, and the number keys for number entry or calculations. The function keys may be much more rarely used, especially when first starting to use computers.

- **Make the most of 'undo' facilities in software.** In many word-processing packages, for example, it is possible to 'undo' a series of keyboard entries. This can be particularly useful when pupils can't remember exactly what they actually did, but know that something has gone wrong. They can also try using the 're-do' command to find out, step-by-step, what they may have done when something went wrong.

- **Encourage your pupils to learn to touch-type.** They may not have time to do this during your lessons, but if they really want to do it, there are good computer-aided learning packages for just such a purpose. Explain that if they use computers a great deal, it's perfectly possible for them to become much faster at keyboarding than they may be at handwriting. Also explain that using the right fingers for the right letters makes keyboarding easier in the long run, even though it has to be learnt in the first place.

- **Consider the possibility of having at least one machine where plastic covers or stick-on labels obscure some or all of the letters on the keyboard.** This is one of the techniques used to help people to develop touch-typing skills. Tell pupils using such machines not to look at their fingers at all, but to watch the letters on the screen as they type. Remind them that it doesn't matter if they type incorrect letters; they can always delete them and try again until they get what they want on the screen.

- **Give your pupils computer-based exercises that require them to enter words or numbers from the keyboard.** Many computer-based learning packages, and also computer-managed assessment programmes, require pupils to use text entry and number entry for their answers to at least some of the interactive elements.

- **Help your pupils to become mouse-trained.** The best way for them to do this is simply to work through computer-based packages which require quite a lot of mouse-work, such as using drop-down menus, double-clicking icons and so on. Explain that it's a bit like learning to drive a car. While there are various kinds of mouse (including roller-balls, trackpads, and various other ways of manipulating the position of the cursor on the screen), once competence has been gained using one system, different systems are relatively easy to learn.

■ **Suggest to your pupils that they may benefit from varying the sensitivity of the mouse.** When they get really competent with a mouse, they are likely to prefer using fast speeds, but using slow speeds can help them gain confidence on the way.

■ **Get pupils to experiment with the size and shape of the on-screen cursor.** The biggest source of anxiety when learning to use a mouse, tends to be associated with 'losing' the cursor on the screen. Altering the colour and size of the cursor, to make it easier to spot, takes away much of this anxiety.

■ **Get your pupils to do some exercises using just the cursor keys on the keyboard.** These can normally do all the cursor movements that are normally done using a mouse, but are usually much slower and more cumbersome. Pupils are then more likely to appreciate the benefits of getting themselves mouse-trained.

■ **Choose some exercises that develop mouse skills.** It can be productive to get your pupils to play with a 'painting' programme, both to draw shapes and objects using the mouse, and to select and fill different areas of their drawings. People who have hang-ups about their artistic skills often find that they exceed their own expectations when trying to draw in a completely new medium.

56. Finding out how computer-assisted learning is going

The danger is that only the *computer* knows how well pupils are learning things from it during computer-assisted learning! The following suggestions may help you to keep track of your pupils' learning, and help you focus your interventions:

■ **Watch carefully as pupils start working through any new computer-assisted program.** Whenever you notice anyone who has become stuck, or who looks puzzled, find out exactly what the stumbling block was. Sometimes, you may *intend* them to become momentarily stuck, so that they work out for themselves what to do next, but at other times you may wish to adjust your briefing instructions, or the program itself, to prevent them getting stuck at such points.

■ **Use any tracking capability already built in to the computer programs.** Many computer-aided learning packages automatically track the various pathways chosen by individual users, and it can be very worthwhile to retrace individual pupils' steps from time to time, to diagnose any aspects of the program that could be causing confusion.

■ **Ask your pupils what they think of the computer-assisted packages.** However, don't just ask general questions; structure your questions to focus in on particular aspects of the packages. In particular, if you already know that a given element of the package seems to cause problems, target that element directly in your questions.

■ **Ask pupils what they like most about the learning package.** It's useful to ask them for a given number of favourite things, two or three for example. Analyse their responses, and look for ways that you can make more use of the things that they like. When selecting new packages, keep their preferences firmly in mind.

■ **Ask directly about what they *don't* like about a package.** Sometimes there will be nothing you can do to change the package itself, but you may still be able to adjust your briefings to pupils about how best to approach using the package. When possible, however, try to adjust the software itself so that the most common grumbles are eliminated.

■ **Consider getting the computer to collect pupils' feedback for you.** It may be possible, for example, to build into the learning package intermittent multiple-choice questions about how pupils are feeling about the package at given stages, and to use the computer to store their selections of options.

■ **Sometimes, use *groups* of pupils to provide you with feedback.** The feedback that you can get from groups can be more valuable than from individuals, as you capture the products of group discussion. For example, ask groups to prioritize what they like best about the package, and what they like least.

■ **Don't ask questions lightly.** However pupils' feedback is being gathered, don't waste their time on questions where you don't want to (or don't need to) know the answers. For example, there's no point gathering information on people's age, gender, occupation and so on unless you *know* that you intend to put to use the information that you gather. Most questionnaires can be reduced significantly without affecting their purpose.

■ **Use tests and exercises to find out how well pupils learnt from computer-based packages.** When you find something that most of them learnt well, try to work out what it was about the particular packages that caused such success. Conversely, if most pupils seem to have had difficult learning something, try to find out why this was also.

■ **Give pupils feedback about their feedback!** If you're just seen to be gathering information rather than doing positive things *with* the data you collect, pupils may not be particularly willing to give you well-thought-out feedback. Show your pupils that you take their feedback seriously. Tell them what you are planning to do as a result of their feedback.

57. Using e-mail to support learning

Electronic communication is addictive! Now, e-mail can be used by just about anyone with access to on-line computer networks or the Internet, and is no longer something just for technophiles. To most people who have already climbed the learning curve of how to use e-mail, the apprehension they may have experienced on their first encounters fades into insignificance. E-mail can be an important medium in learning. The following suggestions may help you to maximize some of the benefits it can offer both to you and to your pupils:

■ **If you haven't already used e-mail, try to find time to learn about it yourself.** In practice, you don't need to be highly experienced with it to be ready to start sharing your expertise with your pupils. When you've just learnt about it yourself, you may be in a better position to help your pupils into it, as you will still be able to remember the things you may have found difficult at first, and how to deal with them.

■ **Make sure that pupils get started with e-mail.** Write careful, step-by-step briefing instructions for your pupils. The computer literate people may hardly do more than glance at these before getting into the swing of using e-mail. However, for those pupils with less confidence or experience with computers, these instructions can be vital and comforting until they become familiar with the medium.

■ **Decide what you really want to do with e-mail.** There are numerous purposes that e-mail can serve, and you need to ensure that the purpose is always clear to your pupils. If they know *what* it is being used for, and *why* e-mail has been chosen for this, they are much more likely to get more out of it.

■ **Show pupils how e-mail can be used to send much more than words.** Although you may just want to use e-mail for routine communication with (and between) pupils, there are many more uses that the medium can lend itself to. Think about the possible uses of sending attached files, such as documents, assignments, digitally stored images, sounds and video-recordings. All of these can be edited or marked and returned to pupils, in the same ways as simple messages.

■ **Make most messages really brief and to the point.** Few people take much notice of long e-mail messages. If something takes more than one screen, most readers either dump them or file them. Encourage your pupils also to make good use of the medium, and to send several short messages rather than try to cram lots of points into a single missive.

■ **Take particular care with your e-mail message titles.** It can take ages to search for a particular e-mail if it's not clear what each message is about. The computer software can sort messages by date, and by sender, but it's more difficult to track down topics. Two or three well-chosen keywords make the most useful titles.

■ **Make the most of the lack of time constraints.** One of the most significant advantages of e-mail as a vehicle for feedback is that pupils can view the feedback when they have time to make sense of it. They can also look at it as often as they wish to, and you can keep copies of exactly what you said to each individual pupil.

■ **Be quick to reply to your pupils!** When pupils are accustomed to e-mail, they expect quick replies to their queries. If you're going to be away from your access to the system for more than a day or two at a time, it's worth letting all your pupils know when you will be back on-line.

■ **Make the most of the speed.** If you are using e-mail to deliver to pupils your feedback comments on work you have marked, the sooner pupils get it, the more likely it is that their own thinking is still fresh in their minds, and the feedback is therefore better understood.

■ **Encourage pupils to reply to your feedback**. This lets you know that it's been received, but more importantly gives them the chance to let you know how they *feel* about the feedback you have given them, or the mark or grade that you may have awarded them.

58. Helping pupils to get started with e-mail

The use of electronic mail has accelerated rapidly in the last few years. People who would not have been thought to be computer literate often take their first steps into the area because they are attracted by the benefits of e-mail. Some, perhaps many, of your pupils are likely to be up to speed with computers and e-mail, but the following suggestions may help you to whet the appetites of those who have not yet become 'mouse-trained':

■ **Mention how unlikely it is that pupils will break the computer!** Some pupils may worry that they may do something drastic and irreversible to expensive equipment. Remind pupils that the only thing they are likely to risk when using computers is losing some of the work they have done with the machine, and even this risk is quite small, with 'undo' commands in most computer software, and with good habits about saving work to disk every few minutes.

■ **Point out that e-mail is a way of practising useful written communication skills.** Getting pupils to communicate with each other, and with you, using e-mail helps them to develop their written command of the language, including payoff in terms of spelling and grammar. Seeing their own words on the screen rather than on paper can make them more aware of their strengths and weaknesses with the language.

■ **Promote the benefits of computer literacy.** The information technology revolution has meant that more and more people need to use computers in their everyday work and lives. Being computer literate also means that people don't have to rely on other people do perform various tasks for them.

■ **Remind pupils that an e-mail message need not be sent until they are completely happy with it.** This allows them to edit and polish their writing. If they were to attempt so much editing on a hand-written message, it could either look very messy, or have to be written out several times before the same amount of adjustments had been achieved.

■ **Remind pupils that e-mail can be viewed as environment-friendly.** The saving of paper can be significant. If the computing facilities are already available, it can be argued that using e-mail incurs negligible costs.

■ **Point out to pupils that they can save and keep their own e-mail communications.** By copying each e-mailed message to their own files or disks, they can keep track of all the messages they have composed and sent. Keeping similar track of hand-written messages is less likely, or would involve the trouble and expense of photocopying. Pupils looking back at a range of e-mails they have composed can see for themselves how their skills with the language are developing.

■ **Help pupils to take that first step.** Probably the best way to do this is for you to *require* all of your pupils to e-mail something short to you, with a time deadline. It can be worth thinking about using a short written exercise for this purpose, in which case you can attach at least some marks to the task. This can make all the difference to pupils who might otherwise not get round to finding out how to log in to the system and send an e-mail.

■ **Make pupils' efforts worthwhile.** If you've asked all members of a group to e-mail something to you, try to respond *immediately* (within a day or two) to each message as it arrives. The fact that pupils get a little individual feedback via e-mail from you, and quickly, helps them to see for themselves the potential of e-mail as a communication medium.

■ **Encourage pupils to write *short* e-mails!** One of the problems with e-mail communication is that people only tend to read the beginning of a message. If an incoming message is too long for immediate reading, people tend either to file it away for later reading (and forget it!) or simply delete it.

■ **Get your pupils to select, then print out, their best e-mails.** These can be part of the evidence that goes into their portfolios of work. Getting them to pick the best ones helps to remind them of what you're trying to get them to do regarding good communication with the medium.

■ **Be aware that it's relatively unlikely that generating enthusiasm will take that much effort.** In fact the only barrier we've come across is not having anybody to write to. Get kids to collect and swap addresses so they all have a potential audience.

59. Giving pupils feedback using e-mail

E-mail is particularly useful as a vehicle for giving pupils individual feedback on assessed work, and can save you time and energy as you mark their work. E-mail feedback can extend usefully, from time to time, to giving pupils feedback on hand-written work that they have submitted for assessment. The following suggestions may help you to exploit the benefits of e-mail, not least to save you time and energy in giving pupils feedback:

■ **Make the most of the comfort of privacy.** When pupils receive feedback by e-mail (as opposed to face-to-face or in class), they have the comfort of being able to read the feedback without anyone (particularly you!) being able to see their reactions to it. This is most useful when you need to give some critical feedback to pupils.

■ **Remember that you can edit your own feedback before you send it.** For example, you may well want to adjust individual feedback comments in the light of pupils' overall performance. It's much harder to edit your own hand-written feedback on pupils' written work. E-mail feedback allows you to type in immediate feedback to things that you see in each pupil's work, and to adjust or delete particular parts of your feedback as you go further into marking their work.

■ **Exploit the space.** Inserting hand-written feedback comments into pupils' written work is limited by the amount of space that there may be for your comments. With e-mail feedback, you don't have to restrict your wording if you need to elaborate on a point.

■ **Consider combining e-mail feedback with written feedback.** Occasionally, for example, you can write on to pupils' work a series of numbers of letters, at the points where you wish to give detailed feedback. The e-mail feedback can then translate these numbers or letters into feedback comments or phrases, so that pupils can see exactly what each element of feedback is telling them. The fact that pupils sometimes have to decode the feedback can help them to think about it more deeply, and learn from it effectively.

■ **Spare yourself from repeated typing.** When designing computer-delivered feedback messages, you should aim towards only having to type each important message once. You can then copy and paste any of the messages when you need to give several pupils the same feedback information. It can be useful to combine this process with numbers or letters which you write on pupils' work, and building up each e-mail to individual pupils by pasting together the feedback messages which go with each of the numbers or letters.

■ **Consider the possibilities of 'global' feedback messages.** For example, you may wish to give all of the pupils in a class the same feedback message about overall matters arising from a test or exercise. The overall message can be pasted into each e-mail before the individual comments addressed to each pupil.

■ **Check that your e-mail feedback is getting through.** Most e-mail systems can be programmed to send you back a message saying when the e-mail was opened, and by whom. This can help you to identify any pupils who are not succeeding at opening their e-mails. It can also be useful sometimes to end each e-mail with a question asking the pupil to reply to you on some point arising from the feedback. This helps to make sure that pupils don't just open their e-mail feedback messages, but have to read them!

■ **Keep records of your e-mail feedback.** It is easy to keep copies on disk of all of your feedback to each pupil, and you can open a folder for each pupil if you wish. This makes it much easier to keep track of your ongoing feedback to individual pupils, than when your hand-written feedback is lost to you when you return their work to them. If you use e-mail a lot for feedback, these collections of feedback save time when you come to writing reports.

■ **Make the most of the technology.** For example, many e-mail systems support spellcheck facilities, which can allow you to type really fast and ignore most of the resulting errors, until you correct them all just before sending your message. This also causes you to re-read each message, which can be very useful for encouraging you to add second thoughts that may have occurred to you as you went further in your assessment of the task.

■ **Use e-mail to gather feedback from your pupils.** Pupils are often bolder sitting at a computer terminal than they are face-to-face with you. Ask your pupils questions about how they are finding selected aspects of their studies, but don't turn it into an obvious routine questionnaire. Include some open-ended questions, so that they feel free to let you know how they are feeling about their own progress, and (if you're brave enough!) about your teaching too.

60. Helping pupils to learn with computer conferencing

There are several parallel names for this, including computer-mediated communication (CMC), computer-supported cooperative learning and, more simply, on-line learning. Whatever we call them, computer conferences can be of great value in learning programmes. Many of the suggestions made about e-mail continue to apply, but in this section we would like to alert you to some of the additional factors to consider with computer conferences.

You can set up computer conferences for special interest topics. Alternatively, it can be useful to set up broader conferences to serve particular identified needs of pupils across a range of groups, or across the whole school, or even in collaboration with other schools. The following suggestions may help you to maximize the benefits that your pupils can derive from computer conferencing:

■ **Note the differences between computer conferencing and other forms of electronic communication.** The distinguishing feature of computer conferencing is that many people can see the same contents, from different places, and at any time. The contents 'grow' as further notes and replies are added by participants. Most systems automatically alert participants to 'new messages' that have been added since they last viewed the conference, and allow these messages to be read first if desired.

- **Regard computer conferences as virtual classrooms, common rooms and libraries.** They can provide a virtual classroom, where the whole pupil group can 'meet'. They can be used to provide a virtual seminar room, closed to all but a small learning group of around six pupils. They can function as virtual libraries, where resource banks and materials are kept. They can also function as pupil-only gossip areas. Each of these ways of using computer conferences can emulate electronically the related best practice in face-to-face learning environments.

- **Get involved in computer-conferencing situations yourself first.** If you have access to e-mail or the Internet, one of the best ways to pave the way towards putting computer conferencing to good use with your pupils is to participate yourself. For example, join some discussion lists and experience at first hand the things that work and the things that go wrong with such means of communication.

- **Explore the computer conferencing systems from which you can choose.** If there is already a system up and running in your school, you will probably need to make the best of it anyway. If you're responsible for choosing the system, it's useful to do your research on this. There are several systems available round the world, each with their own formats, features and idiosyncrasies. If most of your pupils are not particularly computer literate, go for a system that makes it as easy as possible to log-on and to add messages.

- **Sell the idea to your pupils.** Explain the benefits of participating in computer conferences. Pupils can exchange a lot of information, both study-related and social, through such conferences. They can get peer feedback on their own ideas, and even on selected parts of their work. Participating in computer conferences helps pupils to develop computer-related skills, and can quickly help them to speed up their keyboarding skills.

- **Work out definite purposes for each computer conference.** Conferences are much more successful where they are provided to relate to identified needs, or specific intended outcomes.

- **Make sure that all of your pupils will be able to access all the conferences which you want them to.** Ideally, you may also intend them to be able to download and/or print chosen extracts from the conference for their own personal study purposes. You can only build a computer conference into a programme as an essential component if all of your pupils are able to participate. If the conference is just an optional extra for those able to join it, other pupils who can't may be able to claim to have been disadvantaged.

- **Provide good 'start-up' pages.** These are essentially the main topics of the conference, and are listed sequentially in the main directory of the conference. Conferencing takes place when participants add 'replies' to these pages. The replies are normally listed in the sub-directory of each start-up page in the order in which they are received.

- **Make each screen speak for itself.** Especially with 'start-up' pages, which introduce each topic in the conference, it's best that the essence of the main message takes up less than a single screen. Further detail can be added in the next few pages (or 'replies'). Encourage pupils contributing their own replies to keep them to a single screen whenever possible, and to send several replies with different titles rather than one long reply addressing a number of different aspects.

- **Choose the titles of starter pages carefully.** When pupils are looking at the directory of a computer conference, they will see the titles of these pages arranged as an index, in the order in which the pages were originally entered. Aim to make these titles self-explanatory, so that pupils can tell what each section of the conference is about directly from the directory, rather than having to read the whole of a starter page before finding out whether they wish to explore the topic further.

- **Don't cover too much in a starter page.** It's better if each section of the conference is relatively self-contained, and prescribed, rather than having topic pages that cover several different aspects. As new matters arise from pupils' replies to starter pages, decide whether to introduce new starter pages to carry these matters forward separately. Add your own responses directing pupils who may be following the conference themes regarding where in the conference each theme is being developed further.

- **Use the conference as a notice board.** Get into the habit of making the conference *the* best way to keep up with topical developments in the subject of study, as well as administrative matters such as assessment deadlines, guidance for pupils preparing assessments and so on. Try to make it necessary for pupils to log-on to the conference regularly; this will result in a greater extent of active contribution by them.

- **Use the conference as a support mechanism.** This can save a lot of your time. Elements of explanation, advice or counselling that otherwise may have had to be sent individually to several different pupils can be put into the conference once only, and remain available to all. Whenever your reply to an enquiry or problem raised by a pupil warrants a wider audience, the conference is there to do this.

- **Make the conference a resource in its own right.** Add some screens of useful resource material, maybe with 'hot-links' to other Internet sources that are relevant. It's useful if some such material is *only* available through the computer conference; this ensures that all your pupils will make efforts to use it.

- **Try to get pupils discussing and arguing with each other via the conference.** The best computer conferences are not just teacher–pupil debates, but are taken over by the pupils themselves. They can add new topics and bring a social dimension to the conference.

- **Consider having some assessed work entered onto the conference.** If pupils *have to* make some contributions, they are more likely to ascend the learning curve regarding sending in replies, and to do so more readily in non-assessed elements too. One advantage in having an assessed task 'up on the conference' is that each pupil can see everyone else's attempts, and the standards of work improve very rapidly.

■ **Moderate computer conferences rigorously.** For example, remove anything offensive or inappropriate before it is likely to be seen by many pupils. If particular pupils misuse the conference, treat the issue seriously, and seek them out and warn them of the consequences of such actions, for example loss of computer privileges. It's useful to recruit pupil moderators from those pupils who are particularly computer literate, and who may be only too willing to become conference moderators, editing and rearranging contributions to keep the structure of the conference fluent and easy to follow.

61. Using video for learning

Video recordings are widely used in many forms of teaching and learning, and already play valuable roles in helping to show pupils things that they would not be in a position to explore on their own. However, the act of watching material on a television screen is not one of the most powerful ways through which pupils actually learn, unless the video extracts are carefully planned into their learning programme. The following suggestions may help you help your pupils to make the most of video:

■ **Decide whether the video is just for fun.** It's perfectly legitimate to decide that a particular video showing will just be a 'sit back and watch this' occasion, and that pupils will be expected to do no more than enjoy the experience. If this is the case, tell your pupils so. However, such occasions are a luxury, and it's important to tell pupils whether or not a video is an integral part of something that they are learning. The remaining suggestions in this section aim to help you make best use of those videos that are not just for fun.

■ **Decide what the intended learning outcomes directly associated with the video extracts will be.** It's important that any video extracts are not just seen as an optional extra by your pupils. The best way to prevent this from happening is to tell them exactly what they are intended to gain from each extract of video material.

■ **Decide why video is the best medium for your purposes.** Ask yourself, 'What is this video extract doing that could not be done just in print?' Video extracts can be invaluable for showing all sorts of things that pupils could not experience directly, as well as for conveying all of the subtleties that go with body language, facial expression, tone of voice, and interpersonal interactions, skills and techniques.

■ **Decide** *how* **the video material is planned to help your pupils to learn.** Is it primarily intended to whet their appetites and stimulate their motivation? Is it designed to help them to make sense of some important ideas or concepts that are hard to learn without seeing things? Is it designed to give them useful briefings about things they themselves are intended to do after watching the material?

- ■ **Consider whether your pupils could need their own copies of the video.** If they are intended to watch the video a number of times, and at their own choices of points during their learning, you may need to issue them with personal copies, or make them available on loan. Alternatively, you may be able to arrange for the materials to be viewed on demand in a resources centre. If so, make sure that there are mechanisms enabling pupils to book a time-slot when they can see the video material.

- ■ **Decide what your pupils will take away after watching the video.** One of the dangers with video extracts is the 'now you see it, then it's gone' situation. If the video is serving important purposes for your pupils, they will need to have something more permanent to remind them of what they learnt from it. Since, even if they have their own copies of the video material, they are unlikely to find time to revise from it directly, it's important that they have some other kind of summary of what they are expected to remember from it.

- ■ **Work out what (if anything) will be assessed.** If the video is just 'icing on the cake' and there is nothing arising from the video material that will be directly involved in any form of assessment, tell your pupils that this is the case. When things they derive from using the video elements *are* involved in their assessment, explain this to them, to help them give the video materials appropriate attention.

- ■ **Use short extracts at a time.** People are conditioned to watch quite long episodes of television, but to do so in a relatively passive way. Make sure that your pupils approach video extracts in a different way to that which they normally use for watching television. It's better to split up a 30-minute video into half a dozen or so separate episodes if there are several different things you wish your pupils to get out of the material. Some video materials have timings encoded onto the videotape.

- ■ **Set the agenda for your pupils *before* each episode of video.** This can be done by you before showing each of the video extracts, or can be done through accompanying handout materials. Either way, ensure that your pupils are set up with questions in their minds, to which the video extracts will provide answers.

- ■ **Consider giving your pupils things to do *while* they view the video extracts.** You could brief them to note down particular observations, or to make particular decisions, or to extract and record specific facts or figures as they watch the video episodes.

- ■ **Consider asking your pupils to do things *after* they've watched each extract.** This can help them to consolidate what they've gained from watching the extracts. It can also prompt them to try to have a further look, if this is possible, at any extract where they may have slipped into passive viewing mode and missed important points.

■ **Don't underestimate the importance of handout support materials.** To make the most of video elements, pupils need something in another medium to remind them about what they should be getting out of the video, and where it fits into the overall picture of their learning. Video recordings often work best when supported by a task-sheet or workbook, into which pupils write their observations and their interpretations of what they see. Their learning from such handouts can be reviewed by looking again at them, even without looking again at the recording.

62. Using audiotapes for learning

Audiotape is so commonplace and cheap that its potential in learning contexts is easily overlooked. In subject disciplines such as music, where sound is all-important, the use of audiotapes as a learning medium is already well developed. In multimedia packages, sound and images are often combined to good effect, yet audiotape can sometimes play a similar role at much less cost. The use of audiotapes to support learning can be extended to many disciplines. The following suggestions may help you to put audiotape to good use to support your pupils:

■ **Have good reasons for using audiotapes.** Always be in a position to explain to your pupils *why* an audiotape is being used alongside their other learning resource materials. Share with them information on what they should be getting out of using the audiotape.

■ **Most pupils have access to audiotape.** Many pupils have portable cassette players, and may use these when travelling on public transport, or jogging, and in all sorts of circumstances. When elements of learning packages are available as audiotapes, there is the possibility that you will extend their learning to times when they would not otherwise be attempting to study.

■ **Label audiotapes informatively.** People who listen to tapes tend to accumulate lots of them, and it's easy for audiocassettes accompanying learning programmes to get lost amid those used for entertainment.

■ **Disable re-recording.** Remove the tags from the back of each audiotape so that pupils can't accidentally record over the material on the tape. They can still do so deliberately of course, by placing adhesive tape over the tab positions! Always keep several back-up copies of audiotape materials that you issue to pupils, and don't expect to get all of your issued copies back intact!

■ **Keep audiotape extracts short and sharp, and link them to handout materials.** When there are specific intentions about what pupils should get out of listening to audiotapes, extracts should normally last for a few minutes rather than quarter of an hour! It is worth starting each extract with a recorded 'name' such as, 'Extract 3, to go with Section 1, Part 2', and to have the same voice reminding pupils when they have reached the 'End of Extract 3, going with Section 1, Part 2', and so on.

■ **Use audiotape where tone of voice is important.** It can be particularly useful for pupils to hear messages where the emphasis that you place on key words or phrases helps them to make sense of material that would be harder to interpret from a printed page or from a computer screen.

■ **Sound can help pupils into subject-related jargon.** When there is new terminology, for example, it can be hard to tell how to pronounce a word just by seeing it in print, and it can be humiliating for pupils to find when talking to a teacher that they've got their pronunciation wrong! Audiotapes can introduce the vocabulary of a subject to pupils. It goes without saying that audiotapes come into their own when helping pupils to learn the pronunciation of languages.

■ **Use audiotapes to bring learning to life**. Audiotapes can be invaluable for giving pupils the chance to hear people talking, discussing, debating, arguing, persuading, counselling and criticizing, and can capture and pass on to them many experiences and processes which would be difficult to capture in print.

■ **Clarify exactly when a recorded episode should be used.** If you're using audiotape alongside printed materials, it can be useful to have a visual 'flag' to indicate to your pupils when they should listen to a recorded extract.

■ **Turn pupils' listening into an active process.** Listening can all too easily be a passive process. Avoid this by setting your pupils things to think about before listening to a tape extract. Prime them with a few questions, so that they will be searching for the answers from what they hear.

■ **Consider using audiotape to give pupils feedback on their assignments.** It can be quicker to talk for a few minutes into a tape recorder than to write all of your feedback on your pupils' written assignments. The added intimacy of tone of voice can help you to deliver critical feedback in a more acceptable form. Besides, pupils may regard it as something special to have such a distinguished voice talking directly to them! Pupils can also play the tape again and again, until they have understood each part of your recorded feedback. Always try to begin and end with something positive, just as you would do with written feedback.

■ **Combine audio and visual learning.** For example, it can be useful to use audiotape to talk pupils through things that they are looking at in their resource materials. For example, complex diagrams or derivations in printed materials, or graphics, tables, spreadsheets shown on-screen in computer-based materials, can be brought to life by the sound of a human voice explaining what to look for in them.

63. Using multimedia packages for learning

Learning packages can contain, or refer to, an increasing range of other kinds of material. We explored the use of video above, but the present set of suggestions aims to alert you to the questions you should be asking yourself about *any* medium. This could include CD-ROMs, the Internet, intranets, interactive videos, and anything which adds sounds, still pictures, moving images or graphics to the experience of pupils working through learning materials:

- **How does the medium help pupils' motivation?** Ideally, any multimedia component should help pupils to want to learn from it. If there are too many steps to getting going with the multimedia elements, there is the danger that pupils can be put off, and maybe stopped in their tracks.

- **Can the medium be used to provide some learning-by-doing?** Perhaps the biggest danger with some multimedia packages is that however sophisticated the media used, pupils may only be spectators rather than players. Where it's not possible to cause pupils to interact directly with the materials, it remains possible to get them to make decisions, answer questions and summarize conclusions, and to write these down for later reference.

- **Can the medium be used to give pupils feedback?** The danger is that the information presented using multimedia is often fixed, and cannot then respond to what pupils may be thinking about it, or to the problems or misunderstandings that may be in their minds. Multimedia materials that *respond* to pupils immediately after they have done something are more effective at helping to make pupils' learning effective as well as enjoyable.

- **How does the medium help pupils to make sense of things?** There are often excellent answers to this question. For example, sounds, pictures, moving images and colourful graphics can all play useful parts in helping pupils to get their heads round things with which they've been grappling.

- **Why is this medium better than other, cheaper media?** For example, why is a computer-based package better than a print-based one? There are many good answers to this question. The best answers are when the medium chosen does something that just cannot be done by other media, for example moving pictures showing body language and facial expressions where such dimensions are crucially important for getting particular messages or attitudes across to pupils.

- **How relevant will the medium-based element be to the overall learning programme?** One of the dangers with media-based learning is that too much 'nice-to-know' material may be involved, and not enough emphasis placed on 'need-to-know' material, and that pupils may not easily be able to distinguish the two categories.

■ **How will the choice of medium affect pupils' opportunities to learn?** For example, will they only be able to study the particular elements concerned when they are sitting at a networked computer terminal, or when logged on to the Internet? Will this mean that they have frequently to stop learning until they can gain such access? Will there be alternative coverage of these elements of learning for any pupils who have not got easy access to the medium, and can it be guaranteed that they will not end up disadvantaged?

■ **How easy will it be to edit and change the medium-based elements?** Learning materials are never 'finished'. There are always adjustments and changes that are indicated from piloting, feedback from pupils, and from assessments measuring how well pupils actually succeeded in their learning. Some media are much easier to edit and change than others. Changing a CD-ROM or videodisk is a much more complex (and expensive) business than changing a file in a computer-based package.

■ **What *other* media could have been used?** There is rarely just one way to package a particular element of learning. It's useful to explore at least two or three alternative ways of using media to deliver each element of learning, and then to make an informed decision about *why* a particular medium is chosen.

■ **How will pupils revise and consolidate what they have learnt from the medium?** What will they have to take away? Will they be able to make a structured summary of what they learnt while working with the medium, which will bring all the important points back to their minds when looking at it later?

64. Helping pupils to learn from the Internet

The Internet is the electronic highway to the largest collection of information, data and communication ever constructed by the human species. There is information available through the World Wide Web on every imaginable subject. Playing with the Internet is easy, but *learning* from it is not always straightforward. The following suggestions may help you to point your pupils in directions where they will not only enjoy playing with the Internet, but also develop their techniques so that they learn effectively from it too:

■ **Consider starting small.** For example, you might be able to download selected information from the Internet onto individual computers, or a locally networked series of terminals. You can then give your pupils specific 'search' tasks, where it will be relatively easy for them to locate specific information.

■ **Get your pupils to induct each other.** Learning from the Internet need not be a solo activity. Indeed, it can be very useful to have two or three pupils working at each terminal, so that they talk to each other about what they are finding and follow up leads together. Encourage them to take turns at working the keyboard, so that they all develop their confidence at handling the medium, and are then equipped to carry on working on their own.

Help your pupils master the use of search engines. There are many free search engines available on the Internet. Some are faster than others, and some are more successful than others for tracking down particular fields of information. Give your pupils some exercises to help them find out which search engines suit them best.

■ **Give your pupils exercises that help them to improve their selection of search words.** Show them how choosing a single broad search word leads to far too many sources being listed, and make it very slow and boring to go through all of the sources looking for the information they really want. Get them to experiment with different combinations of search words, so that the sources that are located become much more relevant to their search purposes.

■ **Allow your pupils to find out about the different speeds at which information can be found on the Internet.** For example, let them experiment at different times of the day, so they can see when the Internet is heavily used and slower. Also, let them find out for themselves how much slower it can be waiting for graphics to be downloaded than for mainly text materials. Help them to become better at deciding whether to persist with a source that is highly relevant but slow to download, or whether to continue searching for sources that may download more quickly.

■ **Remind your pupils that finding information is only the first step in learning from it.** It is only too easy to discover a wealth of information during an Internet search, only to forget most of it within a very short time.

■ **Help your pupils to learn to keep tabs on what they've found.** Entering 'bookmarks' or 'favourites' is one of the most efficient ways of being able to go back easily to what may have turned out to be the most relevant or valuable source of information during a search. Get your pupils to practise logging the sites that could turn out to be worth returning to. Also help them to practise clearing out bookmarks that turn out to be irrelevant, or that are superseded by later finds.

■ **Give your pupils practice at recording things that they have found during searches**. It can be useful to design worksheets to train them to note down key items of information as they find them, and to teach them to be better at making their own notes as a matter of routine when exploring a topic using the Internet.

■ **Help your pupils to develop their critical skills.** The authenticity and validity of information found using the Internet varies enormously. It's not possible to tell whether information is good or bad just by looking at the apparent quality of it on the screen. Remind your pupils that information on the Internet may not have been subjected to refereeing or other quality-assurance processes normally associated with published information in books or in journal articles.

■ **Remind pupils to balance playing with the Internet and learning from it.** It's perfectly natural and healthy to explore, and to follow up interesting leads, even when they take pupils far away from the purpose of their searches. However, it's useful to develop the skills to ration the amount of random exploration, and to devote 'spurts' of conscious activity to following through the specific purposes of searches.

65. Using the Internet for learning

Pupils may be able to use the Internet at times of their own choice, in their own ways, at their own pace, and from anywhere in school or beyond, where access to it is available to them. That said, this doesn't mean that it's automatically a vehicle for productive and effective learning. Indeed, it's very easy to become side-tracked by all sorts of fascinating things, and to stray well away from any intended learning outcome. The suggestions that follow are not intended as starting points for setting out to *deliver* learning through the Internet, but rather to help pupils to *use* the Internet to obtain material to use in connection with their studies, such as in assignments they are preparing. The following suggestions may help you to help your pupils both to enjoy the Internet *and* to learn well from it:

■ **Play with the Internet yourself.** You need to pick up your own experience of how it feels to tap into such a vast and varied database, before you can design ways of delivering with it to your pupils some meaningful learning experiences.

■ **Decide whether you want your pupils to use the Internet, or an intranet.** An intranet is where a networked set of computers talk to each other, while using Internet conventions, but where the content is not open to the rest of the universe. If you are working in an organization which already has such a network, and if your pupils can make use of this network effectively, there will be some purposes that will be better served by an intranet. You can also have *controlled* access to the Internet via an intranet, such as by using hot-links to predetermined external sites.

■ **Use the Internet to research something yourself.** You may well have done this often already, but if not, give it a try before you think of setting your pupils 'search and retrieve' tasks with the Internet. Set yourself a fixed time, perhaps half-an-hour or even less. Choose a topic that you're going to search for, preferably something a little offbeat. See for yourself how best to use the search engines, and compare the efficiency of different engines. Find out for yourself how to deal with 4593 references to your chosen topic, and how to improve your searching strategy to whittle them down to the 10 that you really want to use!

■ **Don't just use the Internet as a filing cabinet for your own learning resources!** While it's useful in its own way if your pupils can have access to your own notes and resources, this is not really *using* the Internet. Too many materials designed for use in other forms are already cluttering up the Internet. If all you intend your pupils to do is to download your notes and print their own copies, sending them e-mailed attachments would do the same job much more efficiently.

- **Think carefully about your intended learning outcomes.** You may indeed wish to use the Internet as a means whereby your pupils address the existing intended outcomes associated with their subject material. However, it's also worth considering whether you may wish to add further learning outcomes, to do with the processes of searching, selecting, retrieving and analysing subject material. If so, you may also need to think about whether, and how, these additional learning outcomes may be assessed.

- **Give your pupils specific things to do using the Internet.** Make these tasks where it is relevant to have up-to-the-minute data or news, rather than where the 'answers' are already encapsulated in easily accessible books or learning resources.

- **Consider giving your pupils a menu of tasks and activities.** They will feel more ownership if they have a significant degree of choice in their Internet tasks. Where you have a group of pupils working on the same syllabus, it can be worth letting them choose different tasks, and then communicating their main findings to each other (and to you) using a computer conference or by e-mail.

- **Let your pupils know that the process is at least as important as the outcome.** The key skills that they can develop using the Internet include designing an effective search, and making decisions about the quality and authenticity of the evidence they find. It's worth designing tasks where you already know of at least some of the evidence you expect them to locate, and remaining open to the fact that they will each uncover at least as much again!

- **Consider designing your own interactive pages.** You may want to restrict these to an intranet, at least at first. You can then use dialogue boxes to cause your pupils to answer questions, enter data and so on. Putting such pages up for all to see on the Internet may mean that you get a lot of unsolicited replies!

- **Consider getting your pupils to design and enter some pages.** This may be best done restricted to an intranet, at least until your pupils have picked up sufficient skills to develop pages that are worth putting up for all to see. The act of designing their own Internet material is one of the most productive ways to help your pupils develop their critical skills at evaluating materials already on the Internet.

Part 2

Particularly for primary teachers

Classroom management and organization

Curricular responsibilities

Pastoral care

Making and managing resources

Assessment and record keeping

Your professional life

This part of the book was originally written before the advent of the National Strategies for Literacy and Numeracy in the primary sector in England and Wales, and the QCA Schemes of Work were still in their planning stages. The vast majority of the ideas and suggestions are, we believe, as valid as they ever were, though some may have been deprived of a little of their thunder. The classroom organization suggested by these developments means that some of the decision making about classroom management and organization has been taken for us, but there are still a great many decisions that need to be taken. We trust that these tips will help with this process.

CLASSROOM MANAGEMENT AND ORGANIZATION

When working with young children, the way that you set up and run a teaching space is crucial. Young children need to be clear about what's expected of them and how they're supposed to go about their work. A disorganized classroom or constantly changing routines make for chaotic lessons. This section contains some ideas on how to help ensure that your classroom and classroom organization make life as easy and stress free as possible, for you *and* the children in your class.

1. Preparing yourself for a lesson

To be sure of using the time you have with the children in school as efficiently as possible, you have to be properly prepared. This section looks at a range of issues you may need to consider and gives some practical ideas for helping you do this quickly and effectively:

- **Always start positively.** In all aspects of your work, try to approach everything as cheerfully as possible. It usually has a positive effect on those around you too. Children are quick to pick up on a negative atmosphere, and often react badly to it.

- **Know where you're starting from.** This helps to ensure that activities and questions can be pitched at the right level. Once you've had a class for a short time you will quickly develop a good idea of your class's abilities and knowledge. Experience of a year group also counts for a lot, but in the meantime it may help to ask regular class teachers (if you're on teaching practice) or previous class teachers for background data. Also, refer to previous work and records of the children involved. Of course, you could also start by asking the children!

- **Know where you're going.** In your long-term planning you will have identified your long-term aims for a topic or term, but it's essential to identify very short-term objectives for each activity or lesson too. Know in advance exactly what you're hoping the children will have learnt by the end of the lesson. This helps you focus on the sorts of questions, resources and support you may need to build in to the activity.

- **Know what resources you will need.** Consider what resources will make the activity you're working on easier to manage and give appropriate structure so that the children can work independently if necessary, helping to keep them on task.

- **Know where to find these resources.** Much of what you will need for your lesson will be readily available in school. Ask subject coordinators where possible about specific resources. Sometimes your own ideas can be adapted to fit the resources available but if not, you will need to either produce some resources yourself or delegate the task to auxiliaries or trainees if you have them in school. Ensure that you give *precise* instructions.

- **Allow plenty of time to set up.** Having all activities fully prepared and the resources readily available for the children before you begin the lesson will mean that they can settle to their work quickly. Even sharpening the pencils before the lesson means less fuss when the lesson starts! This isn't always appropriate because children do need to learn how to organize themselves too, but even this should be planned for.

- **Make a list of the main points to be included in the lesson.** A list of the main points you wish to cover in discussions with the children or instructions you need to give can help you put your original intentions into practice, even though this is not always that easy!

- **Decide who will work where.** Know where *you* will be working (your focus task). If you have nursery nurses, auxiliaries or parents helping in class, make sure you know what they're going to be doing too. You will need to give them clear and explicit instructions to make the best of their assistance.

- **Have backup activities to hand.** Consider what those children who might finish their work early will do. Try to build extension activities into the normal routines of the day. Having role-play areas, structured work in sand and water or free-writing areas, reading or number games, reading and non-fiction books applicable to the class you're teaching readily available will ensure that children are engaged in worthwhile activities while others finish off.

- **Have a checklist that shows what activities individual children or groups of children will be working on**. It can also show when they start and whether they have finished or not. It will help you keep track and is especially useful if you're running an integrated day.

2. Preparing the children for a lesson

Getting the children in your class prepared for work is essential to get the best from them in the time available. The following ideas might help you to get the children settled and paying attention with the minimum of fuss:

- **Welcome the children in to the class.** This gives you a chance to set the tone for the day. You will be able to welcome them properly but also to establish control and reinforce your expectations of them from the first moment.

- **Settle the children down.** Many classrooms have a collecting or carpeted area, a place to gather the children together for whole-class work and administration. Make clear to the class the rules that apply to the use of these areas. Having story or non-fiction books, puzzles, puppets or toys and some simple games available for the children in these areas gives them something to do and helps prevent disruptive behaviour.

■ **Manage things they might bring from home.** Matters that the children are likely to want to talk about, or items they may wish to play with, will be disrupted if they keep hold of things they've brought with them in class. If you want to encourage children to bring things into class for 'show and tell' sessions, have a space where they might leave their belongings or ask them to leave them in drawers.

■ **Establish the rules for registration.** Be imaginative: registration times can be fun and educational but you will need to be clear and consistent about the rules. Try allowing children to respond in different languages or accents, quietly or loudly, or time how long the register takes, and so on.

■ **Set the scene for an activity**. Start with what the children already know. Sometimes an activity will build on previous work, so remind the children of this work. Introducing new ideas will require more discussion, so allow time for this and consider how best to introduce the idea. Often stories, books or artefacts can be used, but asking children what they already know about a concept establishes a context well too.

■ **Ensure the children know *why* they're doing what they're doing.** Making sure that children know what they're supposed to learn helps them focus on the real point of the activity. Leaving them unsure of what they're trying to achieve means they might get the wrong end of the stick.

■ **Recap on the instructions you have given.** It's worth recapping on the main points of the activity the children will be tackling just before they start. With young children, try to keep the number of different instructions to a minimum.

■ **Give the children the chance to ask questions.** It's a good idea to let the children have the opportunity to check things out if they don't understand what's required of them. You can use this to reinforce the need for them to pay attention. Making it clear that you won't repeat your instructions once the lesson has started encourages good listening skills.

■ **Send the children to their jobs.** Getting the children to settle to their work quickly sets the right tone for the lesson. Sending them off in small groups, or even one by one, helps prevent a crush or arguments over who might sit where. It's worth spending the first few minutes ensuring the children make a good start on their work before getting on with your main focus activity.

■ **Consider the environmental needs of the children.** If the classroom is too warm or too cold, it makes it harder for them to concentrate. Try to get this sorted out before the lesson starts. Every so often, remind the children about others' needs and how important it is to let everyone get on with their work in peace.

3. Organizing an integrated day

Usually running an integrated day means tackling three or four activities covering different areas of the curriculum at the same time. If you're going to use this integrated approach it's usually best to do it on a regular basis so that children get into the routines involved. The following tips offer some routines that might come in useful:

- **Have one focus activity for each work session.** One of the main advantages of integrated activities is that you can structure each work session so that you can work with a small group on a specific task – the thing that you're actually going to teach. Let the children know where you're going to be working too!

- **Prepare other work for the rest of the class.** On the whole, these activities should be consolidatory tasks. Try to plan activities that the children will be able to tackle independently. Consider what resources you will be able to give the children to support them.

- **Organize your classroom for integrated activities.** If you're going to work on integrated activities, your classroom will probably need to be set up in areas where resources that support work in each curriculum area can be collected and made available for the children. You might also want to try to separate potentially noisy or active areas from areas for quieter and more settled activities.

- **Help the children to help you.** To allow you to get on with your focus activity, it's a good idea to instruct in advance those working on other tasks where they should put finished work and what they should do when they have finished, so as to avoid disturbing you. To help them manage their time it's also a good idea now and then to let them know how long they have got left.

- **Remember that not every area of the curriculum has to be tackled each day or even each week**. Trying to squeeze everything into a space where it doesn't comfortably fit might result in a waste of time for all concerned.

- **Be aware that administration of integrated days can be complex.** This is because you have to keep track of a range of different activities at the same time. Having a tick list that tables each child against each activity is virtually essential as is a key that shows when they do what and how far they have progressed.

- **Think about group sizes.** Generally it's easier to split up your class according to broad ability bands, but some activities are inappropriate for (say) 10 children to do at once. Practical activities, scientific investigations, art work, technology and so on may need to be done in smaller groups, so consider what the others might be doing at the same time.

- **Keep instructions simple.** Some children will need to work fairly independently. It's easy to bombard them with too much information. Often there will be points during work on your focus task where you can leave the children in your group to carry on independently. With careful management, you can use these times to give new briefings or reinforce previously delivered instructions or guidance to the other groups, or mark work.

■ **Remember that setting up for integrated days can be time-consuming.** This is because there are more activities to set up than when all of the children are working on one task. Try taking some of the pressure off and getting the children to set up the more practical tasks for you. If they have just done a particular activity they will have a fair idea of what's required, and besides, they love doing it!

■ **Make sure you finish the session as carefully as you started it.** At the end of the session you will probably want to get the children to start tidying up while you try to get round and check work. Having containers and spaces for storage of the equipment they have been using is really useful because it takes away a lot of the pressure of continually giving instructions about where things should go.

4. Providing for practical activities

The sorts of practical activity that you will want to tackle in your class obviously depend on the age of the children, the number in the class and how settled they tend to be. However, there are still some basic, underlying ideas that might help you organize and manage practical work. For ease they have been arranged into the three sections that practical activities tend to fall, but there is some overlap. It may be useful to consider the ideas outlined in 'Organizing an integrated day' too:

Scientific investigation

■ **Provide unstructured opportunities for investigation.** Giving the children the materials that they will be investigating as a 'choosing' activity some time before setting a more structured one gives them a good head start when it comes to trying to answer a specific question. For instance, leave out a range of batteries, wires and bulbs for a week or so, then ask them to try to make a circuit.

■ **Try to make sure that there's an adult to help.** Left to their own devices, children tend to stray from an intended path during investigations. This may be part of the point, but if you or another adult can be on hand to ask questions and listen to the children's responses, you will be able to keep the children focused on the original question.

■ **Consider whether you really need a written record.** The recording of an experiment (what the children observe and appear to find out) doesn't necessarily demonstrate understanding and can disrupt the children's concentration. A verbal report to the class, group recording using an adult as a scribe, a concept keyboard overlay on a computer, diagrams, Cloze procedures, cut-and-stick activities, and so on, can be effective too.

■ **Manage investigations to keep children on task.** You may want a small group to experiment as a group and without adult support. Keeping them on task will need structuring. This could be achieved by the use of worksheets, prompt cards, peer tutoring or something even more imaginative, such as displays or games.

Mathematical investigation

■ **Remember, you can never have too much practical equipment for maths.** This is most especially true when working with very young children and having this equipment on display and accessible to the children is important too. Having small children waiting their turn for equipment may be detrimental to attention and behaviour.

■ **Try to make practical activities relevant to children's lives.** If you want to tackle non-standard measures, comparing the height of the children, their hand spans, foot sizes, reach and so on, comparing spoons, chairs, beds or even eating porridge from different bowls after reading *Goldilocks and the Three Bears* is more relevant and memorable than 'colouring the biggest bowl in the picture'.

Art and technology

■ **Give the children ready access to materials that are available.** If they're able to get at what they need when they need it, they will not have to bother you so often. Set up your areas with as wide a range of materials on show as possible. In the long term this will give them more confidence in choosing appropriate materials too.

■ **For specific artistic activities, you will need to prepare the materials in advance**. If the table is ready for them to get on they will settle more quickly and it will tend to be less messy and a more efficient use of time. When preparing these resources bear in mind the intended outcome.

■ **When working on developing specific skills, select specific resources.** If you want children to work on colour mixing or cutting out in a focused practical task, selecting materials for them in advance will help them achieve the intended outcomes and avoid waste.

■ **Allow access to plenty of materials when working on design-and-making activities.** Where the task is more open-ended and the children have the opportunity to experiment, investigate and solve problems, a wider range of materials should be available. It may be worth taking the time to discuss some of these materials with the children, including their properties, how to join and cut them, and how to avoid waste.

5. Providing for consolidatory activities

Consolidatory tasks should be well thought-out and structured if they're going to be beneficial to the children and allow you the time to concentrate on your focus task. The following are some tried and tested ideas for effective consolidatory activities:

■ **Remember the importance of worksheets.** Just because it's on an A4 piece of paper doesn't mean it's 'death by worksheet'. Well-planned and interesting worksheets help to structure work for young children. They can keep children on task, help them concentrate and work with relatively little support and so assist you to achieve your aims.

■ **Be aware of the alternatives to worksheets.** Work cards might be more appropriate. If the activity requires something to keep the children focused on their work but doesn't have to help them structure the way they record their answers, a work card, backed in clear plastic or laminated to protect it, can be very effective and efficient because it can be used over and over, year after year.

■ **Collect together open-ended resources.** A set of cards with the letters of the alphabet, numbers 0 to 20, common initial letter blends or diagraphs, sight vocabulary words, days, times, seasons and so on come in useful time and again and can be used for a wide range of consolidatory activities without the need for new resources.

■ **Try to get a stock of open-ended worksheets.** Worksheets with no single specific purpose, like blank 100 squares or number pyramids, domino squares, alphabet ladders and so on are invaluable in a range of contexts. Having a stock of as many of these sorts of worksheets as possible and a wide repertoire of activities to go with them means you will never be without something useful to give the children.

■ **Collect jigsaws, dominoes, playing cards, dice and other such activity resources.** They're useful, worthwhile and familiar activities you will use time and time again, in a variety of educational ways.

■ **Children can design and make their own games.** If you've been studying a particular concept in number work or phonics, for example, asking the children to design and make a game about that idea is not only a worthwhile activity, but also a demonstration of exactly what the children have understood about the work you've been doing. It may even produce more resources for the rest of the class.

■ **Recycle resources used in structured activities.** If you've produced resources for an activity to introduce a new concept, you might be able to recycle them for use on a worksheet (for example, pictures on initial letter dominoes could be copied and used on work cards or sheets).

- **Experiment with peer tutoring.** There can be benefits for both parties! Often, when particular children have grasped a concept, then a good way of consolidating their ideas is by getting them to try to explain it to others who are still struggling. Sometimes they do it even better than a teacher, because they have the relevant perspective on the concept which helps the struggler too.

- **Share ideas with colleagues.** If you work in a school with more than one class to each year group, try sharing ideas and resources with the parallel class teacher. You could even split up the jobs to cover twice the ground!

- **Use homework to consolidate skills or concepts covered in class.** This opens up opportunities for parents or carers to tune in to the ways you're working with the children. It's best not to introduce new concepts in homework activities, as you may find that the approach adopted by parents is not in line with your planned way of covering them.

6. Keeping children on task

If you can keep children on task during work sessions, then you can avoid disruption and get on with what you really need to do. But juggling 30-odd children and three or four different activities in five or six groups is no mean feat. Recent strategies make much of whole-class teaching and short, sharp independent work, which should be a big help in itself but the following suggestions might offer some further ideas to help with this:

- **Try to keep to routines.** Children usually like and respond well to routine. If children know what to expect, they tend to stay more settled and concentrate better. As far as possible, try to develop routines for the everyday activities and stick to them.

- **Develop rules to encourage good work habits.** Making rules clear, concise and explicit so the children know what's expected of them is an important part of developing their 'social responsibility'. Sometimes children fail to notice that their behaviour has a significant effect on the rest on the class.

- **Try to group the children to avoid confrontation.** Some children just can't work together. It isn't always easy, but try to group children so that they're sitting and working with children with whom they get on well, but avoid them becoming over-excited.

- **Make the work appropriate and relevant.** This can make a great deal of difference to classroom management. If children are working on tasks that they can manage but that they find interesting then they will settle quickly and concentrate for longer! It's worth taking time to plan and differentiate your activities carefully because, in the long run, it will make your life a lot easier.

■ **Develop good time-keeping skills.** If children are clear about how long they have to finish a task, and you reinforce this throughout work times by letting them know how much time is remaining, it will help them to work more consistently. It's worth letting them know what the consequences of not finishing might be!

■ **Explain why they're doing what they're doing.** If children know what they're supposed to be learning or finding out about, it makes them more confident and so keeps them interested and motivated. Before they go about their work, tell them what you expect them to achieve.

■ **Consider your responses.** The responses you give to the children about their work are obviously really important and provide a good opportunity for motivating the class. A tick and a 'Well done' are fine for every day, but there are many much more imaginative responses. These include star badges, certificates, special jobs, showing work to the rest of the class, showing work to other teachers or to the headteacher, as well as your own comments in response to achievements. The list of tried and tested ways of keeping children interested is endless.

■ **Keep tasks short and sweet.** Some children have real problems concentrating for sustained periods. They may need specific help, and talking to your school's special educational needs coordinator is usually helpful. In the meantime, keeping tasks short, specific and familiar but as stimulating and achievable as possible will help them to stay on task, and children's ensuing successes may help improve their self-esteem.

■ **Try to be aware of the whole class.** Even if you're working on one specific activity, going round and checking work, praising effort and tackling minor problems will reassure children and remind them that what they're doing is still important.

■ **Offer praise and encouragement.** No teacher should be above a bit of 'bribery and corruption'! Setting goals and offering rewards, however simple, can have a positive effect on children's motivation to work.

7. Involving children

Ideas of ownership are closely linked to effective teaching and learning. The whole process is essentially about empowering children and helping them to play a role in their own learning. The following suggestions will possibly include many of the things that you already do in the classroom, but perhaps will give you additional ideas to build on:

■ **Work out as many different ways as possible for children to make inputs into your teaching and their learning.** For example, you could have daily or weekly targets. It'll be up to the children to decide when and how they work towards them, but insist that they must do them!

■ **Show children that you value their views.** When children make suggestions that are not sensible, don't reject them out of hand, but acknowledge them and then get the children to suggest how their ideas might be adapted to fit circumstances better. Build on what they say rather than destroy their confidence.

■ **Get children to brainstorm ideas in class.** Even when starting a new topic, it's useful to involve the class in a brainstorm to collect together the existing knowledge and ideas about the subject. This will give you a clearer idea of where they're starting from, and developing their sense of ownership will help them focus on the work in hand.

■ **Collect feedback from children.** Find out from them details of what they enjoy and why they enjoy it. Similarly find out what they dislike and why they dislike it. Then use this to inform the decisions that you make about classroom activities.

■ **Try to respond positively to any suggestions children make.** Explain to them what you have done in response to their suggestions, or why it has not been possible to do so. Involving them in this way is likely to have a positive effect on their motivation.

■ **Let children set their own deadlines for pieces of work.** It might be possible to let children negotiate with you how long a piece of work may take. Considering what will be required and how much time they will need is an excellent way to help them learn about forward planning, and will encourage them to work to deadlines. It may also act as a great motivator. Be prepared to let them renegotiate, however, if they have been over- (or under-) ambitious in their targets.

■ **Let children get involved in assessing each other's work.** Children will learn a great deal from seeing and discussing their peers' work, good or bad. Obviously it's important to prepare the ground for such an activity, for instance you might agree with the children on how to phrase criticism positively, on avoiding using personal remarks, and on backing up criticism with evidence to avoid hurting anyone's feelings.

■ **Involve children in helping each other to learn.** The process of working with other children is as beneficial for those leading as for those following. Not only will less able pupils learn from the guidance of others, but also the more able are likely to benefit from the reinforcement they derive from explaining things to someone else.

■ **Children can help to evaluate learning resource materials.** Children are likely to be able to tell you the strengths and weaknesses of learning materials and computer packages. The feedback they provide is based on usage by the target group that the materials were designed for, so is likely to be very sound.

■ **Get children involved in daily administrative tasks.** It's useful to let children take responsibility for daily routines such as preparing the milk, returning the register, tidying up, watering plants and sharpening pencils. This can help them develop good working habits and build up their sense of responsibility.

8. Different teaching styles

How effectively you teach is closely related to how you choose to teach, and the ways in which you feel most comfortable working. Different teaching styles are clearly going to be more appropriate for teaching certain concepts than others. Most of the time you will know almost instinctively what is and is not an appropriate way of tackling something, but here are a few ideas about how certain teaching styles can be used effectively:

- **Make the most of whole-class opportunities.** Use them to develop whole-class cohesion as well as for giving instruction, giving demonstrations, asking general questions and reviewing work and what has been learnt. Children like to feel part of a group, and the times when you're working with the class as a whole are the ones when they will develop collective cohesiveness.

- **Children can learn by doing in large groups.** Even as a whole class, children can be given tasks to do independently for a few minutes at a time. This will help to break up the session, and maintain attentiveness.

- **Whole-class sessions can be used to help children make sense of the things they have already learnt**. Through the process of discussing a task and what people found out, think or have learnt, children's confidence will grow as they see that their ideas fit in with those of others. Of course they could also realize that they have got the wrong end of the stick and usefully ask for help.

- **Feedback can be drawn from children in whole-class sessions.** Such sessions can be used to provide a useful barometer of how their learning is progressing. Well-directed and carefully phrased questions will give you an opportunity to make some useful assessments, both for individuals and groups.

- **Put energy and effort into making your whole-class sessions interesting and stimulating.** A well-paced and structured session, that has some visual impact and which involves the children, is a powerful teaching opportunity. It's the kind of occasion that children remember for years to come, and can be really stimulating for teachers too.

- **Think about the different ways of forming groups.** These include, randomly, alphabetically, by friendship, by ability or mixed-ability group. Each method has its advantages and its drawbacks. Try to use a system that suits you and that suits the children. Don't change the groups round so often that the children are unsettled, but provide opportunities for them to work in different groupings, so that they get used to the idea.

- **Help children in their early attempts at collaborative work.** Children naturally don't always work well in groups. Try to manage such work so that you have the chance to help them to assist and cooperate with one another, rather than fight over who does what and when. With a little guidance they can often achieve very productive outcomes.

■ **Try to ensure a balance of participation.** It's important that everyone has the opportunity to gain from and participate in group work. You will always have dominant and recessive children in any group, but with careful management you should be able to give everyone a chance. Try directing questions at individuals, and start with the more confident ones who appear to know what's going on. This gives the less confident children a chance to watch and learn from the others. Start directing questions at those children when they start showing more interest.

■ **Try to manufacture opportunities for one-to-one work.** Working with individual children is important in all kinds of situations, particularly, for example, when hearing them read, and when they're having particular difficulties. If you can get children working independently on familiar tasks, take whatever chances you can to work in this way. You may consider giving up some break times to work with individuals, and may be able to negotiate that you're excused from some assemblies.

■ **Have rules that allow you to work uninterrupted.** Opportunities to work one-to-one during class time have to be planned for and become part of normal classroom routines. Get children used to the idea that you have work to do too, and they should only approach you under certain, predetermined circumstances.

9. Using other adults in the classroom

No matter how good you are, you can always use another pair of hands. Some schools have additional auxiliary support, but encouraging governors, parents, grandparents and others to help out too can really reap dividends. It can also be tricky, but thorough preparation will pay off in terms of additional support for you in your teaching:

■ **You may need to give volunteers quite detailed information.** This is likely to be about the level and kinds of support you want the children to have, or the intended outcomes of the activity. You may need to give guidance about the sorts of questions they should ask or how they might help children to reach a greater understanding of the work they're doing. Making sure they know what they're doing, and why, will mean that you get the best help possible.

■ **Find out what you can about the people who offer to help.** Try to get to know the parents or carers of the children in your class before asking for help, or try asking the class's previous teacher for suggestions. With the best will in the world, not every parent will make the ideal helper in class and asking ones with whom you think you are likely to work well may make life a bit easier.

■ **Check your school's policy on having volunteers in class**. Often volunteers need police clearance before being allowed to work with children, and it's essential you check this out. It's worth going through all the proper procedures, to make sure that your children are in safe hands.

■ | **Check your school's policy on having volunteers *out* of the class.** Asking volunteers to take groups or individuals out of the class or to work in the school grounds or in the local community is usually only acceptable if they're helping you to supervise a group, but again, check your school's policy first. It's best to err on the side of caution.

■ | **Build a good working relationship with volunteers.** It's a good idea to ask them what sorts of activities they might like to work on. If they're enjoying it, the children they work with are more likely to enjoy it too. You can also build on the strengths they can offer, to get the best from the process.

■ | **Get adult helpers to come in a little before the session starts**. This will give you time to introduce them to the activity they will be helping with, and you will be able to consider and discuss the activity properly without interruptions. It will also provide time for them to ask questions and to voice their opinions.

■ | **If you feel a volunteer is not coping with some activities, try something else**. They might struggle working with a group of 10 children on a structured task but have a whale of a time in one-to-one activities developing phonemic awareness or 'number bonds'. It's difficult to tackle a subject like this from cold, so experimenting with activities until you find something that suits you both can be a diplomatic solution.

■ | **Remember that no helper needs to be redundant.** Getting them involved in mounting work, preparing resources, stocking shelves or baskets of resources are always good uses of volunteers' time. Try to save up jobs you can delegate for the times when you have help in the classroom.

■ | **At the end of the session, make sure that the children and the volunteers know who's doing what.** Out of a willingness to be as helpful as possible, volunteers may end up doing jobs that you would prefer the children to do. Clarifying the tasks at the outset will avoid confusion.

■ | **Remember, you're in charge.** The discipline in the class is still your responsibility and if some children working with a volunteer are not behaving as you would expect them to, it's a good idea to just bite the bullet and treat that group in the same way as you would normally, otherwise they may start to take advantage of the situation. More often than not, volunteers and parents appreciate the fact that you're supporting them in their voluntary efforts.

10. Using other professionals in the classroom

Getting the best out of an experienced nursery nurse, auxiliary or student involves developing a different working relationship from those required for working well with parents and volunteers.

These tips relate largely to working with a nursery nurse on a full- or part-time basis, but can also be extended to other professionals working with you in the classroom:

- **Plan your programme of study together**. This is important when working with fellow-professionals, even if they're less qualified than you. For them to work effectively, they have to know what you're both trying to achieve and ideally to agree with those goals too.

- **Share responsibility for the everyday chores.** A nursery nurse, for example, is not there just to do the messy jobs that you don't like doing. If you share out the unpleasant jobs you can share out the nice ones too. This way you will develop a genuine, productive working partnership.

- **Use your respective strengths and interests.** By playing to your strengths, the two of you will be able to cover far more of the curriculum much more effectively. Enthusiasm is infectious and the children will get more out of an activity when the person teaching them is enjoying it too.

- **Share ideas about the design and maintenance of children's records.** Assistants who know what's needed and why in children's records will be better placed to assist you in the collection and filing of evidence. It's important that everyone works to the same system, or confusion can arise.

- **Visit other schools together.** You may be able to pick up new ideas or discuss solutions to problems that you're experiencing, and it may be a pleasant team-building outing for you both.

- **Build in opportunities to review your work together.** Feedback from other trained professionals about how things are going, and where they could go to next, is invaluable. You will find that you can achieve more than twice as much as you would have done on your own.

- **Approach your headteacher about possible training opportunities.** These opportunities should relate to the development of the team. It's important that co-professionals have the chance to get involved in the development of your unit.

- **Use your nursery nurse's previous experience.** They may well have tackled issues or aspects of the curriculum that you haven't, and nothing counts so much as having been through it before! Make the most of your colleagues' ideas, and value contributions from each other.

- **Make sure you both have the chance of doing something different.** Variety is the spice of life and a break from an activity or responsibility can do you both good. Taking turns with activities can stop them becoming monotonous, and it also means that you can cover for each other in emergencies.

- **Use whole-group times effectively.** How many teachers need to be there when the children are watching television or hearing a story? It could be that these times will provide good opportunities for getting other things done, with only one person supervising the whole group.

11. Displaying work

Displaying work is important as it can be used as a focus for discussion, a stimulus for creative work, a recognition of children's achievements and an opportunity to enhance the classroom environment. It may be the most valuable resource you can have:

- **Have a variety of ways and spaces for displaying work.** Don't just consider what you're going to put on which wall, but also how tables, benches, boxes, shelves, fabrics and so on can be used to make the best of a space.

- **Mount work before displaying it.** Work looks significantly better when it's mounted, though whether it's single or double mounted may be determined by availability of resources. You could consider mounting on different sorts of materials, cardboard, tin foil, Christmas wrapping paper, unused wallpaper, fabrics and so on. You can also consider whether you really want everything to be rectangular or not!

- **Plan displays for 3D work carefully.** Think of creative or unusual ways of displaying work. For example, you might try making stacks of cardboard boxes and draping them with fabric (secured with twists of masking tape). Or you could attach small boxes to walls (though staples tend to be problematic) to make small shelves, or hang models from strings stapled to the walls or attached to the ceiling, or make use of benches, window ledges and shelves. Whatever you do is likely to have to suffer small pedestrian traffic, so try to build it to last!

- **Use display work for language development.** Displays can be used as a good way of consolidating or even extending children's understanding of activities they have been working on. Captions to accompany displayed work can explain processes, ask questions, add descriptive detail and generate added interest. They can offer support to reading, written and number work and discussion in ways that can be very productive.

- **Use interactive displays as a stimulus**. Displays can be used as a stimulus and a support for investigative or creative work. For instance, as a class make a map on the wall of the route of Rosie's Walk in the story of the same name, and then use it to help the children sequence the events in the story.

- **Use different kinds of text.** Different sizes and styles of lettering, and different kinds of written information, such as newspaper articles, typed or hand-written captions by you or the children, letters cut out of different coloured papers or fabrics, all help to enhance the impact of a display as well as to extend awareness of the written word.

- **Use your displays.** Encourage children to notice, describe and comment upon them. For instance, 'What have we put on the wall? Why has it been displayed there? How has it has been displayed and what do you think of it? How would you have done it? What do you like and what would you like to change?'

- **Site permanent classroom displays where they will do the most good.** If you have a number line in the class, try to put it where the children working in number can see it. Have book displays in a corner where children can sit quietly; you could have a couple of comfortable chairs and a listening centre there too.

- **Make collections of artefacts.** They are an excellent stimulus, but whether collected by you or the children, they need to be sited in a safe place and children will need to be given specific instructions on what they're allowed to touch and how to handle objects safely. Restricting their interest by stopping them from touching may seem a shame, but it's also important that they know how to treat other people's belongings. Don't forget the safety implications of displays.

- **Try to establish displays that evolve over time.** These sorts of displays tend to hold children's attention for longer and should be referred to and discussed on a regular, even daily basis. Children will enjoy watching a display as it changes and develops, and will learn from the experience too.

CURRICULAR RESPONSIBILITIES

Very few primary teachers are just concerned with what's going on in their own classrooms and if they were that would surely be to their detriment. Most teachers will be given additional responsibility for specific areas of the curriculum or school life, which obviously raises a number of issues, not least how to find the time. Different schools will have very different expectations of curriculum coordinators, as will individual members of staff, so you will need to find ways to balance the needs of the school, the needs of your colleagues, the needs of the children and most importantly, your own needs.

12. Managing time

No matter how efficient you are, any teacher could end up working 24 hours a day, seven days a week. This section suggests some ideas to help you make the best use of your time so you can do what you need to do for your class and still have enough time for yourself at the end of the day. It may help preserve your sanity too!

- **Leave time for yourself.** It's easy to get into the habit of working all the hours available, but enough is enough. If all you do is work then you may well limit the enthusiasm and experiences you can bring into the classroom. Don't feel guilty about having some evenings and parts of weekends to yourself.

- **Get yourself an action plan.** If you can set yourself a detailed but realistic plan of the things you would like to cover in a topic, term, or year, as a subject coordinator or whatever, and then stick to it, it will help you use your time effectively.

- **Be aware that action plans go wrong.** This is probably because you can't predict what might happen. If it becomes obvious that you aren't going to be able to live up to your aspirations, for whatever reason, it's better to adapt or make a new plan than to work yourself silly to keep up! The best action plans are strict enough to keep you to task, but flexible enough to cope with contingencies.

- **Set time in school aside for coordinating your area of the curriculum.** Try to decide upon a time during your week, probably after school, when you can support or meet with colleagues, check and order resources, and do similar tasks. Training yourself and your colleagues to use this time effectively helps!

- **Organize your subject resources.** Doing this so that you know what materials and resources you have got, and where they are, will help you to respond to the needs of your curriculum area efficiently. Persuading colleagues to maintain this organization helps even more.

- **Try to be proactive rather than reactive in the ways you communicate with others.** This is perhaps most important when responding to enquiries or relevant issues. Informing the whole staff at once rather than one by one is more efficient, and keeping them up to date with what you're doing may help to solve issues before they arise. If you know where you're going, it makes responding to issues or questions easier.

- **Delegate whatever you reasonably can.** They say that delegation is the key to good management. Before doing something yourself consider whether you can give the job to nursery nurses, auxiliaries, administrative assistants, trainees, parents and even children. This may help by taking some of the pressure off you, and freeing up time for you to develop new activities and initiatives.

- **Take time to check what resources and materials are already available in school.** It might save you having to make your own. While checking resource cupboards and files will give you the information you need, try asking your colleagues first; it's quicker than wading through it all by yourself.

- **Don't reinvent the wheel.** Even if the resources you can get hold of don't give you exactly what you want, they may be adaptable and could save you a lot of planning time, which is often the hardest bit. Be wary of the 'not invented here' syndrome, and be open to modifying resources when they're nearly what you want.

- **Get the children active.** Children love the responsibility of sharpening pencils, bringing in the milk, emptying the water tray, taking messages, even photocopying worksheets, so let them. You might even be able to set up a helper system in school where the older children act as aids to teachers of younger children in lunch times, where this can be beneficial to all parties.

13. Coordinating a curriculum area

Many primary or infant teachers are given an area of the curriculum, or an aspect of a school's management to coordinate. Sometimes this may be related to a personal interest or to an individual's educational background, but sometimes it isn't. In smaller schools, teachers may have responsibility for several aspects of school life. Whatever the set-up in your school, you'll need to see that whatever you're coordinating is undertaken efficiently and professionally:

- **Start with the resources.** It's a relatively manageable thing to tackle. Find out what you have got and where it is. Make a list or a catalogue. These can be useful for informing other staff about what is available and where it is. It will also help you to identify what you lack, so you can take steps to obtain what you need.

- **Organize your resources.** If you have a designated storage area for your resources, sort them out and if possible get the school secretary to make up labels so that every box, shelf, drawer or cupboard says on the outside what it holds on the inside. This can save enormous amounts of time, especially if you can persuade the rest of the staff to put things back where they came from!

- **Maintain resources for your curriculum area.** This is likely to be your responsibility. Some schools delegate parts of their budget to curriculum areas and others ask you to submit requisitions, but either way, a good place to start is by looking at last year's orders and, of course, what you've got left.

- **Consider how resources might help move your curriculum area forward.** Ask your colleagues what they think would help them teach your subject. Looking through educational catalogues can also give you a few good ideas for opportunities for new activities. Be cautious about buying resources without having a clear idea about using them, however.

- **Get yourself trained**. It may come down to you to help support colleagues with the development of your curriculum area. Your Local Education Authority and local universities will probably run educational training courses. Ask your headteacher about allowing you to attend some of these. They may not be exactly what you need, but just having the time to discuss ideas with others in the same situation can be very useful.

- **Offer In-Service Training.** Running informal workshops can be a productive way of offering colleagues support. You may be called upon to offer your colleagues advice and training and, if you're keen to make improvements in your curricular area, you will have to put in a lot of effort. There's never enough time for training, but giving staff a chance to come to you by offering workshop sessions after school can help.

- **Map out a progression of skills for your subject.** This can give you a good overview of what you're trying to achieve. With the help of management or experienced staff, sit down and plan the broad aspects of what children should experience in your subject across the whole school. This will help you to decide on realistic and achievable goals.

■ **Help staff to plan your subject carefully.** By developing activities that match the themes you have outlined in the progression charts, you can make sure that all the areas that you want to cover get covered. Detailed plans do not have to be inflexible, but should set out guidelines for action.

■ **Tackle one issue at a time.** Otherwise you end up juggling half a dozen different things at the same time and not really doing any of them properly. Finishing what you start can be tricky when there are so many other things to keep track of in a classroom. Keep aspects of your curricular responsibilities to small, manageable chunks.

■ **Tread carefully!** Other members of staff may not be as enthusiastic about changes and advice as you are yourself, not least because it may mean extra work. Diplomacy is essential if you want to achieve your goals. Take time to explain why you're trying to implement changes, and spell out to everyone details of the benefits that should accrue.

14. Covering the National Curriculum

Part of your responsibility as a class teacher is to ensure that the National Curriculum is delivered to the children in your class. The fact that your own education may not have equipped you to feel confident in teaching all the subjects in the National Curriculum can compound an already complex problem. So where do you find the support and information you need to do your job properly?

■ **Track down established schemes of work.** Some schools have a system of support that could map out what you teach and when you teach it. Though this may seem rather rigid, it does help a school to ensure that it offers exactly what it should. If your school works to this kind of system, get hold of schemes of work before you start planning!

■ **Establish the focus of a topic before you plan.** Different topics give opportunities for focusing on different subject areas. Before you plan, make sure you know what the intended focus of your topic is! The danger is that your provision will be diffused if you don't have a clear vision to start with.

■ **Find out if your school has already mapped out the curriculum areas.** If it has, then planning for activities that cover the skills and concepts that have already been mapped out for you will ensure that you're tackling activities that are worthwhile and that fit into an overall plan for each subject.

■ **If you don't have schemes of work, try to get hold of old planning and record sheets.** Ensuring that you're not needlessly repeating work that has already been covered in a previous class will be your responsibility. Check through these records to get an idea of what your class has already covered.

■ **Remember that a lot of the National Curriculum is just common sense.** Looking at the core subjects, if you have an idea about what the next step should be in helping the children to acquire the knowledge and skills they need to become competent at using numbers or language, then it will almost certainly fit with the National Curriculum.

■ **Find out what others are doing.** Comparing notes with other teachers on how they are addressing areas of the National Curriculum, can be most helpful. You may then be in a position to return the favour with something that may be taxing your colleagues' ingenuity.

■ **Network wherever you can.** Talk about National Curriculum issues with colleagues you meet at training events, members of your social circle who are involved in primary school teaching, and others whose brains you can pick, to help you to make sense of the requirements.

■ **Get along to the library.** Read what others have written about implementing the National Curriculum. You may find journal articles, books and items on the Internet that will further familiarize you with what you need to know.

■ **Use the National Curriculum framework creatively.** Don't let it be a straitjacket, preventing you from introducing innovative ideas and approaches into your teaching. Explore how you can satisfy the requirements in ways that fit your own context and individual approaches.

■ **You don't have to know the National Curriculum inside out to be able to teach it effectively.** Planning stimulating and appropriate experiences for the children will probably be more than adequate, and making these sorts of experiences part of the normal daily or weekly routines will help you cover most of what you need to.

15. Ensuring continuity and progression

This is really a whole-school issue, but some schools don't tackle it effectively. You may still need to take steps to ensure that you're not repeating work your class has already done, and also ensure that what you plan will extend their skills and understanding, enabling the children to make real progress:

■ **Make sure that you're familiar with the records that already exist.** You'll need to build on prior achievement if you are to demonstrate children's progression from the base-line data.

■ **Get an idea of the range of abilities in the class.** A class's previous teacher may be able to give you an idea of the levels achieved by the more able, the average and the less able children in a class, and the sorts of work that the children could be expected to do next.

■ **Find out about the sorts of routines the children are used to.** Children, especially those who are less able, rely on and respond well to established routines. Work that is presented and tackled in a similar way but which extends children's knowledge is easier to manage in the classroom. Beware of boredom setting in though, and build in the unexpected from time to time.

■ **Establish the kinds of support materials they're used to.** Maintaining a consistent approach to supporting children's independent work makes things easier for you and less stressful for the children. If children are used to using number lines to 20 there's little point in giving them 100 squares and expecting them to be able to use them without introduction and support from you.

■ **Consider where they should be by the end of the year**. While knowing where the children are coming from is very important, discussing where they should be by the end of the year with a teacher in the year above might give you a better idea of what you're trying to achieve.

■ **Keep reasonably detailed records of what you have done.** These will be useful to hand on to your class's next teacher, who can then build on what you've started. Keeping such records can also help you to remember from year to year details of what you did, and may save you preparation time.

■ **Consider whether to group.** Grouping your class by ability is not universally regarded ideal, but doing so may make it easier to differentiate the work you give children, and to provide the sorts of resources that support the way they need to work.

■ **Keep a tick list to help you keep track.** A matrix listing of the children in your class, against the work that they have tackled, will help you keep track of what they're doing and when, and will provide a really good record of what they have achieved, for future reference.

■ **Concentrate on the basic skills.** This is especially important early on in the primary age range, where number and literacy skills can be developed in a fairly progressive way. Here, keeping track of what's going on and where the work should go next is fairly simple. Concepts related to Humanities or Science can usefully stand much more repetition because they're not so developmental.

■ **Make sure that any repetition is deliberate.** Repeating activities and areas of work can provide useful consolidation, but repetition due to the teacher having no records of previous work, is rarely beneficial.

16. Extracurricular activities

Many schools offer a range of extracurricular activities. Some offer them within the normal school timetable through club or activity sessions, and others offer opportunities outside the normal school day or at lunch times. Whichever your school offers may affect the amount of choice you have in whether or not to offer extracurricular activities, and what kind you're likely to be involved in. These tips are designed to help you make the most of the opportunity, by asking the right kinds of question:

- **Consider what you're going to do.** Just because you're good at something doesn't mean you necessarily want to spend your free time doing it with 30 lively, demanding children, so be selective about what you offer.

- **Consider when you're going to do it.** Your time as a teacher is precious, so don't offer too much at first. For example, football matches, leagues, cup ties, training and the like can take up vast amounts of time, so don't make too many commitments until you know you can keep them!

- **Consider where you're going to do it.** Check with cleaners, caretakers and headteachers (in descending order of importance) about whether your plans are going to interfere with theirs. Plans can be readily sabotaged by uncooperative support staff, so make sure that you take their needs into account from the outset.

- **Consider how many are going to do it with you.** Pick a manageable number of children, and stick to it (always err on the side of caution!). It's easy to get pressured into taking on more than you want to, and you need to ask yourself whether you and they will still enjoy it if you take on too many.

- **Consider whether you have the space.** If you're running a creative activity, technology or art work, consider how much space you have available before deciding on the numbers you intend to take on. Consider also where work might be stored from one week to the next! Sometimes your solutions to the space problem can be quite creative.

- **Consider who might want to do it too.** Working alongside another member of staff is more fun and probably safer for you. Ask other members of staff if they fancy helping out, and look for other potential helpers from your classroom volunteers.

- **Consider who needs to know.** Obviously, the head, other teachers whose pupils might be involved and the parents or carers of those children, will need to be aware of your plans. Most schools also insist that parents be informed of the arrangements in writing, and that you get permission slips from them.

- **Consider whether you have a mission.** Setting yourself a goal, such as a performance or display, may seem like a good way of focusing your activities, but it can also become a pressure. Sometimes, just doing things for the fun of it's more enjoyable for both the children and for you, and less stressful for all concerned.

- **Consider what you need to know.** You should check if your school has a policy on extracurricular activities. If it has, read it, and try to ensure that your plan articulates with it.

- **Think of the transport implications.** If you're running the activities after school, find out and record how the children will get home. Alternatively, if they're going to be picked up at school, find out who you can expect to collect them. It's also important to make sure you know they have indeed been picked up at the end of the evening.

17. Getting the most from In-Service Training (INSET)

Whether you're intending to benefit from INSET from someone else, or hoping others will benefit from what you have to offer, INSET can be rather a hit-or-miss affair. But here are some things that you can do to avoid wasting time – yours or everybody else's!

- **Identify your own developmental needs**. Despite pressures to the contrary, you can't be the perfect teacher in every aspect of the curriculum, so prioritize your own professional needs as far as you can. Don't be tempted to take training just because it's on offer. Make sure you think it's going to be worthwhile and relevant before you enrol.

- **Seek help if you aren't sure what your needs are.** Consult with your mentor or appointed appraiser, line manager or your close colleagues. You could also talk to your head or deputy or even your Local Education Authority advisory teacher. They may be able to observe your teaching and make suggestions that help you identify your own needs. You'll also get feedback sooner or later from your OFSTED inspection.

- **Ask your headteacher where the best place to get help might be.** It may be the case that support can be offered from within the school, from another member of staff who has received training or has experience in that particular field. Otherwise your Local Education Authority advisory service or local further education colleges and universities may offer continuing professional development courses that are suitable.

- **When reading details of courses, check the small print.** Read prospectuses from providers of training to make sure you know what the course will offer. Titles can be misleading, and you may well be limited to a fairly restricted number of courses per year, for financial reasons. Make sure that the ones you choose are right for you.

- **If the small print doesn't tell you enough, try to find out more.** Get in touch with the institution or preferably the individual who will be running the course to get clarification of exactly what's on offer and whether it will help you. This kind of research pays dividends in the long run.

- **Ask other colleagues.** They may have attended similar courses on previous occasions or may have encountered the trainer before (especially where Local Education Authority advisory service training is concerned). They can help you find out if its going to be worthwhile for you.

- **Try to match your needs with what's on offer.** This will help to ensure you don't waste your own time and the school's resources on inappropriate training that doesn't cover your developmental needs.

- **Remember that if it's worth doing, it's worth investing time in.** Attending a one-off course may help tackle immediate, short-term issues and raise your awareness, but it won't help raise your skills all that much. Sometimes, only a concerted effort will suffice. Attending a series of courses after school, reading relevant books, or giving yourself time to practise on a weekly basis will have a significant long-term impact.

- **Use educational journals and magazines constructively.** They are often packed full of practical activities on how to develop specific ideas or skills in the classroom. Although they may not appear to be training materials in themselves, they often give you access to what the 'experts' consider good practice as well as tried and tested learning experiences for the children.

- **Make use of informal training opportunities.** Most of the best training comes from the staff room. This is especially true if you have a friendly staff. Much of the talk in staff rooms seems to be about how teachers handle situations, how they tackle problems, how they teach different concepts and how they cope with a particularly difficult child. So spend your coffee and lunch breaks in the staff room and enjoy a good chat, because it's not idle gossip – it's professional development!

18. Offering INSET

Most primary school teachers are now expected not only to be teachers but also to be 'curriculum experts'. As a curriculum expert you may be asked to devise INSET or courses, or you may feel that you're competent to offer your colleagues training in your field of expertise. Further ideas about training are covered in the section 'Coordinating a curriculum area' but here we suggest some basic ideas that could prove helpful:

- **Identify training needs for your curriculum area.** You can do this yourself, based on how you feel things are going in your subject or through a curriculum audit. However, probably the best and least threatening way is through the school development plan, if you have one. If so, get hold of it and see if your curriculum area is identified as needing attention as a whole, or in specific areas.

- **Don't rush in!** Once you think you've established a training need, it might be tempting to go ahead and organize some INSET. However, it's well worth taking a step back and considering why this need has arisen. It could be that a lack of resources is more to blame, or it could be that there's a lack of progression and problems are being experienced because the ground work is not being undertaken effectively. Changes in staffing, sickness, unfamiliarity with resources, inconsistent interpretation of attainment targets and so on could be the source of the problem, and so training needs should be clarified at an early stage.

- **Find out if there's someone better placed than you to help.** If the problem seems to be limited to a small number of staff or to a single, isolated problem, you might be able to tackle it effectively by yourself. However, if it's a more complex issue, why not ask if you can invite your Local Education Authority advisor or another qualified person in to tackle the problem on your behalf.

- **If you think you can do it yourself, don't get carried away.** Set yourself very specific and achievable targets. How much work you do to support staff in attaining those targets is up to you, but writing a specific brief and telling the staff what this is before you start helps keep everything clearly focused. It also means that it's less likely that you will set up expectations that you can't satisfy.

- **If someone else (for example your headteacher) thinks you can do it yourself, ask them to help you set specific targets.** Once you have jointly established goals, it may be worth discussing their feasibility, and how you might go about tackling them in practice.

- **Ask for time to get ready.** Arranging whole-staff INSET is a very time-consuming job and many school managers will try to give their staff time to organize it. However, if the offer isn't forthcoming, set out what you think you will have to do and approach your headteacher with your proposals. Once it's apparent what's involved, it's more likely that you will make your case to good effect.

- **Keep notes on the INSET you provide.** Much of the INSET you offer will be one-to-one, because most of the time it's a question of you helping another teacher with a particular problem, especially if you have a specific area of curriculum responsibility. This sort of work tends to go unnoticed, so keep a note of what you've done as evidence of achievement in your own area of specialization.

- **If you keep getting individual requests about the same issues, try to tackle it in a whole-staff group.** You might be in a position to offer a session that is more convenient to you, and it will be a more efficient use of your time if you can impart your pearls of wisdom to a collected audience.

■ **Don't expect to perform miracles.** When running INSET courses, it's tempting to try to provide really ambitious programmes, but taking on board a lot of new ideas in one go is hard. Providing notes and visual prompts about what you're talking about will help considerably. Many staff are happy if they just have something to take away with them that's well presented, provides useful guidance, and acts as a memory jogger. Try to break areas for development down into small, manageable steps.

■ **As far as possible, keep INSET sessions practical.** Listening to one person for an hour or so becomes boring. Practical activities tend to be easier to remember and often make more sense. Ensure that your INSET sessions are as well planned, interactive and professional as your classroom teaching.

19. Communicating with colleagues

Effective communication can sometimes fall by the wayside in the rush of a school day, but effective communication can also save a lot of wasted time. This set of tips addresses how you can keep one another informed and keep up with what's going on without getting bogged down in unimportant detail:

■ **Use the staff room notice board.** It's easy to just walk straight past but it can be a most effective communication tool if used well. Try moving things round and remove all the old notices, because a change makes a board more eye-catching. Use all of your creative display skills to draw attention to important information.

■ **Suggest to your colleagues that you should circulate a weekly diary.** This could let all staff know the main events of the week in advance. It helps raise awareness about what's going on in the rest of the school, and helps colleagues plan and coordinate activities effectively.

■ **Make the most of your opportunities at staff meetings.** They sometimes seem to be primarily forums for management to talk while teachers listen, but they're much more effective if used to keep one another informed. Take your chances at the end of the meeting, under 'Any other business' to circulate ideas or raise questions.

■ **Keep an eye out for Local Education Authority advisory service network meetings.** These are run for curriculum coordinators and interested parties. They are a good opportunity to find out what's going on within your authority and to collect good ideas that have been tried out and work in classrooms. You can also build useful networks of colleagues who are interested in the same kinds of areas as yourself.

■ **Take the ideas raised at network meetings back to your own school.** Many schools ask staff to report back on such meetings. If you aren't required to but nevertheless feel you have information worth sharing, you could put together an information sheet to circulate, or ask for a few minutes at the end of a staff meeting to give an oral report.

■ **Try to use appraisal as a communication opportunity.** Appraisal can seem a bit daunting, especially to new teachers, but if you prepare for it, it can be a positive developmental opportunity. Consider carefully what you would like to concentrate on and why. If there's an aspect of your work that you're unsure of, ask for this to be the focus of your appraisal. It's your responsibility to prioritize what will be looked at, so don't be afraid to take the lead.

■ **Keep careful notes about what you do as curriculum coordinator**. Reporting progress is likely to be part of your duties as a curriculum coordinator. Keep notes about requests you've received, action you've taken, resources you've ordered or organized and any other jobs you've undertaken. These will demonstrate what you've done and act as a good memory jogger for you and your colleagues.

■ **Try to keep a record of any dealings with outside agencies.** When communicating with services such as Educational Support Services or Equipment Maintenance, make sure you keep a record of who you talk to, when you talked to them, how to get in touch with them, and what you discussed. This can be invaluable later on when follow-up action may be required.

■ **Start communicating with the schools into which your children will be moving.** Often this is simply a question of telling them what you think they want to know about children they will be taking. Get them to write down what they want and when they want it. Ask for such details as early in the year as possible, to give you plenty of time to get all the information together. Try to establish a rapport with 'feeder schools' because there are bound to be things with which you can help one another.

■ **Keep minutes or action notes of all meetings.** Even if it's just a small sub-group meeting, it's still a good idea to keep a written record, however informal. Apart from anything else, it will remind everyone of what they agreed to, and what they promised to do!

20. Policies and schemes of work

Schools often have a surfeit of policy statements and schemes of work. Policies are put in place for good reasons, however, and it's as well to know what you need to know, and what responsibilities you have regarding policies and schemes of work. The following suggestions should help with this:

Policy statements for your curriculum area

■ **If the policy statement exists, check if it's up to date.** Many policy statements state how often they should be reviewed. It's important that a policy statement is relevant, recent and read. It's pointless to work to a historic document.

■ **If the policy doesn't exist, check if you need to write one.** More often than not the answer will be yes! If it is, you'll need to establish clear terms of reference, and make clear where the responsibilities for direction and implementation lie.

■ **Get hold of other policy statements.** They'll give you the sorts of headings and statements that you need to put together your own policy. Schools sometimes have a 'house style' which you should adopt for your own statements too, without letting it be a straitjacket.

■ **Seek advice from your advisory service.** That is one of the things that they're there for. They should be able to tell you whether a draft statement covers all the areas that it should, or give you a skeleton policy statement and examples of good policy documents for you to emulate.

■ **Ask other colleagues within the authority.** Take your opportunities, either at network or pyramid meetings (other members of staff at your school might be able to help out here) to find examples of what others have found to be effective policies.

Schemes of work for your curriculum area

■ **Check that any scheme of work is the current version.** If not, it should still be fairly simple to update your scheme but again, getting hold of other schemes, either from nearby schools or from the Local Education Authority might help you identify weaknesses or gaps within your own documentation.

■ **If there is no scheme, use your contacts to obtain sample schemes from elsewhere.** Find them from within the school or from the Local Education Authority, to give you a framework and headings to work from. You will of course need to customize any schemes you borrow, for your own particular contexts.

■ **Remember that schemes of work should be dynamic.** This is especially the case because they're rather complex documents. They should evolve from what's already going on in school. By comparing what is already going on with what you and the National Curriculum require, a scheme can be used to identify and fill gaps or weaknesses. But don't expect to produce one in a couple of days. Care taken at this stage will save problems from occurring later.

■ **If you want your scheme to work well, keep it straightforward.** It must be easy to use, easy to read and accessible. If teachers don't have a scheme on hand when planning activities, the chances are that they'll ignore the process altogether and carry on doing it in the ways they're used to.

■ **Cut your coat according to your cloth**. It would be easy to think that once you've got a copy of someone else's scheme your problems will be entirely solved, but you have to tailor any scheme to the needs and the resources available in your school.

21. Making learning processes meaningful to children

One of the most important factors that can predetermine success in learning is confidence. It's important to give children every chance to gain this confidence and one of the best ways of helping them to do so is to help them gain greater control over the processes they apply during their learning. These tips are designed to enable you to help children to make sense of how they're learning:

■ **Cultivate the want to learn.** Children need to be motivated to learn things. They may need to be helped to increase their motivation by showing them what the benefits are. When possible, make learning fun, interesting and rewarding. Don't mistake lack of confidence for lack of motivation.

■ **Learning by doing is important.** Most learning happens when children practice things, have a go and learn by making mistakes and finding out why. It's important to ensure that children are given early opportunities to try out and apply new things that they've been introduced to. There is no substitute for focused, practical experience.

■ **Feedback is essential.** Children need to find out how their learning is actually going. They may feel that they have understood something but can't be certain until you let them know. Feedback must be well timed if it's to be of use to children, and needs to be given to them in forms that they can readily understand and accept.

■ **Needing to learn something can be almost as productive as wanting to learn it.** When children know why something will be useful to them, even if they find it difficult, they're more likely to maintain their efforts until they succeed. Help them to understand the value of what they're doing, so they can make the most of the opportunity.

■ **Children need to try to make sense of what they're learning.** It's of little value learning things by rote, or becoming able to do things, without knowing why or how. It's also important that they have lots of opportunities to apply their new learning at an early stage. Putting things they have learnt into practice helps them 'get their heads round' the new ideas.

■ **Learning is not just a matter of storing up further knowledge.** Successful learning is about being able to use what has been learnt, not just in familiar situations but also in new contexts. Help children to see how their learning can be transferable.

■ **Children take cues about how they're expected to learn from the ways in which we teach them.** If we concentrate on supplying them with information, they're likely simply to try to store it. If we structure our teaching so that they're practising, applying, extending, comparing and evaluating, they're more likely to see these processes as central to the ways in which they need to work.

■ **Learning is not just an independent activity.** While much can be learnt by children working on their own with various learning resource materials, they can also learn a great deal by talking to each other and tackling tasks and activities jointly. Help them to gain benefit from working productively in pairs, threes and small groups.

■ **Becoming better at learning is important.** The most important learning outcomes in primary schools are not topic-based, but are the outcomes of being better able to learn new skills. Learning skills are among the most important of transferable life skills.

■ **Try to tune in to children's learning styles.** Sometimes children struggle because the way they're taught and the way they learn are in conflict. If you try different approaches to your classroom work, you're more likely to be able to keep some of the people happy all of the time! Some children will learn more from things they hear, others from things they see; some from tackling things alone, others from working collaboratively. The more variety you can bring into the learning experiences you provide them with, the better each child's learning style will be accommodated.

22. Planning a new topic

Planning a new topic or unit of work from scratch can be a daunting task, but it can also be a rewarding experience, and a chance to enjoy the creativity that such a task involves. While you will still have to stick quite rigidly to curriculum guidelines, you can approach them in a wide variety of ways, using your initiative and following your own interests at least to some extent. Here we offer a few practical guidelines, many of which are expanded upon elsewhere in this book:

■ **Clarify the key skills that the topic should cover.** You need to have a really clear idea about how you will ensure that the relevant key skills fit into your chosen topic. Check your other topics to see if you can identify gaps that you could try to tackle through your new topic.

■ **Identify basic concepts that could be covered by your topic.** These will be the 'meat on the bones' of your topic, and will give it a subject focus, whether it is, for example, a scientifically or historically driven topic.

■ **Identify key questions that you want children to be able to answer.** These key questions will really be the starting points for the development of the skills and concepts identified above, and they will also provide you with the perfect assessment criteria. These will lead you naturally to the incorporation of the relevant learning outcomes, which you can identify by breaking down the basic concepts and key questions into simple steps. These learning outcomes can then shape the activities you will plan.

■ **Sort out what resources you will need.** Can most of your resourcing provision be found from inside school? Where could you go to get the resources you need? What visits/visitors could you arrange? Will other Local Education Authority services be able to help? Will you be given any kind of budget?

■ **Decide upon a time frame.** Though this may be dictated by existing arrangements, it's important to bear in mind the length of time you can afford to spend on a topic. You may be able to base this simply on how long you think you can sustain the children's interest, but other external factors, such as school events like sports days, open days and school trips, can also impact on your plans, and need to be taken into account.

■ **Consider the range of possible teaching and learning strategies.** Consider whether each activity will be most effectively tackled as a whole class, in small groups, or one-to-one. Consider whether each one should be tackled collaboratively or independently, with or without adult supervision and so on. Identifying these points at the planning stage might help you decide upon resources and time-scales.

■ **Decide whether, and how, the learning outcomes might be assessed.** Much of your assessment will probably be continuous and informal, but some tasks may offer opportunities for more formal assessment, which you can build in to your overall assessment strategy.

■ **Consider the possibility of visits.** Do you know of any local sites suitable for field trips? Do any of your colleagues? Will the costs, in time and money, make it worthwhile? Can you get out to have a look for yourself? How can you make sure that the visit will be a really worthwhile learning experience?

■ **Think about inviting in 'expert witnesses'.** If you're doing an historical topic, for example, asking grandparents or great-grandparents in to talk about their childhood can be very interesting for the children, and can bring the topic to life.

■ **Pick your best ideas as starting points and as conclusions.** Starting and finishing strongly gives a topic definition and purpose. An interesting visit to start with gives plenty of good ideas and motivation; a celebratory event such as a teddy bears' picnic at the end provides a good incentive.

PASTORAL CARE

One of the most rewarding and demanding aspects of teaching young children is that you have an opportunity to build up a fairly close working relationship with a small number of children (relative to the numbers of children a secondary teacher may have to try to keep track of). Building this relationship can take a lot of time and effort and is an aspect of teaching that's difficult to teach anyone else to do. It's a very personal thing but considering other people's approaches and points of view can help us tackle it in our own way with more confidence.

23. Dealing with upset children

When working with young children, you're bound to have to deal with emotional upsets as there are any number of reasons why children might get themselves into states. How you deal with these situations is very much a personal thing and depends greatly on your experience of the child concerned, but possibly the most important thing is to calm the situation down quickly so you can get to the cause of the problem. These tips are designed to help you to take control of the situation promptly and effectively:

- **Be firm but gentle!** When children become upset the most important thing is to get them settled as quickly as possible, so you can get to the bottom of it all. Telling them firmly that they need to calm down usually works more quickly than a lot of sympathy, which can inflame emotions further.

- **Act quickly to settle children who don't want to be left at school by their parents or carers.** They may cling to whoever has brought them in. However, being firm usually sorts the problem out more quickly than prolonging the situation. Try telling the child exactly what they're going to do; more often than not in these cases children will do as they're told.

- **If a child is upset, don't change your expectations.** If children think that they might get special favours or wriggle out of something they don't want to do just because they appear to be upset, then there is no incentive for them to calm down. Obviously, you have to be sensitive to the situation, but as a general rule, letting children off the hook doesn't help in the long run.

- **If an upset child becomes disruptive, send for help.** If possible get another child to find help, in the shape of an auxiliary, nursery nurse or perhaps even the headteacher, because the child needs to be removed from the class to avoid disrupting the rest of the class. You may have to restrain the child to prevent harm to the child or others, but take extreme care never to use excessive physical force, which cannot ever be condoned.

- **Give a child time and space to calm down.** Sometimes getting upset might make children feel that they have lost face with the rest of the class. Giving them a little time and space by themselves affords them a chance to recover their composure and their dignity.

- **Keep other children away.** A crowd isn't always conducive to getting an angry or distressed child to calm down; the sympathy seems to make them feel even more sorry for themselves. Again, it's a matter of being sensitive to the situation but generally, removing such children from the centre of attention helps them recover more quickly.

- **Your experience of the children is the most important thing.** Knowing the children individually, the kinds of things they're interested in, and what makes them laugh, can be very useful. Sometimes all that's required is that you distract children from the cause of their upset and get them to focus on something that's much more fun!

- **Don't expect children to be able to explain why they're upset.** Sometimes they simply can't find the words to explain the way they feel. If children seem reluctant to talk about why they're upset or say they don't know why, it may simply be a matter of getting them calm and offering reassurance.

- **If your discipline of children upsets them, don't let them get away with things for the sake of a quiet life!** Instead it can be a good idea to get them to sit quietly on their own and think about what they've done. This ensures that you haven't climbed down but it also ensures that you don't end up upsetting the children further.

- **Tell the children: 'You can tell me about anything.'** Getting children to bring their problems to you, instead of bottling them up or dealing with them by themselves, is usually a good idea. This may make more work for you, but reassuring the children that you're on their side is important. Striking a balance between genuine support and perpetually sorting out petty disputes can be a bit tricky though! Nevertheless, it's important to provide opportunities for children to work through whatever concerns them, especially if it means you're alerted to serious problems which you may need to refer on for specialist help.

24. Play times

Supervising children at play times is part of most teachers' duties and is rarely, if ever, a dull affair! The potential for having a fistful of incidents all cropping up at once is high, but you still have to deal with them quickly and efficiently to make sure that things don't get out of hand. No teacher can expect to monitor everything that goes on, but these tips are designed to help you deal with play times to the best of your ability:

■ **Be clear in your own mind what is, and what is not, permitted.** Are the children allowed footballs or skipping ropes? Are they allowed on the field (if you have one)? If you don't know you may open yourself up to a lot of persuasion and protest from the children. Ideally these decisions should be made by management and their dictates communicated to the children and to you. It's useful if the lunch-time supervisors know them too to keep everything consistent.

■ **Check if there's a policy on the supervision of children at play time.** If there is, then it will probably give you guidance on how children are taken out of and brought back into school, on who should be available as back up (the designated first-aider, for example), and on what to do in case of accidents (by way of recording incidents and informing parents or carers, and management) or who might supervise those children who have had play times suspended as a punishment.

■ **If there is no official policy, check if there is an unofficial one.** This information is useful because if your expectations are the same as the children's, it's all going to be much more straightforward. Check this out with the most established teachers in the school, who will normally be happy to share their wisdom with you.

■ **Once you know the rules of the game, stick to them!** Even if you disagree with some of the methods or procedures used, go along with them, because dealing with a large number of children can be hard work. If you have concerns, raise them at a staff meeting and reach a consensus before making changes off your own bat.

■ **Try to enjoy yourself.** Play times tend to be less formal than classroom situations, and are good opportunities to get to know the children a little better, and for them to get to know you better too. While you're entitled to let your hair down a bit, make sure that you maintain your high expectations about how the children behave around and with you so as to avoid any misunderstanding. Excessive high spirits can spill over into classroom activities if you're not careful.

■ **Find out who could/should be on hand to help you when things go wrong.** You may have a great number of children to supervise, and you won't be able to attend to an injury or pursue someone who has decided they've had enough of school for the day. Make sure that you know who to send for as back up, and where they're likely to be, so another child can be sent with a message.

■ **Check the Local Education Authority's policies and practices before treating injuries yourself.** Most, if not all authorities have clear guidelines on the treatment of injuries, including such things as the administration of a sticking plaster being done only by a designated first-aid trained member of staff. Make sure you know who this member of staff is, and if you're in any doubt about what you should do, send for help!

■ **Buy your own whistle.** This is a wonderful way of gaining attention in a noisy playground. Keep it safe because, most certainly, someone will what to borrow it come play time and if there is a 'communal whistle' the chances are that the football coach will have borrowed it the previous night, and no one will know where it is!

- ■ **Try not to overuse a whistle.** Children stop paying it any attention if it gets blown too often. Change your strategy by blowing the whistle then using your voice to reinforce the whistle's command. Then praise good behaviour, then single out bad behaviour, and you will probably achieve more impact than by repeated whistle-blowing.

- ■ **Send your own class in from the playground last.** Otherwise they will find themselves unsupervised in an empty classroom. While they're with you they remain under your supervision; they may even see it as a kind of bonus.

25. Making children feel secure and comfortable

Children need to feel safe in your care. If you don't have their trust, getting them to make progress in your class is going to be an uphill struggle. It's not a question of wrapping them in cotton wool, however. Ideally you would want every child to feel comfortable in the classroom from day one, but building this relationship can take time with some children. Here are some ideas for you to establish the right kind of climate:

- ■ **Be consistent.** Treating all children the same way as consistently as possible is vital. If they know what to expect from you, and their expectations are justified, they will at least know where they stand, and that goes a long way to making them feel comfortable. Inconsistency is unfair to children, and lies at the root of a lot of poor behaviour, when children don't feel that they understand the rules of the game.

- ■ **Be fair.** This goes hand in hand with being consistent. In a busy classroom, it's all too easy to settle for an easy solution, but it's worth taking a step back and counting to 10. There will always be one or two children in the class who cause you more bother than all the rest, but they need to be dealt with fairly too if you're going to gain their trust. You may often, nevertheless, feel in need of the wisdom of Solomon!

- ■ **Remember that children often feel more comfortable in the presence of 'strict' teachers.** Although initially a firm teacher may be frightening, when the children discover that you're strict with those who don't do as they're asked, but perfectly lovely to those who get on and try hard, they will feel at ease. It's all about establishing clear boundaries.

- ■ **Children need to know that they can rely on you.** Most of all, they need to know that they can trust you to listen to what they have to say, and to help them tackle their problems. Children need a lot of reminders about this, and using anecdotes about how you have helped children in the past can help them to be assured of your trustworthiness.

- **Children hate changes, and often find them unsettling.** Try not to move furniture or working groups around too often. Avoid changes in the timetable as far as possible, and take the time to explain when things do need to be changed. Many children begin to panic when things aren't following their normal pattern. If major changes need to take place, for example when buildings are refurbished, try to give the children as long as possible a lead time to prepare.

- **Take your opportunities for reinforcing the idea that you're on their side!** If you have successfully dealt with a problem or concern, get the child concerned to tell the story of what happened and what was done about it. If it would embarrass them, then tell it on their behalf and anonymously. These stories help foster the idea that when things go wrong, there is something that can be done.

- **Make the classroom environment as reassuring as possible.** Cover the walls; many children think that bare walls are scary. Putting up a bit of 'dazzle roll' or cheap wallpaper makes a classroom a much more inviting place. Try to get something interesting on the walls before introducing a new class to their new classroom.

- **Try to give the children a space of their own.** A drawer and a peg to hang their coats – something they have ownership of – seems to be something of a touchstone for younger children. It can also be the source of argument and disruption, so you need to foster the idea that personal spaces such as work drawers are to be respected by others.

- **Get down to their level.** When working with small children, they often seem to feel more comfortable when you're on their level, rather than physically, and possibly metaphorically, talking down to them. Making eye contact will often be easier when you're sitting on a low chair, or kneeling beside them.

- **Don't be excessively rigid.** Though you may have set clear guidelines about who certain children work with, or where they're expected to work, you may need to be flexible once in a while. However, you need to make sure this doesn't get out of hand. Try negotiating with the children so they get what they want in return for trying harder at something else. This way it isn't something they're likely to try to exploit.

26. Helping children to build self-esteem

Children who suffer badly from a lack of self-esteem often need a lot of support and fail to make good progress. Everyone needs a pat on the back once in a while, perhaps especially the really bright children. This doesn't have to be something that takes huge amounts of planning and preparation; it just takes a bit of thought and making the most of your opportunities:

■ **Give praise at every opportunity.** This will help not just the slower learners; everybody needs to be encouraged. Don't say something is good if it's not, however, as children seem able to see through this. If it *is* good, and the child concerned knows this is the case, then your praise has even greater impact.

■ **If your school has built-in reward systems, like 'show and tell' sessions, use them.** Keep a record of who takes work to show to the rest of the class, and try to keep a balance. Again, it means a lot more if everyone feels they have an equal chance. Try to ensure that the kinds of things that are celebrated are as diverse as possible, so it's not always the same ones who get the kudos.

■ **Consider whether ability grouping can help.** Children naturally compare themselves and their work to others in their class. If children are working with others of similar ability, then there's less likelihood that they will begin to worry about their own abilities. This way, everyone is likely to be kept reasonably happy.

■ **Put it on the wall.** Displaying a piece of work by mounting it and putting it on the wall can be an extremely good way of praising work and helping to build self-esteem. If you actually take the time and trouble to make a point of showing children's individual work on new displays, this could be the icing on the cake for them.

■ **As far as possible, make sure everyone gets something onto the wall.** This will ensure that all members of the class feel valued. Don't, however, start to put up work that doesn't demonstrate at least a good effort, otherwise the children themselves might be highly critical of poor achievement.

■ **Differentiate tasks and activities to avoid frustration.** If tasks are chosen to be appropriate to the children's levels, then the work they do will extend their abilities. However, avoid knocking their self-esteem by underestimating their potential.

■ **Manage stressful situations.** When working on assessment tasks the children may have to work independently. This can cause some to panic, so explain why you're getting them to work this way, and that you don't mind if their work is right or wrong, as long as they try their best and do their own work.

■ **Be straight, especially with the strugglers.** It's hard to be honest with them when work is not up to scratch simply because you want to be positive. Two things are important here. First, say what you have to say without embarrassing the child; as far as possible, do it discreetly. Secondly, try to make sure that you end on a high note, for example using the tried and tested comment: 'I know you can do so much better.'

■ **Sometimes it's worth enlisting others' support.** If a piece of work represents a significant effort, and you want to take this opportunity to really encourage a child, you could let them choose to take the work to another teacher to show off. You may even be able to send them to the headteacher with good news.

■ **Pair or group children to facilitate success.** Sometimes getting a maths whiz to work with someone who is struggling, or a technological genius to work with one who is all fingers and thumbs, can help both parties. The able children often benefit a lot, in terms of their own self-esteem, for being seen as an 'expert'. The less able gain from the individual attention.

27. Dealing with bad behaviour

Dealing with bad behaviour could be something you have to do day-in and day-out, or it may be something that fortunately only crops up from time to time. Either way, it needs to be handled firmly, confidently and consistently:

■ **Start with your school's policy on behaviour.** Knowing what procedures are in place and are supported by the school management will help you deal with bad behaviour consistently and positively. It's important for everyone in the school to sing to the same song sheet.

■ **Make sure there's consistency between teachers on what is, and what is not, acceptable.** Even disruptive and badly behaved children know the difference between a teacher who chops and changes, and one who always handles things firmly and fairly, and they respond accordingly. If they think there's a chance of getting a different reaction, they might try to provoke one!

■ **Keep the class informed when disruption occurs.** It can be useful to tell the rest of the class exactly what has taken place, although care should be taken not to embarrass the child concerned unduly. This serves two purposes: it reinforces the consequences of poor behaviour, and it stops gossip running rife, which could prolong the discomfort of the child concerned.

■ **Avoid open confrontation as far as possible.** It could be that children will become distressed or even violent when faced with having to deal with the consequences of their own behaviour. They may feel threatened and foolish, and being given time out to draw back from the brink is usually a good idea.

■ **You can say an awful lot with body language.** Often that's all that's required to avert potentially disruptive behaviour. A look, a raised eyebrow or a gesture can remind children of what's expected of them without making a big deal of it. Experienced teachers learn a range of non-verbal language to communicate effectively with naughty children.

■ **Never issue an ultimatum that you can't stand by.** If you warn a child that you will do something, and then don't do it, you will lose your credibility and inflame the situation further.

■ **Use different voices for different circumstances.** The tone of your voice may well say a lot more than the words you're speaking. Your voice can express a wide range of emotions, and this can influence children's behaviour profoundly. Children seem to respond more to the way in which something is said than to *what* is said.

- **Don't always blame yourself.** If a child behaves badly in class, there's often an underlying reason that has nothing to do with your expertise in managing behaviour in the classroom. Recognize that children behave badly for all kinds of reasons, and it's not always in your power to influence the causes of such behaviour.

- **If a problem continues, seek support.** If a child's behaviour becomes too disruptive, over a considerable period of time, remember that it's not just your problem. Approach your headteacher, special needs coordinator or mentor about how this bad behaviour could be managed more effectively.

- **Remember your responsibility to yourself.** If persistent bad behaviour is getting you down, approach your headteacher, or someone who can help you manage the situation professionally. You should not feel that you have to cope alone.

MAKING AND MANAGING RESOURCES

Primary teaching often seems to be a very resource-driven task. Producing stimulating, relevant and beneficial aids to help you teach is obviously essential but can also become extremely time-consuming and is not necessarily the key to being a good teacher. The most important resource in your classroom is you and your experience, but having the right teaching and learning aids to hand will make you a more efficient and confident teacher. This section aims to give ideas about what's worth doing, how to do it efficiently and how to use it to its best advantage.

28. Obtaining resources

All schools have a wide variety of resources that might help you in your teaching and in the management of your class. Finding out what they have and where it's stored is another matter. You may find much of what you need, but you will probably have to make or borrow some of it for yourself:

- **If you're new to a school, try to get in before school starts.** It's always a good idea to try to get into school well before the beginning of term and have a look through resource rooms and cupboards in your classroom. Keep a note of the resources that you think might come in useful, and start thinking how you can use or adapt them for your own purposes.

■ **Review the topics that you will be teaching, and what you need to do about planning for those topics.** This will give you a much better idea of what resources you might need, making any lists of available resources you keep even more useful. You can then quickly locate and use material that's immediately relevant and useful.

■ **Try to consider the resources you'll need for the other work you might cover.** Think about what you might be dealing with in number, practical maths, phonics, technology, science and so on. See if you can collect resources for these subjects to kit out your classroom before you need it all.

■ **Learn how to laminate your paper resources.** If you make any work cards, get them laminated or 'Shire Sealed' to protect them from the rigours of classroom life. Even sealing master copies of worksheets that you intend to photocopy is a good idea, as they don't tend to get dog-eared so quickly. Colleagues and children are also more likely to return laminated resources than paper sheets.

■ **Store master copies of work sheets in plastic wallets.** If your school doesn't have them, then buying them in boxes of 100 from office supplies stores is fairly cheap to do. Storing sheets in special files for different subjects or topics is a good idea too. The better you index your materials, the less time you'll spend hunting for them.

■ **Using work cards saves on photocopying.** They allow you to give children slightly different tasks, cutting down on copying in class too. However, they take a lot of time and effort to make, so preserve the investment by keeping master copies and photocopy the master onto card. Keep the master copy in a safe (separate) place, just in case!

■ **Try to share resources.** If you work in a two- or three-form entry school, it's likely that you and your year group colleagues will be duplicating resources. Get together and plan who will produce what and cut the time you spend on making resources in half (or double the number of resources you can produce). Otherwise you might be able to borrow resources, or at least glean good ideas from teachers who have worked in your year group in previous years.

■ **Bear in mind that preparing too far in advance might be counter-productive.** It's tempting to use a summer holiday to get prepared for the whole year, but producing or collecting resources too far in advance can be a waste of time, because you may find that they're inappropriate or even irrelevant, especially if you're relatively new. You may need to spend a little time tuning in to what the children in a new class need.

■ **Buying a computer with a reasonable printer, for home use, will save you huge amounts of time in the long run.** Making multiple versions of slightly varying resources is so much easier when you don't have to start from scratch each time, and this is what computers are good at! It's also advantageous to be able to work at your own pace when you feel like it, rather than having to do everything on the school premises.

■ **The very best resources are the ones that can be used flexibly in many different ways.** Blank 100 Squares, number spirals, number squares, alphabet ladders, letter and number cards are worth their weight in gold because they can be used in so many different ways. Building up stocks of these sorts of resources can prove useful over and over again.

29. Choosing and using printed learning resources

The array of printed resources available to children in school can be bewildering. Children need to be helped (or taught) to use these resources effectively, and you'll need to make sure that the resources are well managed and maintained so as to get the best out of them:

■ **Identify the intended learning outcome from each resource.** Many learning packages already contain explicit learning objectives but you may need to customize these depending on the context of your topic, and on the abilities of your children. Being very clear about what you want to achieve with learning resources is crucial to success.

■ **Plan in advance what you might be intending to assess.** Will you be able to use the materials you have chosen to inform your planning and to fulfil assessment tasks? Make sure that you tailor assessments to the identified goals you have set yourself, to give your children the best possible opportunities to show their best work in assessed tasks.

■ **Give children the chance to develop appropriate self-help skills.** Different resources can be used to develop different approaches, especially if they're accessible and well displayed. Give responsibility where you can to children, to select and use resources in a variety of ways.

■ **Try to strike a balance between independent and collaborative work.** There are considerable advantages in planning work in small groups, especially when resources and materials are limited. However, being able to work independently is important, not least for assessment of each child's understanding. Ideally, use learning resources to give children the chance to work both cooperatively and independently.

■ **Help children to put the skills they gain into a context.** It helps children if they know why the things they're learning will be of value to them. For example, being able to find a book at school has relevance to how to use libraries outside. Being able to use the contents page will help them find what they're looking for quickly, and is an invaluable skill. Being able to load a computer program at school has relevance at home and perhaps later in their working lives.

■ **Try to find out how well materials have already worked elsewhere.** Try to get feedback from other teachers. Ask them whether they were really worth the money? Did they help cut down the work load? Did they help with assessment? Did they remain current, or did they start to date quickly? Did the children enjoy using them?

- **Consider whether the materials will be self-supporting and self-sufficient.** Some learning packages rely on the availability of other resources, such as textbooks, others don't. Before you purchase them, it's worth asking whether you have sufficient or if further resources are required.

- **Look for materials that can be freely copied.** Photocopied materials can work out cheaper than a one-off learning package. Be very careful to ensure that you don't infringe copyright, as legislation is quite strict in this domain.

- **Be aware of 'apparent' quality.** Some materials look impressive but it's more important that the actual learning opportunities are sound and relevant. 'All that glisters is not gold.' Glossy production can sometimes be used to mask poorly thought-out learning materials.

- **Monitor children's learning from resources.** Do they find it easy to use them effectively? Do they enjoy using them? Do they affect the quality of their work? Are they eager to work with them, or are they reluctant to use them? If you do discover that you have purchased something that children hate, it's as well to cut your losses rather than persevere with materials that are plainly unsuitable.

30. Deciding on what's most important for you to do

Simply because there will never be enough time to do all the things that you might want to do, it's important that you prioritize your jobs. Sometimes it's obvious what must be done first, especially in the short term, but planning ahead and prioritizing your work well in advance will help you avoid wasting valuable time:

- **Remember that you're the most valuable resource in your classroom.** Your first responsibility is to yourself because you're the person who keeps your classroom running smoothly. Make time for yourself, and consider your own needs as well as those of the children.

- **At the end of a school day, first relax, then tidy up.** Perhaps get yourself a cup of tea and then set the classroom straight! It's amazing how much better things look when you know your classroom is sorted out and your records are up to date. It's also easy to feel that there are more important things to do first, but if you neglect your classroom then it's likely that the children will too. Avoid as far as possible leaving it all to the next day, when other priorities are likely to impinge.

- **Get the most immediate things done first.** If you can develop the discipline of getting your paperwork sorted out before you do anything else, then you know that you can afford to devote what ever time there is left in the day to less immediate things.

■ **Remember that making absolutely perfect resources for tomorrow's lesson might be unachievable.** Having well-presented, immaculate worksheets is a target to strive for, and they're always nice to have, but remember that you do the teaching, not the worksheet. It's better to compromise with reasonable quality than to struggle for perfection to the point of exhaustion.

■ **Recognize that making good resources for the next day's lesson might save you a lot of time.** They can help you to use your time in the classroom more effectively because children will have a better chance of using them unaided, allowing you more time to focus on what you want to do. Use the time you have available to make the most of what you have.

■ **Use your record keeping and planning to help prioritize essential jobs.** At the topic planning stage, it might be a good idea to make a list of resources you think you will need, and to decide roughly when you will need them. If you have any spare time or a willing helper, working through the list might help you actually get ahead of yourself!

■ **At the topic-planning stage, get hold of catalogues as well as resource books.** They will give you lots of good ideas and identify useful resources you might need, well ahead of time, so you can order them in advance. If you're really organized you can also submit requisitions and get photocopying done in advance too.

■ **Plan in advance to make the best of opportunities to beautify your classroom.** Again, at the planning stage, make a list of displays and activities that you would like to have in your classroom. Order, collect or scrounge what you're likely to need for them. This means that you'll never be stuck to know what to do next and that you'll always have a list of jobs ready for any helper who might offer.

■ **Consider what are the best uses of your time.** You may sometimes have to decide between keeping your paperwork and records up to date, or preparing resources for the next lesson. It's a difficult balancing act, but often short-term priorities will have to win, for pragmatic reasons.

■ **Recognize that you can't achieve everything that you might wish to do.** You may, for example, want to reorganize and label the resources by the water tray, or set up an interactive display for number investigation. However, you need to accept that such activities, although an important part of making your classroom a stimulating place to learn, are luxuries rather than essentials.

31. Identifying and filling in the gaps

Whether you're working in a school that has meticulous planning and record-keeping procedures, or one that barely offers any guidance at all, you will still come across gaps in the provision of National

Curriculum requirements, resources, guidance, your area of responsibility and in your classroom work. Identifying and filling in those gaps is a long process but will help you ensure that you do your job properly:

- **In long-term planning, cross-reference activities with learning outcomes.** If you're working with existing planning guidelines, photocopy the guidance notes and keep them in a prominent place. Tick off the learning outcomes as you plan an activity that covers them. This will help you to monitor continuously what you are achieving.

- **In short-term planning, cross-reference actual work with planned work.** Keep an additional photocopy of your planning sheets and tick off each activity as you do it. This way you avoid creating gaps in the first place. It also gives you a great sense of personal satisfaction, as the sheets get progressively busier!

- **In planning for your curriculum area, cross-reference planned outcomes against National Curriculum requirements.** If you're planning or reviewing the provision for your curriculum area, get a copy of the programme of study from the National Curriculum, and tick off each part as you identify it within the whole-school plan.

- **Nothing beats effective record keeping.** If your records are thorough and up-to-date, identifying the gaps will be so much easier. If there's a system for record keeping in your school, use it. If not, make your own: it isn't just a matter of being well prepared for OFSTED inspections, it's part of being a professional.

- **When trying to plug the gaps, use every other source possible.** If you've identified a gap in provision while reviewing your curriculum area, look through source books, catalogues, the library, and talk to colleagues and other staff concerned for ideas on how they cover these areas.

- **Consult the rest of the staff when planning changes that are to be made.** If, having completed a review of provision for your curriculum area, you identify gaps in provision and need to add to existing plans, it's diplomatic to approach the staff concerned with some ideas, and the paperwork that shows where the gap exists, before making any firm decisions. Involve them in decision making, and you're more likely to take them along with you in any changes you initiate.

- **Try bringing up issues in the staff room.** The biggest database of ideas that will help you fill gaps in your planning is the experience of the rest of the staff, and 99 times out of 100 someone will have tackled the problem before. Use your colleagues as a resource, to help you to bridge gaps, rectify omissions and correct for oversights.

- **Approach the subject coordinator for assistance.** If you come across a gap in provision that you don't feel you have the expertise to fill as effectively as you should, ask the subject coordinator. Such colleagues might not always be able to help, but they should be able to put you in touch with someone who can.

■ **Use your Local Education Authority advisory service.** Although they're usually only available for assistance with school-wide issues, they can help you ensure that the provision in your school is complete, and can help with ideas and resources to remedy deficiencies. They also have a wealth of expertise and experience you can draw on.

■ **Map basic skills across the curriculum.** While mapping skills progression across the whole school and the whole curriculum is a highly complex task, breaking it down into Key Stages, or even year groups, can make it more manageable, and can give guidance to staff and help to ensure continuity of provision.

32. Using other people to produce classroom resources

If you have access to parents, governors or members of the community who are willing to help, you would be mad not to at least consider the opportunity. Be aware also that some people who would like to help can't give time to work in the classroom, but may be able to offer support in the production of classroom resources:

■ **Cast your net wide.** Sometimes people are reluctant to come forward and offer help, so send out a letter or put up posters making it clear that there are many ways in which people can assist. These don't necessarily involve working alongside you in the classroom.

■ **Use positive influence to get assistance whenever possible.** If you're trying to press-gang a few into helping out, foster the idea that the school can only work well with help from the community. Point out that even someone with just a half an hour to spare can be of use. Foster a sense that children's learning is the responsibility of everyone concerned, not just teachers.

■ **Give helpers an example of what you want.** If you're getting others to make or prepare resources for you, it's often easier to show them rather than to explain what's required. It may also give them confidence to watch what you do, and to practice while you're there to give them feedback (and lots of praise and thanks).

■ **Only provide sufficient resources to complete the task.** With the best will in the world, helpers often forget how precious and limited school resources are. Making sure that you give the right amount of resources will help preserve stocks and make your requirements clear.

■ **Be realistic about setting time goals.** Both in and out of the classroom, giving people a clear idea of how long it should all take will help ensure that the task is done in the way you want. Some people offering help might otherwise strive to achieve unrealistically high levels of perfection, and then become fed up, ultimately withdrawing their support.

- **Train your helpers to be aware of everyday chores.** You might even want to draw up a list of jobs linked to learning resources that are always in need of attention, such as sharpening pencils, cleaning paint pots, sorting shelves, tidying and cataloguing resources and so on. This way you will be able to make the best use of helpers' time.

- **Ask helpers to *support* the children in the management of resources.** Children need to learn not to waste resources unnecessarily, and to tidy up after themselves. Classroom helpers can reinforce this.

- **Try not to depend excessively on voluntary help.** Sometimes it won't become apparent until the eleventh hour that the help you had expected isn't going to materialize. When you plan activities that will rely on such help, spare a thought for what will happen if you're let down. Have contingency plans to cope with the situation.

- **Get volunteers to keep their eyes open.** If you keep parents and helpers up to date with what's happening in the classroom, they can keep an eye out for materials and resources that might come in useful, or offer suggestions for valuable, additional opportunities to extend your work. They often have access to all kinds of free or cheap materials that can supplement your restricted stock.

- **Consider sending jobs home.** Some parents or volunteers might be able to tackle jobs such as sewing, mounting work, laminating or 'Shire Sealing' work cards or books, doing such tasks better at home than in the classroom. Make sure, however, that you let them know if the job is urgent!

33. Access to resources

Life in the classroom tends to be happier and more productive if the children know where to find things, and if they can access what they need, when they need it. How you set up and manage this will depend on the facilities you have available, and what options you have about where and how things are stored. The following suggestions give some general principles you might bear in mind, to make life easier for yourself:

- **Put as much as possible out on show where the children can see it.** You may have shelving in your classroom that will help you display the resources you have, but you otherwise might need to resort to taking cupboard doors off fixed units, to give you more accessible shelf space.

- **Organize resources according to curriculum areas.** It makes sense to collect resources for one subject in one area. Materials can be further categorized by having resources specifically for number work or supporting written work, for example, grouped separately.

■ **Have your categories clearly identified.** If you colour-code the containers in which you keep your resources according to the subject that they support, it'll be easier for the children to work out where resources should be put back, and what kinds of work they're likely to be used for.

■ **'Shadow' and label your shelves.** If every resource container is clearly labelled with the name of what should be placed there, clearly marked in the space from which it came, children will know what to put where. If your shelves are 'shadowed' and labelled they will know where resources should go, but most importantly, you will be able to see precisely what's missing when tidying up hasn't been done properly.

■ **Use pictorial cues where possible.** Labels and shadow labels may not help if children can't read. Providing visual cues to containers' or shelves' contents, as well as the relevant title will supports those with poor reading skills, and may help reinforce useful vocabulary.

■ **Draw the children's attention to what's available.** It's easy to assume that, just because things are on display, the children will know where they are. Point out to them what's there for their use. Discuss why it's sorted and stored in the way that it is. Ask them what they think those particular resources might be for.

■ **Collect and display resources for investigation.** Getting children to think about investigation and raise questions, isn't always easy. Having interesting resources out on show for them to explore, discuss, handle and look at may provide opportunities for exactly that.

■ **Don't expect role-play areas to run themselves.** Providing a beautiful home corner, or an exquisite post office for the children to play in, isn't enough in itself. If you don't have time to play in there too, talk to the children about what things are for, what they could do, read relevant stories, show videos, indeed use anything you can to give them ideas to try out in their play.

■ **Put resources at child height.** If the children can't see the resources left out on shelves or in cupboards, because they're too high up, it will rarely occur to them to try and use them. Worse still, they may get into danger if they try to climb up to get them down.

■ **Label things that can't readily be looked in to.** If resources that are stored in plastic boxes or cupboards are for the children to use, then label them clearly and, if possible, put some kind of visual clue on the front too. This will help to draw things to their attention and possibly stimulate their interest.

34. Accessing materials and resources outside school

Resources, materials and support are widely available if you know where to look and you're not afraid to ask. Some sources will be linked to your Local Education Authority and others will be private ventures. All are worth plundering in order to stock your classroom and enhance your curriculum:

- **Remember that local shops are worth a visit.** Some companies set aside an amount of stock to donate to schools and charities. Asking for raffle prizes or tombola supplies can take time but can also be rewarding. It's amazing what people can give you for free, if you're cheeky enough to ask. Be sure to speak to the managers or supervisors, however, who usually have authority to write off stock. Junior staff may just dismiss your request out of hand, because they don't know company policy or are not authorized to made decisions of this sort.

- **Don't be afraid of your computer.** Most authorities have a Technology Development and Support Centre. They will be able to advise you about hardware and software, and will usually have hardware for you to try out on loan. They also may be able to advise you about how to get hold of equipment that has been declared superfluous or redundant, but which may be just right for your needs.

- **Plunder schools library services to boost topic resources**. You're likely to be able to borrow from a wide range of project collections that usually include maps, posters and booklets as well as books. This can extend the stock of resources you have in school, and can provide a greater variety of materials for you and your children.

- **See if you can borrow things from local museums.** Many museums have education departments that will lend objects to schools, or staff to bring objects in to school and talk about them. Obviously, you'll need to take care of whatever is lent to you, but children are often stimulated and excited by real artefacts.

- **Find out if you have a multicultural resource centre.** Centres can provide resources as well as offer training courses. They're likely to offer specialist services and materials, which will extend your repertoire and provide valuable diversity in the classroom.

- **Try to get experts into school.** You may be able to persuade parents or people from local religious and social groups to visit the school and talk to the children. They will need briefing carefully about the level of the work done by the children and what you hope to achieve, but the benefit to all parties is likely to be high.

- **Take opportunities to work with others who teach in the same age range as you.** Many LEAs run 'Early Years' meetings (among others) where you can meet regularly to discuss planning and working styles and share ideas with other schools around you. These can provide invaluable networking opportunities, and may help you to feel less alone in your work if you're new to the job.

- **Find out about local resource centres.** Many councils bring together under one roof a variety of resources and materials that have been donated from other areas of the council and businesses. It's amazing what a treasure-trove you can often access in this way.

■ **Don't be afraid to beg, scrounge and plead.** Local businesses whose raw materials could be of use to you can often be persuaded to provide materials free of charge, as long as you'll take what you're given and collect it yourself. What are, to them, often waste materials, such as off-cuts, roll-ends and so on, can provide super materials for the classroom. Take special care, however, that what you bring into your school is safe for children to use.

■ **Try to visit jumble sales and car boot sales.** Or get a parent or helper to go for you. It's amazing how many costumes and props you can find for next to nothing! You will, of course, need to check everything carefully, to make sure it's clean, serviceable and safe.

ASSESSMENT AND RECORD KEEPING

Effective assessment and record keeping are essential for effective teaching. Without good and consistent assessment of your pupils' abilities, you can't plan or provide work that moves the children on at the right rate. Similarly, without efficient and effective record keeping, you can't be sure that your pupils are progressing as well as they should. This section offers some practical suggestions about how to do both without them becoming too much of a chore.

35. Keeping track of progress

Keeping your records and documentation in order will help you to keep track of many of the things that go on in a busy classroom, both in the long and short term. They're useful not only in terms of good management, but also in terms of demonstrating to other interested parties what's going on:

■ **Think about how best to use matrices and tick sheets.** Draw up a list of the names of the children in your class against a blank grid, and then photocopy it several times. This sort of grid can be used in any number of ways and situations to record vital information.

■ **Keep records of each child's individual activities, as well as of those of the class as a whole.** Tick sheets can give a good overview of what's going on in a classroom if used to record and plan the tasks the children have undertaken, and can provide a record of what they've achieved. You can also then keep track of each child's progress in important areas.

■ **Use tick sheets as an assessment tool.** Each activity described on your matrix will have a learning outcome identified in your planning. Use them to record whether you feel that each individual has actually understood what has been done. It will also help you to build evidence of individual achievement for formative assessment.

- **Get advice on keeping formal recording procedures.** Many schools will have some form of standardized record keeping and assessment. Seek advice from a mentor or appropriate coordinator on how to use them and try to get ideas about how different people use them and keep them up to date. Sometimes the job is not as onerous as it first seems.

- **Keep your records as simple as possible.** If you're not required to keep records of individuals' achievements against National Curriculum targets, but feel it would be useful, simply photocopy relevant pages from the National Curriculum documentation, and highlight those aspects of the level descriptions a child has attained. This will provide you with a clear overview of achievement.

- **Identify opportunities for assessment as you go.** You can use any and every task as an assessment task, if it seems appropriate and sensible. If you always decide what you want the children to learn before you decide the activity you're going to use to teach it, you will automatically have identified what it is that you could assess through that work.

- **Manage your class so that you have time to spend with every child.** Keeping track of what everyone in the class is doing is very tricky, especially if you're running an integrated day. Concentrate on one job at a time and train the children to expect that you'll be there to support them at all times, but that you'll share your time out between them. This helps prevent you from being interrupted, unless it's an emergency. Get the children used to the idea that normally you will approach them, rather than vice-versa.

- **Use the observations of helpers in your class.** If auxiliaries or parents have been well briefed about activities that are undertaken with groups of children, they will know what you're looking for and their observations and comments will be useful in helping you to monitor activities and achievements.

- **Get the children to do some of the recording for you.** Older children should be well able to take responsibility for recording what they have achieved in class, so they could fill in record sheets for you. With younger children the same thing could be achieved but will require an imaginative approach. You could, for example, ask them to put stickers onto a wall chart once they have completed a task which has a specific outcome which you could review later.

- **Grow eyes in the back of your head.** Or at least try to tune in to the more unusual sounds or movements in the classroom. If they're unusual, then they probably shouldn't be happening! The price of peace is eternal vigilance.

36. Assessment and planning

The ideal situation in the organization of your teaching is that you should teach what the children need to know, find out if they have understood it or not and then continue to the next area. This link between planning and assessment can be tricky to establish, so you need to adopt systematic structures to ensure that such connections are established:

- **Don't be afraid to use your intuition.** One of the most useful forms of assessment is the impression you build up about the children in your class, what their needs are and where they're going. Such informal assessment, however, should be supplemented by evidence of achievement, as described in the section on 'Keeping track of progress', to avoid subjectivity swaying your judgement.

- **Don't be afraid of going over the same ground.** Children can't be relied upon to learn in a developmental way. If you feel that a child hasn't grasped an idea, giving the same task presented in a different way will be valid and valuable reinforcement. Classroom assessment should never be a 'sudden death' situation, where only one attempt is permitted.

- **Don't reinvent the wheel.** There are plenty of good ideas for assessment opportunities and planning strategies in source books and magazines. If they suit your purpose, use them; if they aren't a perfect match, just adapt them. Creative recycling is an excellent pedagogical principle!

- **Try keeping planning for topic work and core skills separate.** If you tie core skills to topic planning, you might find that progress through the topic dictates progress through core skills. It should be your informal assessment of progress in these skills that determines what happens next.

- **Don't underestimate the value of formal assessment as a record of achievement.** Although formal assessment may not appear to help you plan and teach, it's a good way of charting children's progress and identifying trends that may indicate problems. It may also provide base-line data against which you can make comparisons.

- **Don't overestimate the value of formal assessment for informing planning.** Many schools undertake a programme of formal assessment over and above those that are statutorily required. While, in theory, these assessments should assist you in your planning, in reality they often only serve to confirm your expectations. When the findings don't ring true with your gut feelings, take them with a pinch of salt, while keeping an open mind about whether your hunches might have been wrong.

- **Keep formal assessment manageable.** When carrying out formal assessment tasks, try to make them as similar as possible to those relating to ordinary classroom situations. It's probably better to annotate a piece of work outlining how it was completed, and then take this into account when grading it, than to force children to do it under 'exam conditions' where they might perform very badly.

■ **Remember that planning may need to be flexible.** If your assessments indicate that your long-term planning was over-optimistic, or isn't stretching the children enough, make a note of it and go with what your observations indicate to be a most useful course of action. All action planning should be dynamic and responsive to changing situations, otherwise it becomes merely an exercise.

■ **Ask questions.** Conversations with children about the work that they've been doing will reveal far more about their understanding of the work they're undertaking than a formal test. Their responses to questions can reveal whether a good work is mainly due to a good comprehension of the concept or task, or due to a lucky guess.

■ **Try to remember that the most under-used question is 'Why?'** If children are able to explain what they've done and why they've done it, it's a sure sign that they understand the concept well.

37. Learning outcomes

Recording specific learning objectives provides a systematic way of planning how the required elements of the curriculum will be delivered and evaluated. More and more teachers have to justify what they're planning to do in terms of what children will learn, and how they intend to assess whether that outcome has been understood. Many people do find learning outcomes hard to come to terms with however, so these tips are designed to smooth the way:

■ **Start from what you hope your children would be able to achieve by the end of a unit of work.** You may well be working with a topic that's already planned in terms of objectives or outcomes, but it's worth thinking about your goals for each session and how these will be achieved. If everything went absolutely to plan, what would the ultimate outcomes be like? Then you can start planning how to get there.

■ **Remember the difference between an aim and an objective.** An aim is a long-term goal that may take several weeks or even a term to fulfil. This is usually achieved by breaking the aim down into a series of short-term, specific objectives and working through them. So an aim might be, 'To develop children's familiarity with traditional stories' and linked objectives might be, 'To listen to the story of…', 'Sequence the main events in the story of…' and so on.

■ **Express learning outcomes in terms of actions.** Use lively action verbs such as 'Know…', 'Be able to…', 'Know the difference between…', 'Know why…' or 'Respond appropriately to…', to demonstrate exactly what it is that the children are expected to become able to do.

- **Work out how children will demonstrate their understanding.** Will this be through discussion, filling in a worksheet, a tally or pro forma, through written work, charts or diagrams, or simply getting the answer right in a classroom task? If you're clear about the evidence that you require to demonstrate achievement, the children will be too.

- **Be selective about the evidence of achievement that you require.** You may be able to think of several ways a child might be able to demonstrate understanding, but pick the one that you think will be the most appropriate, and stick to just that single activity. This will make it easier for you to manage, and will prevent children being overwhelmed by assessment requirements.

- **Decide what constitutes comprehension and what doesn't.** Your learning outcome may not contain quite enough information to act as a strict guide to assessment. Consider whether '8 out of 10' is enough, or whether to demonstrate proficiency, children need to get everything right.

- **Keep learning outcomes specific and very short term.** Units of work can usually be broken down into specific outcomes. These can often be tackled by having one outcome taught through one activity in one session. Outcomes should never be multiple, vague, or internally contradictory.

- **Consider whether one task might be able to assess many outcomes.** Combining assessments in this way will keep the work more manageable for you, and more interesting for the children. You will probably find that developing integrative assessment tasks is really productive and creative.

- **Don't be afraid of using the same outcome more than once.** Many aspects of classroom work have to be repetitive to be effective, so when a learning outcome is particularly important, it's likely to recur in a variety of different guises.

- **Keep the language of learning outcomes simple.** Don't feel that you need to dress them up in complex vocabulary: write outcomes that are clearly understandable by your colleagues, support staff, volunteers, helpers, and ideally, by the children themselves.

38. National Curriculum assessment

In the UK there are nationally standardized curriculum descriptors for schools, which outline what should be taught and assessed in all state schools. Feelings about these are mixed, but they have become part of every state school teacher's working life. These tips are designed to make National Curriculum assessment tasks of greatest possible benefit to you and to your children:

- **Have faith in your own experience.** Almost inevitably there are going to be times when children either under- or over-perform in national tests. Don't feel undermined by these results if you disagree with what they suggest. All kinds of factors impinge on children's achievements in formal tests, and they don't always perform to your expectations, or to their own potential.

- **Have faith in the children.** The chances are that they will know something unusual is going on when taking an important assessment. It might be best to just tell them exactly what's going on, without overplaying the test's importance. Children won't be fooled if you just pretend that nothing special is happening.

- **Consider the possibility that the children might actually enjoy the experience.** Sometimes the novelty value of a situation can make it a positive experience for the children. Try playing on this and make it an occasion: special pencils, new erasers, a new room and so on.

- **Don't feel that coaching in 'exam technique' is cheating.** In fact, to give children a fair crack of the whip, they will do better in the tests if you introduce ideas such as timed written work, or discussion of the possible interpretations of a maths problem. Rehearsal opportunities in stress-free contexts will help them get used to what's expected of them, and may lead to better performance. However, don't let preparation for tests take over the life of the classroom.

- **Try to get yourself trained.** Many Education Authorities offer support and training for staff undertaking Standard Assessment Tasks (SATs). Even if you have used SATs before, you might benefit from such an opportunity to learn more about the tests and how they impact on children.

- **Try a couple of dummy runs.** It takes a little while for teachers to understand the format and required procedures for certain tasks in Key Stage 1 SATs. You could try out the process on a couple of children who won't be being assessed that year, say from another class, in advance of giving the tests to your own class, so that if you get muddled or confused, it won't affect the performance of the children when it really matters.

- **Get hold of past papers.** You don't have to use them under test conditions but try including them as normal classroom activities. You'll have opportunities to help children to think their way through the problems they encounter and they'll get used to the format of the papers.

- **With one-to-one tests, leave your lower attainers until last.** Some of the tests are spread out over a number of weeks. Leaving your lower attainers until last might give them a little more time, to make the difference between one level and another.

- **Encourage children to 'have a go' at questions that they find difficult.** The more you can encourage the idea that a guess is better than no answer at all, the better the children's chances of picking up the odd additional mark. Sometimes children can be fearful of looking silly, so may keep quiet rather than risk a wrong answer.

■ **Keep parents or carers informed.** Once times and dates are confirmed for testing procedures, it might be as well to pass this information on to parents or carers. They're bound to be curious and will want to know what's going on. It will also give you the opportunity to explain the school perspective, and hopefully avoid rumours getting out of control. Of course this information could be used against the interests of the testing process, but it may still be worth the effort. It may also mean that parents are less likely to choose the day of the SATs for a dentist appointment, or an out-of-term holiday.

39. Assessing work

Using Statements of Attainment and level descriptors from the National Curriculum to grade and assess children's work is a job most teachers have to do somewhere along the line. Often interpreting these Statements, and turning them into meaningful classroom assignments, is hard work. These tips aim to help you to do this appropriately:

■ **Stick to the Statements as they are written.** Many National Curriculum Statements appear at first sight to be vague or impenetrable, but you should avoid the temptation to read something in to them that isn't actually there. Discuss with colleagues, mentors or any others that you're unsure about, and try to get at what's really required.

■ **Don't do it alone.** If you have a colleague in a parallel class or who you get on well with, you could try moderating one another's work. Another person's perspective, interpretation and opinion of your class's work is valuable, and gives you confidence in the quality of your own judgements. If there are no internal colleagues working at the right level, network outside your school to find people with whom you can set up mutually supportive arrangements.

■ **Use your school's portfolio of assessed work.** Many schools now have a collection of assessed work for at least the core subject areas. These portfolios show examples of work that demonstrate clear attainment at each relevant level of the National Curriculum. If your school has one, use it to compare to the work you're assessing. If it hasn't, it may be worth considering establishing one. Ask senior management for opinions and guidance on this.

■ **Use Statements of Attainment wherever possible.** The more familiar you are with the types of Statement used in national documentation, the easier it is to use them. Many of the Statements and descriptions are well written and concise. Try using them in your planning and possibly in your feedback to children, colleagues and parents or carers.

■ **Keep in mind that your professional opinion matters.** While national documentation and school portfolios are intended to help teachers to make standardized assessments of work, your professional judgement remains paramount. Trust your judgement and maintain a balanced view.

- **Consult avidly your school's assessment policy.** There may be clear guidance on how work should be selected, annotated and assessed. There may be examples of the sorts of statement that are required or felt to be useful. These will be a good starting point, especially for teachers new to the job.

- **Find out what assessing the children's work is supposed to achieve.** Sometimes it might seem that formal assessment of work is a waste of time. Different schools have different reasons for, and methods of, assessing work. Having an agreed purpose will give you a clear idea of what to include and what to leave out.

- **Find out what will happen to the assessed outcomes.** If you know your intended audience, it's easier to decide upon the sort of language and jargon to use. Some formally assessed work may be for parental consumption, and some for specific purposes in school. Knowing who will be reading your evaluations will help you tailor your comments accordingly.

- **If work will be sent to secondary schools into which your children feed, check what their requirements are.** Schools that will be taking your children may use the work you send them as a guide to help them stream pupils. If you know what their purpose is, it will help you decide what should and should not be included.

- **Find out if you're looking for 'value added' information in your assessments.** 'Value added' assessment should clearly show what progress children have made. This may involve repeating the same assessment procedure or by getting children to work under exactly the same conditions on similar tasks at given intervals. Obviously it's important to know this so that tests and criteria are applied consistently.

40. Formal and informal assessment

Assessment can take up enormous amounts of time and effort. To make the best of opportunities for assessment, it's worth considering what exactly it is that you're trying to achieve, and what might be the least complicated and stress-free way to get what you need:

- **Be aware that assessment's primary functions are to support and enable learning.** Without continuous assessment opportunities, you cannot know what the children have understood, and what they need to learn to make progress. It's all too easy to let the assessment become an end in itself, and to forget that it's only one part of the educational process.

- **Remember that the best assessment is often the easiest to manage.** To make realistic use of assessment it has to be manageable and consistent. Keep track of how children perform on a simple tick list and use that as your primary assessment record. Look for ways of streamlining assessment to get the maximum benefit for your efforts.

■ **It's easy to become obsessive about assessment.** If assessment isn't helping you to do your job better, then it can be a waste of time. Assessment is something you will always have to do, so try to devote time and effort in proportion to the potential benefits to be gained by everyone through the process.

■ **Try to make formal assessment tasks valuable.** Of course they're important in terms of the assessment requirements laid upon you, but try to make them valuable from the children's point of view too. If the task is worthwhile in terms of learning it's more likely to be worthwhile in terms of assessment.

■ **Make sure that any formal assessments that you undertake are really necessary.** If you know that they're going to serve your purpose, then go for it. If you're doing them only because you have to, check the school's documentation or discuss with management before putting yourself through it all.

■ **Try to keep assessment tasks as stress-free as possible.** This is important from your point of view and from the children's. A task that's too stressful for you won't be judged fairly and one that's too stressful for the children won't reflect their true ability. Don't work children up into a frenzy of nerves by over-stressing the importance of formal tests.

■ **Try to keep the format of assessment tasks you design familiar.** If you have to spend a lot of time preparing children for a task because it's presented in a way that they find hard to understand, then it may be more a test of their ability to understand the task, not the concept. Keeping the presentation, style and apparent purpose familiar will help to avoid this problem, by helping children to feel comfortable about what they're doing.

■ **Try to manage assessment tasks as straightforwardly as possible.** Formal assessment will often seem to be a slightly alien way of working with children. Even very young children seem to be able to understand when you explain to them what will be different and why. If they feel they know what's going on, they're more likely to undertake what's required of them without fuss.

■ **Keep notes while hearing children read.** This may be the best reading assessment evidence that you can gather, because it can capture significant detail, give examples, give a snapshot of skills and abilities and give a clearer indication of progress. You're also more likely to get an accurate view of children's abilities when they're in a less formal situation.

■ **Break down level descriptors into easily identifiable targets.** For instance 'mainly demarcated by capital letters and full stops' might be quantified as an average of two in every three sentences demarcated this way. Work on defining these descriptors as a school if possible, to achieve consensus. If your school has a portfolio of achievement, use this as a point of reference against which you can check your decisions.

41. Evidence of achievement

Over a period of time a body of evidence may be collected, which records and demonstrates a child's ability and attainment across all or important parts of the curriculum. The best person to collect such information is the teacher. To help make the collection of evidence a beneficial and efficient use of your time, we offer some guidelines on how to do it well:

- **Have an eye or ear out for evidence all the time.** One way of collecting evidence of a child's best work or highest achievement is to make the collection of such work an ongoing process. It's difficult in a busy classroom but, with practice, can become part of the way you work day-to-day.

- **Try putting some of the responsibility onto the children.** Especially with older children, the collection and selection of examples of their best work could become an interesting activity, perhaps towards the end of each term. You can also ask children to help each other to choose work that shows the best that they can do.

- **Common tasks could be used for all the class at given points in the year.** While collecting evidence this way may not always gather examples of a child's full potential, it will provide a consistent and continuous body of evidence. It also means that you have samples of work from every child, as a basis for individual evidence collections.

- **Include your own comments and observations.** A piece of work on its own may not tell the whole story. By adding notes about how the children tackled the exercise, and how much help they sought, the resources they used, etc, you can give a more complete picture. Try to keep such notes concise; you don't want to make extra work if you don't have to, and you're more likely to refer later to brief, pithy comments, than to extended pieces of prose.

- **Include information about aspects of attainment that have been demonstrated.** If a piece of work has been assessed against formal criteria and will be used as evidence, it's a good idea to note which aspects of a given level descriptor have been shown to have been attained through that piece of work.

- **Consider carefully the purpose for which evidence will be used, before gathering additional evidence.** If there is no requirement that you collect evidence of attainment, you need to decide what purposes it will serve before you start collecting it. The effort expended may not be paid back. Look for guidance in school documentation and from management.

- **Remember that your everyday documentation is good evidence.** If your planning and recording show what work children have undertaken, and perhaps an idea of their performance, then that is first rate evidence, which you may not need to supplement further.

- **Consider other ways of gathering evidence.** Many aspects of the curriculum are hard to collect evidence for. A record of your observations or opinions is usually sufficient, but you might also want to try using photography, video, art work or tape recordings too, to add diversity and breadth to your evidence.

- **Put the date on everything!** Try to get into the habit of putting the date on all work, and most especially on work that will be used as evidence. Having a file full of evidence is fairly useless unless it can be viewed chronologically, as you can't track progression meaningfully without time scales.

- **Make sure you know what the evidence will be used for in your school.** It may be that your school only requires work to demonstrate ability and not to map progress. If this is the case, then a large body of work accumulated over a period of time may not be necessary. Perhaps only one or two examples of good work are needed, or perhaps work needs to be kept to serve several purposes. Find out before you give yourself additional work.

42. Marking work and giving feedback

How you respond to children's work is an important aspect of communication between you and your class. It establishes expectations, emphasizes targets, praises and encourages achievement, supports and extends children's work, and has a profound effect on how they feel about it, and so is worthy of careful consideration. These tips are designed to help you to make the most of feedback to foster learning:

- **Consider what form of response is most appropriate.** Writing detailed comments on a piece of work in a reception class won't help the child concerned all that much, although might still be appropriate as a reference for an adult with an interest in what has gone on. With younger or less able children, oral feedback directly to the child will clearly be more appropriate than written remarks. More detailed comments in Year 6 can clearly serve an important role.

- **Don't be afraid to make negative comments.** Many people feel duty bound to only make positive comments, but if a piece of work is not up to scratch the child will not learn from it unless you point out the shortcomings. Use tact and diplomacy to avoid making your comments come across as destructive, however. Honesty without cruelty is the key.

- **Try to end on a positive or encouraging note.** If you've found it necessary to make a negative response to a piece of work, a simple comment indicating that the child is capable of doing better gives the child somewhere to go, and a safety net for dignity.

- ■ **Give oral feedback whenever possible.** For younger children, oral feedback is essential, whereas with older children work may be commented upon in writing after school. Nevertheless, if you can find time to offer oral feedback to children of any age at some point, especially if it's positive or related to an important issue, this is likely to have more impact than a written message.

- ■ **Keep written feedback concise.** If written feedback is too long, it may be disregarded, and not serve the purposes for which it was intended. Try to pick out one issue, one strength and give a brief general comment about it. It's better to focus on relatively few issues than to overwhelm children with too much.

- ■ **Date the work as you mark it.** Having the date on every piece of work is useful, especially if your children work on loose-leaf paper a lot. It also helps you to keep track of children's progression when you compare work over a period of time.

- ■ **Consider whether words are enough!** Children get a real buzz out of showing others how well they've done, and nothing counts like the approval of somebody new. For a real pat on the back try showing the rest of the class, send them to another teacher, the head, even to assembly or a 'Show and Tell' session. If your school has a system of points or assertive discipline, use it because it only works when everyone contributes.

- ■ **Use examples of good work as an example for everyone.** If a piece of work demonstrates the qualities you're looking for, discuss it with the rest of the class. Encourage them to think about why it looks nice, what makes it clear, well structured, neatly presented and so on. Let them learn more about what's expected from them, by showing them the standards that can be achieved.

- ■ **Display work that you feel demonstrates significant achievement.** Even if you weren't planning a display for that work, having a display that's simply for good work may provide a good incentive.

- ■ **When marking work, keep a focus on the intended learning outcomes.** Use them as your criteria for making evaluations. On the whole, the intended learning outcome of the task you're marking will give you a focus for your comments about the completed work. These comments will also act as a record for future reference of what the child was supposed to be focusing on.

43. Self-assessment

Encouraging children to think about their work and reflect upon how they could do better are widely regarded as being good practice. This isn't just a matter of letting children mark themselves, but a way of helping children to make realistic evaluations of their own achievements. It can be a powerful way of building children's self-esteem and of motivating them to work. However, some children find it difficult, so managing the situation takes some thought and some preparation. These tips are designed to help you get children involved in their own assessment:

■ **Start to train children as soon as possible.** Children can find it very difficult to reflect on their own work. Starting the process while they're young may seem to have limited immediate benefit, but the ability to critique one's own work is a difficult skill to develop and takes time.

■ **Get a progressive format for self-assessment.** To help children reflect in any kind of detail, worksheets that act as a guide or prompt may help. The form these sheets take could remain similar across the whole school, increasing in detail and complexity as the children's familiarity with the tasks and their overall abilities improve.

■ **Avoid regurgitation of your assessment of work.** Given the chance, children will simply repeat in their own words what you say in your responses to their work. To avoid this, you could simply ask them to select a piece of their work they're proud of and get them to explain why they think they did well and what they like about it.

■ **Scribe for younger or less able children.** To get any sort of relevant detail in self-assessment, you may have to act as scribe for younger children. While it would be nice to write down their comments verbatim, you may find you have to précis what they say to keep it manageable. You may also be able to use support staff or classroom volunteers to assist with the scribing.

■ **Consider how creative written work may give insight into children's ideas about themselves.** A piece of work entitled 'Why I like to be Me', 'A list of 10 things I am good at', or 'A Best Day of My Life' and so on, could provide a wonderful task, but also act as a valuable self-assessment tool. Be aware, however, that some children with low self-esteem might find the task very frightening.

■ **Try to strike a balance between positive and negative reflections.** While you will naturally want to get the children to focus on positive things about themselves and their work, it's important to get them to think about what they would like to do better, or how they could improve aspects of their work. This awareness of where they need to develop can help them set realistic goals for achievement.

■ **Reflect on what children have learnt at the end of a topic.** Sometimes children move quickly from one topic to another without noticing the transition. At the end of a short topic, you could get them to think about what they have learnt, what they enjoyed and perhaps what they didn't like doing too. This can give a defined ending to the topic as well as providing good personal assessment evidence.

■ **Review work with the children.** When looking back at a piece or a body of work, it might be a good idea to discuss the responses the children have made with them too. You could add comments that reinforce and extend the children's own thoughts. This is likely to provide opportunities for genuine dialogue, and insights into children's values of themselves.

■ **Consider how and where self-assessed work will be stored.** You may want to build up a file of work that each child is proud of. What will it be? Who will have ownership of it? Who decides what goes in and what doesn't? Where and how will it be stored? How can you ensure that it's available for reference when needed (which may not be the case if it goes home)?

■ **Allow time for children to look back over their achievements.** One of the nicest things about collecting work the children are proud of is watching their reactions to it a little further down the line. Giving them access to such work is a rewarding experience for them as well as for you!

44. Assessing children with special needs

Children may come into your class already identified as having special educational needs (SEN) or may for any number of reasons become a cause for concern while in your class. The chances are that it will be your responsibility to handle much of the work for assessing them initially, maintaining paper work, preparing and delivering individual education programmes and so on. UK state schools have specific procedures to follow, and this section applies primarily to these:

■ **Be alert to children's needs and potential problems.** Being responsible for the initial identification of children who might have SEN is a daunting and rather frightening matter. Whether you're a nursery teacher or in Year 6, it's important to be alert to potential problems.

■ **Be aware of both ends of the ability spectrum.** You need to be on the look out for those very bright, but possibly bored children who may need to be stretched, as well as for those who might be struggling and could need extra support to keep up.

■ **Look out for any worrying behaviour.** Bad behaviour is sometimes a result of boredom and under-stimulation or an inability to cope with the work being given. As well as dealing with the behaviour, consider what might be the underlying causes of it.

■ **Listen carefully.** Language skills, both expressive and receptive, can be a good indication of a child's real understanding of what's going on around them. If you become concerned about a child's ability to use language, it's a good indicator that you might need to seek extra help.

■ **Don't go it alone.** If you don't feel confident about identifying children, consult your SEN coordinator, who will help you with the kinds of points and issues you need to put in your 'Initial Concern' paperwork. You can also talk to others in the school, who may have more experience than you of SEN, or who may be familiar with the child causing you concern.

- **Use published assessment tasks.** There are many tests available that can highlight particular strengths or weaknesses, such as auditory memory, visual memory, expressive language, receptive language, hand-eye coordination and so on. Once an area of difficulty has been specifically identified, it will help you to fill in the appropriate level of paperwork, and seek the right kind of help.

- **Use the correct terminology.** When completing the necessary forms, keep your points short, tightly observed and covering only the main areas of concern. However, make sure that the vocabulary you use is precise, and explains explicitly what you're worried about.

- **When writing descriptors to help you define SEN, make them short-term and specific.** When filling in your individual education programmes, you must be clear in your targets. 'Will be able to use prepositions accurately' is rather woolly and unfocused. Try instead, 'Will be able to use: *in, on* and *under,* in a consistent and accurate manner'. This makes assessment and progress much easier to measure and record.

- **Keep parents or carers informed.** Once you have filled in an 'Initial Concern' form, you have to record whether you have had any contact with the parents or carers on this matter. Although it's not a legal requirement at this stage, it may be better to let parents or carers know early on what your concerns are and what could be done about them. This is better than risking them feeling marginalized later.

- **Be over-cautious.** If you're not sure, but think there may be a problem, even if you think it might sort itself out, fill in the paperwork and register your concern. It's better to be safe than to let a potential problem rumble on indefinitely.

45. Differentiation

With large, mixed-ability classes, delivering an effective curriculum is not possible without differentiation of tasks and the outcomes that children are expected to achieve. It's a tricky balancing act to match work to ability, in order to ensure that children are working at a level that they can cope with, but that also stretches them. Nevertheless, teachers need to be able to do this, to ensure that every child has a good chance to learn and develop:

- **Be realistic about how much differentiation is manageable.** In most situations, catering for three groups, higher, average and lower attainers, is about as much as can be achieved. This may not be perfect, but it will avoid getting bound up too often in the needs of small groups or even individuals.

- **Differentiate the activity, not the learning outcome.** In many cases it's possible to tackle the same goal at three different levels. Although this isn't always achievable, do it when you can, because it means you can discuss concepts as a class but tailor actual tasks to meet the children's individual needs, and it helps keep planning simple. It also helps less able children to avoid feeling marginalized to the same extent.

■ **Keep your assessment tasks differentiated.** If you set differentiated work it makes sense to use differentiated assessments too. Making assessment tasks fit the ways the children are able to work independently may initially make more work for you, but it will make for a more effective assessment for the children.

■ **Use different groupings for different subjects**. Someone who is below average in language may be above average in maths. It isn't always possible to group children in several different ways at different times in the day, but where it is, using different groupings will allow you to cater better for individual needs.

■ **Be prepared to change groupings.** Rates of progress differ and it may become apparent that some children are either racing ahead or getting left behind. Changing their groups will help them cope better. It may also be prudent to change groupings if behaviour gets out of hand, or if you're concerned about the effect that one child is having on another.

■ **Challenge children.** It's clearly important to stretch children to prevent them from getting bored. Knowing how much stretching they can take is very difficult, but setting them a challenge, one that you think only the most able will achieve, can be a good way of finding out how well individual children can cope and persevere. Try it as a class activity and share ideas and possible solutions.

■ **Try not to let a lack of basic skills hold children back in other ways.** A child may have poor pencil control, or be unable to read without support, but these things do not indicate a lack of ability in other areas. As far as possible, try to support those aspects of the work with which they struggle, but stretch them in other aspects of the curriculum.

■ **When putting children into groups, draw up a set of criteria for group formation.** How you decide upon who goes where, and who works with who can be tricky. Having a set of criteria can help take some of the guesswork out of the process, but be aware that sticking rigidly to criteria can make life more complicated, and may not give you the result that you intend.

■ **Differentiate whole-class teaching.** One of the appealing things about whole-class teaching for some, is that everyone is doing the same thing at the same time. This style of teaching can still incorporate differentiated elements. Even if it's simply the expected outcome that's differentiated, as long as these expectations are recorded, it's still a valuable way of enabling children to work at levels at which they can succeed.

■ **Differentiate the support you offer.** Another way of using similar activities, but still ensuring that they're tailored to meet different children's needs, is to differentiate the level of support that they will have in order to complete the task. Be careful, however, that children who don't need support don't feel ignored.

YOUR PROFESSIONAL LIFE

There is a great deal more to being a teacher than just teaching. Every teacher will be faced with an array of additional duties that, in time, will become second nature. However, early in a career they can cause quite a strain, not least because nobody seems to have thought to tell you what's involved until too late! Forewarned is at least partially forearmed.

46. Inspection

Many teachers find the idea of having someone else in the classroom, watching over their teaching, a daunting prospect. Nevertheless, such visits are part of the professional life of every teacher nowadays. Such occasions don't have to be traumatic, however. If you prepare well you can make the experience less stressful and more useful. These tips are designed to help you to make inspection as positive an experience as possible:

- **Recognize that it's worth spending time preparing.** It's all too easy to be so busy with everyday matters that it's tempting to take the attitude, 'They'll have to take us as they find us.' Taking the time to make sure that you're ready for the visit will pay off in terms of your own confidence.

- **Prepare well in advance.** It's never too early to start preparing. Get an action plan, including target dates, and take responsibility for the things that you think you can manage. Avoid the 'groundrush' effect, as in parachuting, where everything seems to speed up horribly towards the end.

- **Prepare for an inspection, even if one isn't actually imminent.** If you work day-to-day towards narrowing the gap between where you are and where you think you need to be, the anxiety of the actual date should diminish. The more your record-keeping and good professional practice is a matter of routine, the less stressful an inspection visit will be.

- **Let everyone know.** Coping well with an inspection needs to be a team effort. Don't make the mistake of assuming that everyone, including cleaners, caretakers and non-teaching staff know about it. Tell them and help them to feel part of it all. After all, everyone will have an important part to play in building a good impression of the school.

- **Talk about it.** Discussing worries or concerns that you may have with other professionals will probably lighten the load, just because you have got them off your chest. You may even discover that there's a lot you can help one another with.

- **Make full use of other people who've done it before.** You may well know other teachers who've been visited, or even people who are trained inspectors. Use their experience and pick their brains because they may well have some good advice, examples that you could borrow and adapt, or encouraging words: it all helps!

- **Avoid complacency based on previous successes.** Even if you or your school has had a successful inspection on an earlier occasion, don't make the mistake of assuming that the next one will be equally positive. The goalposts may well have been moved, and certainly it will involve different people with different perspectives. Treat each inspection as a new occasion to demonstrate your approach to teaching.

- **Avoid despair based on previous negative experiences.** Even if you have had an inspection or pre-inspection that was traumatic, it doesn't mean that the next one will be. Because things change, and you've been busy, you may not have had the chance to reflect upon how much progress you've really made. Additionally, if you have seriously addressed the comments made in a previous less successful visit, you will have plenty of evidence to demonstrate commitment to improve.

- **Get the team spirit going.** When colleagues get together and work as a team, they create a positive attitude and a favourable impression, rather than conflicting attitudes or approaches. When everyone pulls together, preparing for inspection can be a positive team-building experience.

- **Don't get it out of proportion.** Lengthy meetings in preparation for a visit often end up being unproductive and negative. It's better to have frequent, short meetings with tight agendas and specific goals. Strong leadership doesn't hurt either, so be prepared to take the bull by the horns, if your role requires it. Or be prepared to knuckle down and really work for the sake of the school, if you're asked to do so.

- **Make distinctions between what's urgent and what's important.** Not everything that is important is urgent, and vice versa. Decide upon what's important and then try to work out which of these important things is urgent. Then you can concentrate on your highest priorities to get ready for inspection.

- **You can't solve every problem overnight.** It may be more sensible to make an action plan to tackle a problem you have identified, than to implement a hasty solution immediately. Often inspection looks more favourably on a considered and measured response that's still being implemented, than on a rush job or a cover up!

47. Appraisal

Appraisal is an established part of school and personal development in teaching professions, although sometimes accepted simply because it's inevitable! The aim is to help you as a teacher, and to help the school as a whole. Approach it confidently and positively, using it as a chance to evaluate your own performance, with support, to look forward to developmental opportunities, and to review where you need to go next:

- **Have confidence.** The first and most important thing to remember is that appraisal is designed to help you perform more effectively as a teacher and to give your best to the job. If you find it intimidating, take time to discuss this with your appraiser. Good ones will take your concerns seriously, and address them as part of their negotiation with you.

- **Take the opportunity to discuss the focus of the appraisal before you start.** You should aim to have the opportunity to plan what your appraiser should focus on in your appraisal in advance. Try to make sure that you talk to your appraiser in advance of the appraisal, to set an agenda that suits you both. If your appraiser doesn't raise the subject with you, you may need to tackle it yourself.

- **All feedback is potentially useful.** Without impartial feedback, getting better at your job is very difficult. Appraisal aims to make impartial advice and constructive criticism available to all teachers, so try to make it an occasion to listen, take what's said on board, and move towards positive development.

- **Be prepared to receive positive feedback.** Don't be embarrassed about receiving praise, but listen carefully. Knowing what your strengths are can help you to capitalize on them and, as such, is a vital aspect of appraisal. Don't dismiss or underplay what's said to you; take it at face value.

- **Be prepared to receive negative feedback.** What you at first hear as criticism can actually be valuable feedback. It's difficult for an appraiser to say things that they know you don't want to hear, which makes the fact that they felt it important all the more pressing. Knowing where your weaknesses are is as important as having confidence in your strengths. Don't let natural reactions to the less positive things you hear stop you from using this feedback to build plans for future improvements to your teaching.

- **Be prepared to try to elicit feedback.** If an agenda for your appraisal has been set and comments, one way or another are not forthcoming, be prepared to press your appraiser on these points. It's not a bad idea to have prepared in advance some specific questions you would like answered about your teaching.

- **Use the feedback to set yourself targets.** Take the opportunity to discuss potential ways forward and, in conjunction with your appraiser, set yourself targets or suggested routes for tackling issues.

■ **Take reassurance from the fact that all appraisal is confidential.** The advice and feedback given to you will not become common currency in the staff room, unless you choose that it should.

■ **Look for developmental opportunities.** The appraisal is often your best opportunity to discuss what you feel are your professional training needs, in order to help you to do your job better. Appraisal is designed to look forwards as well as backwards. Consider, for example, how you can use chances to observe others teach, as an opportunity for your own personal development.

■ **Remember that everyone's in the same boat.** Everyone in your school should be the subject of appraisal, from headteachers to Newly Qualified Teachers, so there's no reason to feel that you're under special scrutiny or that you're being treated differently to other members of staff.

48. Mentoring and supporting student teachers

The chances are that at some point in your career you will be asked to support other people's professional development. With more and more of a student teachers' time being spent in school, and the increasing use of mentoring in the continuation of the learning process for Newly Qualified Teachers (NQTs), this role is more likely than ever to be part of your professional duties:

■ **Get as much information about your students as possible, in advance.** Universities and colleges might not be very forthcoming with information about the students, how they have performed on the course so far, and any issues that might be useful to know about in advance. Try to get to talk to the student's tutor before the practice begins.

■ **Be prepared to give practical demonstrations.** Learning the tricks of managing a classroom takes time, and students and NQTs might need to watch you in action in order to be able to develop or reflect upon these skills for themselves. If possible, give them a running commentary; they may not otherwise notice some of the things you do automatically.

■ **Start students off with non-threatening situations.** Give them the chance to get involved in simple activities that they can plan and manage for themselves, such as reading a story or focusing on an aspect of small-group work. This will help give them the confidence they need before tackling bigger things.

■ **Let them know what you will be looking for.** There will be times when you'll have to make formal observations of students and possibly NQTs. Let them know what you will be focusing on and what you will be looking for in advance, so they have the best possible chance of meeting your expectations.

- **Encourage students and NQTs to observe different teachers.** Any opportunities for picking up ideas about teaching and managing a classroom, in as many different contexts as possible, can only be good. It will also take some of the pressure off you.

- **Let the students evaluate their performance first.** If students can identify good and bad points in their teaching, then 90 per cent of the work is done already. You may still need to highlight points they have missed, but letting them come up with the majority of the issues makes for a more comfortable experience for both of you. Be aware that they're likely to be extremely self-critical at first, however.

- **Plan together.** If you leave sole responsibility for planning to students, then problems that could have been identified, solved and avoided at the planning stage, may surface in the classroom, having detrimental effects on their teaching and their confidence and on your class! Joint planning also provides opportunities for students to understand the mechanics of how you go about preparing for classroom activities.

- **Be prepared to let them make mistakes.** It's tempting to quietly intervene when you spot early-warning signs of potential problems that your student has missed. Identifying and tackling one's own mistakes is a valuable learning experience for students. If you intervene, they will not see, for example, the consequences of allowing minor disruptions to go unchallenged. Obviously, if something is going seriously wrong, don't just leave them to suffer the consequences; intervene with tact and diplomacy.

- **Remember that students need encouragement and reassurance.** Sometimes they need more than the children themselves. It's difficult and stressful being put in the position of doing an experienced person's job while that person watches you. Help them to remember that you went through the process yourself when you were being trained.

- **Make sure that you don't over-commit yourself to other tasks.** Someone might be taking responsibility for your class for eight weeks, but that doesn't mean you're going to be free to get on with all those jobs that have stacked up over the term. In fact you may be amazed by how little free time you get out of being out of the class, while a student is with your children.

- **Prepare for a failing student.** If you feel that a student or NQT isn't coping, hard though it is, it will be your responsibility to broach this with them. Discuss your concerns with university tutors, your headteacher, and the students themselves. Try to come up with strategies for dealing with the situation, setting small, manageable targets and monitoring them daily, take back overall responsibility for the class, arrange for additional auxiliary support for a short while, or whatever.

- **Remember that mentoring can be a rewarding experience for you as well.** It may give you opportunities to focus on your own teaching styles, it will make you think more carefully about what you do and why you do it. Though it can be hard work, the benefits should outweigh the drawbacks.

49. Being a newly qualified teacher (NQT)

As an NQT you may feel swamped with information, bewildered by all the frantic comings and going, left out, or perhaps the butt of the jokes and the banter, and terrified of the prospect of flying without a co-pilot. Here are some things that you can do before you start and, in the early days and weeks, that might help you find your feet:

- **Aim to visit the school if you can, when it's in session, before you start.** Nothing can prepare you better than looking around your new school while it's in full swing. Having a feel for the place, its routines, its layout and the people that are in it before you start is a real confidence booster. If at all possible, once you're appointed, get in before the holidays start.

- **Try to get hold of useful information about your school.** This is likely to include copies of the school prospectus, staff lists, a map of the building, a timetable, the sorts of information that the parents or carers will be receiving and asking questions about, and how the register should be filled in. Get anything that you think might come in handy, and spend some time perusing it so you know the right kinds of questions to ask before you start to teach.

- **Get hold of copies of school policy documentation and schemes of work.** Many of the policies will not appear to be instantly relevant; ignore them for the time being but file them for later reference. With those that will affect the way you work from the first day, take the time to read them before term starts and look at how they will impact on your day-to-day life.

- **Check discipline strategies.** Knowing the range of sanctions available to you is important for your own confidence, as well as for managing the behaviour of your new class. If you can achieve consistency from day one, then so much the better.

- **Read assessment, marking and recording policies.** This will give you a good insight into the kinds of areas that you may need to ask about, and will help you keep appropriate records up to date right from the outset.

- **Gather pupil records.** It helps if you're familiar with the names of the children in your class, and have an idea of their personalities. Be careful not to label children though, as they tend to live up to expectations. Keep a healthy scepticism about what you're told about pupils: some views you hear may be jaundiced!

- **Ensure that your lesson plans are well prepared.** This will give you confidence. Also prepare teaching materials well in advance. Most new teachers prepare far too much material at first, but it's better to have too much than too little. You will also normally be able to use any surplus later.

- **Be ready to ask colleagues for help.** You will probably be assigned a mentor. You should use this person to good effect. In the unlikely event of you using too much of their time, they'll let you know. Make use also of informal mentors, and others who are close enough to newly qualified status to remember what it's like to be just starting out.

- **Take opportunities for support.** You may be offered training to extend your skills early on, and you will probably be offered opportunities to meet with fellow NQTs from elsewhere. Go along: it's good to exchange stories of disaster and success. You will find that everyone is in the same boat, and that you can learn a lot from each other.

- **Be prepared to be observed.** Your headteacher or mentor will almost certainly want to observe your teaching from time to time. The areas they will want to look at will probably include class management, relevant subject expertise, appropriate teaching skills and styles, use of resources, your understanding of the needs of the pupils, and your ability to establish appropriate relationships with both pupils and colleagues.

- **Keep a sense of humour.** It isn't worth dwelling for long on lessons that don't go as well as you would wish. You mustn't expect to get it right straightaway. Try not to take every minor setback to heart. Use each seeming disaster as a learning opportunity.

- **Eat and sleep well.** You will probably spend most of your first term feeling exhausted. Avoid taking on anything more than you absolutely have to. It's important not to get too tired.

- **Be prepared for minor illnesses.** Many new teachers find they pick up every germ going around a school, so stock up in advance with cold remedies, throat sweets, and perhaps even treatments for head lice.

- **Give yourself time to relax at home.** Avoid talking about school all the time in your leisure hours; you need time away. Try to keep a proper balance between being well-enough prepared to be comfortable in your work, and having some chances to forget all about school for a while.

- **Arrive with plenty of time to spare.** Finding resources and setting up can take longer than you might think. It's worth getting out of bed an hour earlier than you would otherwise have done, so that if travel arrangements go wrong you still have some leeway.

- **Take a classroom survival kit.** Having a supply, for example, of erasers, pencil-sharpeners, a staple gun and staples, coloured biros, a whistle and a craft knife could all help save your neck on the first day.

- **Put together a personal survival kit.** You may need spare clothes in case of spills and messy accidents, for example. In many staff rooms you will be more welcome if you bring your own mug on the first day, and a small supply of tea and coffee, until you suss out the coffee fund. Many teachers also like a Walkman and a tape of calming music for the times when the children are out of the class, and preparation or tidying-up work needs to be done.

■ **Don't try to reorganize everything on your first day!** You will have a lot to cope with in the early weeks, so it might be as well to live with your classroom as it is at first, until you and the children have a chance to settle down.

■ **Make friends with the non-teaching staff.** They are often your best allies. The nursery nurses, auxiliaries, cleaners and caretaker, the dinner ladies and kitchen staff can be great resources and support. You may get useful information about the children (and about other staff) from them too.

■ **Keep a journal of your first year of teaching.** In this, you can record what went well and not so well, and this will help you to plan and prepare for the subsequent year. It's also helpful in preparing for your first appraisal, and can provide terrific reading to look back on when you're an old hand at the job.

50. Working with outside agencies

As a teacher you will probably need to liaise with a growing number of outside agencies. These might include doctors, nurses, social workers, members of the police force, educational psychologists, speech therapists, university and college staff, family support units, multicultural support workers, educational support services staff and colleagues from other schools. These tips aim to help you to develop a fully professional approach to working with any of these people:

■ **Check school procedures for dealing with 'externals'.** There may be clearly defined steps that you need to follow, for a variety of different issues. It's important that you're aware of these, and abide by the guidelines that are set down for inter-agency interaction.

■ **Find out what your responsibilities are.** Are you the best person to make contact with externals? Is it your responsibility to make the first approach? Who else from the school needs to be involved? Where does your responsibility start and finish?

■ **Find out whose job it is to keep everyone else informed.** When working on a particular case, it's important to find this out. It may be your responsibility, or that of your special educational needs coordinator, or that of the school's administrative assistant or even the headteacher.

■ **Keep individual records up to date.** When liaising with any outside agencies, it's vital to have accurate and up-to-date information on the child in question. This will enable the child to get the best support possible, and you will be above reproach in your dealings. You may need to fill in and maintain special reports or documentation. These will be important in most procedures that involve outside agencies.

■ **Keep notes about any communication.** If you talk on the phone, keep a record of dates, times, content, contact name and so on. These notes and any other correspondence should be kept with the rest of the case notes. Don't try to rely on your memory. Your life is much too busy to remember all the details you may need.

■ **Be prepared to express your opinions.** If called to a meeting about a child, you will almost certainly be called upon to give your professional opinion, as you spend proportionally more time with the child than any other professional. Rely on your records and stick to what you *know* to be true. Try to back assertions with evidence of some kind, for example, notes from incidents, which illustrate the problem as you see it.

■ **Be ready to speak in front of parents or carers.** What you're going to say, or need to say, may not be what the parents want to hear, for a variety of reasons. It's part of your job to say what's necessary, however hard this may seem. Stick to facts and try to support them with evidence, dates and so on. At the same time, remember how painful this is likely to be for the parents or carers, and use all of your tact and diplomacy.

■ **Keep a case diary.** Any relevant incidents or occurrences should be noted carefully. It's amazing how fast you forget the details of incidents, particularly if they're unpleasant, as you may wish to put them out of your mind.

■ **Get support from your colleagues.** Your mentor (if you have one), special educational needs coordinator and headteacher should all be able to give you advice about who to talk to and when to do it. Especially if you're new to the job, don't feel that you need to tackle everything yourself.

■ **Don't take it all home with you.** It's very difficult when you care about the children you teach, not to continue to worry about them outside the teaching situation. It's natural to be concerned, but once you have done everything that you can in identifying problems, seeking specialist support, and pressing for appropriate action to take, try not to let such problems take over your life. You'll be better able to look after the children in your care if you also look after yourself.

51. Liaising with parents or carers

An aspect of teaching that's difficult to get used to, and impossible to predict, is liaising with parents or carers. They may seek your advice, press you for information, confront you, perhaps even cry on your shoulder, and most of it won't wait until open night, so be prepared! Even experienced teachers often find working with parents a complex part of the job, so these tips are designed to prepare the ground for it:

■ **Remember that most parents or carers are on your side.** Most of the time, most parents realize what a difficult job teaching is, and that their child may be far from an angel. Most parents will be happy to cooperate with what you suggest, as they know you have the interests of their child at heart.

■ **Prepare in advance for open night.** Making notes that are specific and accurate to each child can help jog your memory. Have work to hand that may demonstrate the main points. If you have a lot of children, it can help to have an annotated class photograph to help you to make sure that you're talking about the right child, especially if several children share the same first name.

■ **Remember that some parents find speaking to teachers a real trial.** This is especially true of those who have had unhappy experiences of school themselves. Some parents find the whole atmosphere of school traumatic. Even parents who did well at school can find parents' evenings nerve-racking experiences.

■ **Don't forget that although you teach lots of children, parents are only really interested in their own.** Parents can be concerned to the point of obsession about their own children, and are often hungry for information about what goes on in school.

■ **Avoid making comparisons between children to parents.** You should focus on the child under discussion, rather than their best friends, or the brightest child in the class, or a sibling. In this context particularly, comparisons are odious!

■ **Focus on behaviour rather than on personality.** Parents are likely to be receptive to requests to help change behaviour, but may feel threatened if you concentrate on personality. They may feel you're being very critical of them; after all, personality types often run in families.

■ **Have a system to prevent some parents taking up all the time you have.** Concerned parents are very time-consuming, and it may be difficult to bring an interview to an end. Try timed appointments at parents' evenings, even though they always tend to over-run. If you're seeing individual parents out of school time in the classroom, you may sometimes need to arrange for a colleague to 'interrupt' you after a suitable time, say 20 minutes.

■ **If you're confronted by an angry or upset parent, remain calm.** Listen to what they have to say, and give them time to get it off their chests. Often aggression is related to fear, and the parent may be upset and worried about what you will do or say. Try to get to the root of the problem: it may well be something that's easy to sort out. In any case, you need to get a clear picture of what the central issue is.

■ **Don't let yourself be intimidated.** If a parent wants to talk to you in an inappropriate manner, or at an inappropriate time, or about something inappropriate, don't let them. Try to arrange an appointment with a more suitable person or at a more suitable time. However, do not ignore the problem, as that could make matters worse. If offering to arrange an appointment doesn't work, try to send for help, preferably from a member of senior management.

■ | **Have any relevant data written down.** If you do have to confront unhelpful parents or carers with news of bad behaviour or poor work, have something concrete in front of you, as a basis for discussion. You might be surprised how calming irrefutable evidence can be.

■ | **Avoid embarrassing parents or carers.** Many issues can be sorted out quickly at the beginning or at the end of the day. However trivial or mundane the matter may seem to you, a parent may not thank you for discussing problems you may be having with their child in public. Respect confidentiality, and you're likely to get a more cooperative response.

■ | **If you suspect a meeting may become awkward, get back up.** Have another adult in the classroom or within shouting distance. You probably won't need them but it will give valuable moral support.

■ | **Be as positive as you can.** Parents or carers, like children, respond well to praise, but make sure that you also tell the truth. If you have something unpalatable to say, try to think of something good you can say at the beginning of the conversation. Ideally, end the discussion with suggestions about positive action, something concrete that you would like the child or the parent to do.

■ | **Be honest.** Don't try to cover up a potential problem. Most parents or carers would rather face a problem and try to deal with it, than come to feel at a later date that you had not been totally honest with them.

■ | **Check school procedures on parent–teacher interactions.** This will make sure that you're assured of the school's support if anything should go wrong, and will mean that you're confident that you're acting within the appropriate framework.

52. Looking after yourself

In your life as a primary school teacher, you have to look after yourself because nobody is going to do it for you. Teaching is an exhausting and demanding job, despite popular rumours to the contrary, but taking the time and trouble to help yourself to cope and to manage stressful situations is time well spent. Here are some tried and tested ideas for helping to look after yourself:

■ | **Remind yourself of why you started teaching.** You may have discovered that the pay isn't up to much any more, and holidays get shorter and shorter as work takes over, but there are aspects of the job that are exciting and stimulating. Try to dwell on these things more, and the not-so-wonderful bits less!

■ | **Be realistic about taking work home.** Few teachers can get by without taking some work home, but taking too much home isn't a good idea. Try to strike a balance: only take what's essential and try to get as much as possible done before leaving school. If you can, try to keep it down to just one job a night! It just becomes depressing if you keep on taking the same tasks backwards and forwards between home and school.

- **Try to make space for your personal development.** You will be expected to update your skills and knowledge as a teacher. Try to take opportunities for training that also give you skills that might help you to keep on top of the job too. Any form of training where you meet others is likely to help you to build important networks, which will be useful to you. It can also be a real boost to be in the company of a group of adults, since most of your life is spent with children.

- **Be aware of your strengths and weaknesses.** Try to be realistic about yourself: take pride in your strengths and enjoy the benefits these strengths bring. Try to tackle your weaknesses but also give yourself permission to be imperfect. Just because you have a weakness it doesn't mean that you have to work three times as hard at it to keep up.

- **Keep learning about teaching.** The more you can learn about teaching, the more tips and experience you can pick up along the way, the more efficiently you can learn to do your job. Read the 'trade papers', try to allocate time to keep up with current thinking about teaching, and use every opportunity you can to learn from people with more experience than you.

- **Don't ignore stress.** There aren't any prizes for keeping going until you drop, in fact quite the reverse, so it's much better to face the fact that you're stressed and try to do something about it. If you begin to suffer from sleeplessness, weight gain or loss, eating problems, headaches, irritability or other signs of stress, try to identify the causes of your stress and find ways to tackle them.

- **Allow yourself to feel angry.** Anger is a common reaction to stress and is often not clearly directed at anything in particular. People often feel powerless and this makes them frustrated. It's important not to bottle anger up, but try to let it out in situations that will not simply pass your stress on to the children or to colleagues. Exercise, do some vigorous gardening, take a long walk, buy a pet, or try smashing something that will make a satisfying noise, but won't hurt you or your wallet!

- **Have some fun.** Try to find was to de-stress yourself by doing things that make you happy. A little hedonism goes a long way. Think about the sorts of things that you enjoy such as cooking, reading, walking in the countryside, roller blading, hang gliding, spending time with friends, moderate drinking, whatever; and make time for them!

- **Don't be afraid to go to the doctor.** Severe stress can often be helped by medication in the short term. Just because there may not be any physical signs of illness doesn't mean that the doctor won't be able to help. At least give yourself the chance to find out if there's anything that might help.

■ **Get a life outside school.** Family and friends still need you, and you need them if you give yourself the time to think about it. Try not to neglect them, indulge yourself in your hobbies every once in a while, plan (and take) a short break or holiday. Use anything you can to help you keep everything in perspective.

53. Coping with your workload

Many people assume that the point of being a teacher is to teach, but more and more it seems that teaching is just one small part of your professional commitments. Once you have filled in your planning sheets, evaluations, assessments, Individual Educational Plans, arranged a meeting with Educational Support Services, updated your schemes of work, and so on, there seems to be little time left for teaching. Of course, all these things are supposed to help you do your job properly, but how do you manage to juggle all these aspects of your work effectively?

■ **Prioritize your work.** Ask yourself which of the things you need to do are urgent *and* important? Deal quickly with urgent work or materials you need for the next day, and leave record and assessment work until you have a space to fit them in. Don't ignore them, however; try to block out some time to catch up with administrative work. If you leave it all on the back boiler, this will become a cause of stress in itself.

■ **Use your administrative support staff.** Their jobs make them more likely to able to efficiently process standard paperwork, and to do typing or to copy work. Try to ensure that you don't do things you don't have to do, if someone else can.

■ **Make good use of existing learning resource materials.** There are a great many print-based resources that give children the opportunity to 'learn by doing'. Making the most of these resources may free up more of your time to spend with individuals or small groups.

■ **Manage your marking.** Try to spread out heavy marking loads evenly through the week. Where possible, plan when homework should be handed in so that it doesn't all arrive in one lump on Monday morning. If you phase the handing-in of work, you can spread it out over a period of time, rather than rushing it all together. There are few things more daunting than a big pile of marking lurking on the corner of your desk.

■ **Keep files, not piles.** If you think how long you can spend rifling through piles of work for a particular paper, you will know in your heart that spending time organizing a decent filing system is time well spent. There's also a great deal of satisfaction to be gained by establishing your own particular system that works well for you.

■ **Keep your, and everyone else's, paperwork to a minimum.** Your colleagues will be grateful if you don't add paper to their load. Keep any written documents short and clearly focused.

Make it explicit what should be done with these documents. You could have headers for all documentation that show where each piece of paper goes or what should be done with it.

■ | **Don't carry your workload around in your head.** You can only really do one thing at a time, so try to avoid letting yourself be side-tracked. If you're teaching, teach, If you're marking, mark. Getting a job out of the way makes you feel ready to tackle the next one, whereas half-completed jobs just pile up and often never get finished. Use lists to help you to make sure that you don't forget things. Consider carrying a small notebook with you at all times, so you can jot down reminders to yourself anytime.

■ | **Photocopy whatever you can.** Don't rewrite what can be reused. This applies to planning, assessment, worksheets and so on. Nevertheless, be really careful not to infringe copyright, as this can carry heavy penalties both for you and for the school.

■ | **Set specific times for specific preparation jobs.** Give yourself a set time to do a job and stick to it. If you decide that you're going to work until 10 o'clock, only work until 10 o'clock. If you only want to spend Sunday afternoon preparing for Monday morning, only spend Sunday afternoon. Try not to let work spill over into every part of your life.

■ | **Make sure a job is worthwhile.** Will it be time well spent? Will it cut your workload? Is it important that this job be completed in the near future? If not, is it really necessary? You may need to be ruthless in your task management if you're to keep on top of your work.

54. Being an effective colleague

Working in a school can be really miserable if the people around you are not supportive and helpful. Try to start by ensuring that the people around you find you a helpful and supportive colleague; you might be delighted at how the condition can spread:

■ | **Help out when the going gets tough.** If someone in your school is struggling with a time-consuming or monotonous task, it can make a big difference if you're prepared to roll up your sleeves and lend a hand. With luck they will reciprocate when you're having a tough time too.

■ | **Don't spring surprises on colleagues unnecessarily.** If you need to get colleagues to do something for you, such as make contributions to a new scheme of work, complete a curriculum audit or produce work for a display, give them plenty of time and as much guidance as you can. It may even be possible to get part of a staff meeting set aside to do the task collectively, which may save everyone's time.

■ | **Keep to deadlines, especially when they have an impact on others.** If your contribution is late you may inadvertently disrupt your colleagues' plans. If it becomes apparent that you aren't going to be able to meet a deadline, let others know as soon as possible. This will give them a chance to reorganize or redistribute the work.

■ **Note what your colleagues appreciate in what you do.** Try to do more of these things whenever you can! This will be wonderful for the atmosphere of the school, and will probably give you a rosy glow too.

■ **Try to be sensitive to how your colleagues are feeling.** It's easy to forget to take the trouble to pay others a little attention. You may be able to help them with a worry or problem simply by being available and aware of what's going on. A good listener is a valuable colleague, and everyone needs some help from time to time.

■ **Don't wade in where angels fear to tread.** Everyone has teaching days that they would rather forget. Support colleagues when they want support, but be ready to let them deal with things at their own pace and in their own style. If you make an offer and it's refused, withdraw gently and don't take offence. People often need to sort out things for themselves.

■ **Be considerate when sharing teaching areas.** Storage space may be limited and work space will easily become cluttered. Remember that setting up takes long enough without having to clear up other people's mess. As far as possible, negotiate in advance how space will be used, and what your joint guidelines will be.

■ **Be punctual for meetings.** Try to be on time so that others are not kept waiting. If it transpires that you're going to be late, try to send a message or inform the chair of the meeting to make a start without you. If you're the chair then try to delegate where possible. No one likes to be kept waiting, especially when everyone has 101 jobs that need doing.

■ **Keep colleagues informed about what you're doing.** Others need to know what you're up to, what changes you might be making to displays in shared areas, or to the furniture layout. There's nothing worse than coming into a shared area to find that all has changed with no prior consultation.

■ **Leave teaching spaces as you found them, or better.** If you move furniture or use a display board or use messy resources, try to leave the room ready to be used by others. Encourage the children to clear up their own mess and to leave the space tidy.

55. Working with administrative and support staff

Non-teaching staff play an increasingly important role in the effective running of your school. Developing a cooperative and mutually considerate working relationship with your support staff and nursery nurses makes a critical contribution to your being able to cope with your workload:

- **Never neglect the courtesies.** After all, you're both trained professionals in the classroom, bringing particular expertise and abilities to your respective work. Even if individual members of your support staff can be difficult or inflexible, you will find it useful to gain their respect and cooperation. Ask rather than instruct and offer genuine thanks for the work that they have done.

- **Get feedback from support staff on the way that you work with them.** Get them to say which parts of the way that you work are helpful to them, and which give them cause for concern. Apart from improving the effectiveness of the relationship, it will also help you with your own self-evaluation of your performance.

- **Encourage your nursery nurses or support staff to get together with others.** Their own professional updating and exposure to best practice is as important as your own. Information about opportunities for nursery nurses and auxiliaries is scarce, but your headteacher should be able to provide some suggestions. You can also use your own networks to put support staff in touch with others in neighbouring schools, to their mutual benefit.

- **Describe the precise nature and priority of each task you ask them to do.** When do you need it? How many do you need? Who else needs them? How long should it take? Don't expect your colleagues to be mind readers, who automatically know what you want. If you do, you're likely to be disappointed.

- **Don't expect disorganization on your part to produce furious activity on theirs.** Try to give fair notice of tasks you want them to do for you. Provide a clear statement of what you need doing. Check that they understand what's required of them, and that the task is achievable in the time you've given them. Your own professional behaviour is likely to be conducive to good working relationships.

- **Make sure that they get credit for what they do.** Praise is always a good motivator, but don't keep it private. If their contribution has been particularly good or critical to success, give your support staff public acknowledgement and credit. This pays high dividends in the long term.

- **Treat your support staff as equal partners.** If there are cultural or status barriers between you, do what you can to break them down. Remember that effective teamwork includes everyone regardless of job description.

- **Help them to do a decent job.** Give them all the information and paperwork that they need. The art of effective delegation is to give people responsibility for what they do, but also to provide support and inspiration to help them do their job well. Be sure also to give them opportunities to try out their own ideas and make a creative input into the work.

- **Play to their strengths.** First of all, find out about the talents they bring to the classroom. It might be that you can share tasks and play to your respective strengths and abilities. Make the most of what they can offer.

■ **Include them in training and social events.** A whole-school training session should ideally be exactly that. It's tempting to get the auxiliaries to do sorting out or tidying up tasks, while everyone else sits in a meeting or a training session, but auxiliaries and nursery nurses are responsible for the children's education too. However, you need to think carefully about how support staff can be included to best effect – don't make them sit through sessions that have no relevance to them.

56. Ten things you should never do

Throughout this part of the book we have endeavoured to be as positive and encouraging as possible. We all know, however, that when we start teaching there's always plenty of advice on what not to do. The following set of tips, based on the collective wisdom of teachers through the centuries, is offered tongue-in-cheek. All of them are apocryphal, and all of them are at least partially true. We follow these with some home truths that may seem like clichés, but actually contain a lot of genuine wisdom!

■ **Don't fall out with the really important people.** These include the school administrative assistant, the caretaker, the cleaner and most importantly of all, the person who holds the key to the stock cupboard! You can probably get away with falling out with just about anyone else for a short time, but if ever a rift or disagreement with any of the above should begin to show itself, you need to act fast. Offer flowers, chocolates, tickets to the match! You might just about get away with it.

■ **Don't pass personal comments about other members of staff in front of the children.** Such 'slips of the tongue' have an unfortunate tendency to pass from one child to another until they find their way right back to the very person who was *not* meant to hear them! Children, in their innocence, make all-too-faithful messengers.

■ **Don't be surprised by how well you can be misquoted.** Children have an incredible ability to completely misinterpret, twist and quote out of context. The stories that get back to parents about the things you have done and said could make your hair curl! Fortunately, most of the time, parents are aware of the problem – they may well have heard the gossip about the things they're supposed to have done and said that has been going around school too, and so are not unsympathetic to the situation.

■ **Don't believe 90 per cent of the tales children tell you about their parents.** Many a Mum has been horrified to read about herself in her children's news books, and has been amazed to discover the ability of her child to create a whole imaginative world that she completely fails to recognize as life at home.

- **Don't rely on the children to forget.** Children seem to have an unnerving knack of remembering all those incidents and rash promises you would rather they *did* forget and forgetting all those things that they really need to remember. Never make a rash promise you can't keep; you will be reminded of it forever afterwards.

- **Don't smile before Christmas.** Clearly this tip can't be taken literally, but its essence can. It's really about maintaining an air of mystery, keeping your cards close to your chest, and keeping the children guessing until you've got their measure and they've got yours. Perhaps it should be, 'Don't smile at anyone, unless they have earned it, before Christmas.'

- **Don't be surprised if children behave badly on windy days.** Nobody knows why this is the case, but everyone swears it's true. Be prepared for a bumpy ride on a stormy day, as children seem to get wilder the stronger the breezes blow.

- **Never forget to be really grateful for your Christmas presents.** Children love to buy their teachers presents at Christmas. They like to choose them themselves. Frequently they're not precisely what you would choose for yourself. But look at it this way: you'll never have to buy bathsalts again. And you will be made very welcome at your local Oxfam shop.

- **Never take at face value the child who says, 'It wasn't me!'** Many teachers could be rich if they had a pound for every time they had heard this assertion. Take it with a pinch of salt, and investigate further before you punish the assumed culprits.

- **Never wear white in the classroom.** You can guarantee that the day you dress in cool, pale colours, will be the day you have to mop up 'accidents', come into contact with the paint pots, and have a close encounter with the toner from the photocopier. Go for machine-washable, dark colours, with an uneven pattern, or buy shares in a dry cleaning shop.

57. Home truths

- **Don't forget what it's like to be a child.** If you can dredge up such memories it will, of course, help you present your lessons in a more interesting and appropriate manner. But more importantly it will also help you to forgive. If you can remember what it's like you will also remember that, for the children, all this education business doesn't seem all that important or relevant. If you can remember that, it's much easier to cope with how impossibly frustrating children can sometimes be.

- **Don't forget how much fun learning can be.** As a teacher it's easy to get wrapped up in how to teach, so much so that we can forget how to learn too. The children, often and unwittingly, give us so many things to think about, learn about and enjoy. Perhaps they can teach us as many things that are really important as we can teach them!

■ **Don't take it all too seriously.** There are a great many reasons to take teaching too seriously – parents, policies, pupils and politicians to name but a few – but if you do take it all too seriously it soon becomes a very stressful and unpleasant job. For your sake and the sake of the children you teach, try to relax and enjoy the good times. Young children really can be the most rewarding people to work with.

■ **Remember there is always another day.** However tough the going is, and however exhausted and disheartened you may feel, it often all looks better in the morning. Try to start each day anew, leaving behind the disillusionment of the day before, and you may be amazed how much better it all appears.

Part 3

Information Technology

Coping with ICT in the primary classroom

IT as a discrete subject

IT as a cross-curricular subject

Supporting special educational needs with IT

Resources for teaching IT and ICT

Resources for the implementation of ICT

Trouble-shooting, top good habits, and home–school links

In this part of the book we offer practical suggestions to help you to get into using computers in school. The content is very much based on some of the particular developments that have happened in primary education in England and Wales, where there is a National Curriculum for schools. This curriculum includes Information Technology as a discrete subject and QCA schemes of work that show how ICT should be used across the curriculum, but we trust that many of our suggestions will be equally relevant to parts of the world where similar conditions exist and where computers are being introduced into primary education in similar ways.

In Britain, the term Information Technology (IT) has recently evolved into Information and Communications Technologies (ICT). In this part we try to use ICT when talking about Information and Communications Technologies generally. When we use IT, it often refers more specifically to the England and Wales National Curriculum for Information Technology. We have tried to be consistent in this inconsistency!

The emphasis now seems to be upon getting 'connected' and making the best of the information and communications revolution of the late 20th and early 21st centuries. We could say that we are seeing two separate and parallel revolutions. One is an information explosion, where the amount of available information on just about everything has increased dramatically, and the range of formats through which this information is available has expanded rapidly. The other is the communications revolution, whereby information of all sorts can be communicated locally, nationally and world-wide by ever more sophisticated electronic means, and with great speed and increasing reliability. Children who are now in primary schools will need to be able to survive and thrive in this new world of information and communications technologies. Already, many young people are proving to be more able than most of their predecessors (including parents and teachers) at embracing the effects of this revolution.

In the UK, government initiatives are driving hard to meet the newly emerging needs associated with the communications and information technology revolution. The Superhighways initiative has been superseded by the National Grid for Learning and extended by the New Opportunities Fund training for currently practising teachers. It's envisaged that every pupil will have access to e-mail in the first decade of the third millennium. The Virtual Teachers Centre will offer speedy access to a wealth of curriculum resources for teachers. Some people even seem to believe we'll have computers instead of teachers in the near future. However, such predictions were made decades ago when the first teaching machines and early forms of open and flexible learning were introduced, and the value of human beings as resources to facilitate learning has never been eroded in practice, and indeed has become enhanced.

Our aim in this part of the book is to offer support, encouragement and practical ideas to teachers wishing to develop both their personal ICT skills and their teaching skills. Alternatively, to mix metaphors, we hope that some of the ideas will help teachers and IT coordinators to 'get on their bikes', or perhaps pedal a little faster, both in terms of tackling new skills and in trying out different approaches to using ICT in the classroom.

At times the style is certainly somewhat tongue-in-cheek but is definitely intended to be on the side of the teachers, who may sometimes feel that the world is conspiring to make more difficult their mission of helping children to learn and develop. However, if the tone helps to make the absurd amount of jargon bandied around in the area of ICT more understandable through gentle irony, then so much the better! We hope that most of the wry smiles that may be engendered will be accompanied by useful learning points.

COPING WITH ICT IN THE PRIMARY CLASSROOM

There are a great many problems associated with teaching ICT in schools. This is especially true in primary classrooms, where children require high levels of support and structure in order to facilitate learning. In addition, so often there is only one computer, limited software and limited time to actually teach the skills needed to use the computer. As a result, in many primary classrooms ICT is reduced to a 'choosing activity' for much of the time. This picture is likely to change very rapidly in the next decade or two, but meanwhile, we offer practical suggestions to help you make the most of the facilities that you may already have.

In this section we offer practical support and ideas for managing and teaching IT effectively, and subsequently for getting the best out of the time and the equipment available.

1. Getting to grips with hardware and software

There is never enough time to do this properly, but that doesn't mean that it's OK to ignore the whole issue. Even computer gurus will only be experts in a small area of educational ICT use. The secret is to start by doing a *little*, and doing it regularly, then accepting that you'll keep up to date with *some* of what is available:

- ■ **Borrow the class computer for a holiday.** Try to learn *one* new program for use after the holiday. Borrow some children (if you don't have any of the appropriate age) to try out what you have learnt, or so that you can get them to teach you what to do.

- ■ **Get some staff training.** Over the next few years in the UK there will be hundreds of millions of pounds spent on ICT training for teachers. Think about what your needs are and try to make sure you get your share of the training on offer, and that what you get matches what *you* need to learn.

- ■ **Just have a go!** Adults, in general, are more reluctant than children to try things out with computers in case they get it 'wrong'. Learning from mistakes is often the quickest way to get into new computer software. You won't be able to learn effectively unless you play about and try things out.

- ■ **Be clear about what you want your pupils to learn.** Identify how you expect their IT capability (in National Curriculum speak) to be developed with the software you have. Then learn how to use just those particular applications. Your school's scheme of work may well help here.

- ■ **Use a backup program.** Make sure you have a backup of each program in school, and that you're not using the original disks. Companies that have found ways to prevent copying of disks will usually supply new disks on receipt of any corrupted ones you send them.

- ■ **Try out programs as you would expect a pupil to.** Find out what happens when you deliberately do something wrong. It'll help you to rescue pupils who get stuck when working in the classroom. You may also find features of programs you didn't know about. Some programs offer good help on screen too.

■ **Ask for a student teacher who is good at ICT.** Teacher training institutions must ensure that their students are fully trained in ICT. They should also have access to good-quality resources and support. Most of them work in partnership with local schools and they can be a valuable source of help. This will not only help you keep your knowledge up to date but will be a chance for your pupils to learn from someone else.

■ **Get your own computer.** This is not a cheap option, but you'll need practice at using technology if you wish to develop your own skills. There is no quick route to becoming an ICT expert. Ideally, get the same sort of machine that you'll be using in the classroom, so you'll be learning skills and procedures that will help you to teach. However, it'll also be useful in other areas of teaching if your own machine can perform other tasks such as reasonable quality desktop publishing if you want to use it to produce resources. Alternatively you might want to consider how you'll get access to the Internet. Some primary schools are now using presentation packages for teachers so that they can do demonstrations to a whole class, with a projector connected to a laptop computer.

■ **Learn to use effective programs.** These are ones which can be used in more than one situation, or which can support a range of tasks and abilities, rather than one which has a limited use. The types of applications which may be suitable include a word processor suitable for the age you teach, a graphing program or a spreadsheet program for Key Stage 2, or a program around which you can develop a range of identified skills or activities.

■ **Find ways to keep up to date.** As computers have become more sophisticated so has the software they run. This means that new programs tend to be more complex and take longer to learn than older programs. It's debatable whether the newer programs are always more effective at supporting learning! However, if you don't become familiar with newer software as it becomes available you'll have a bigger jump to get up to date at a later stage. Your IT coordinator or local IT centre should be able to advise you on what to look at. The IT centre may have different versions of popular programs to try out, as may your local teacher training institution. Some companies also have an approval scheme for viewing software. Realistically, this might mean that you try to look at one new program a term.

2. Managing IT work in the classroom

There's no simple prescription for effective management in the classroom and you'll need to review what you do regularly as things change. The increasing emphasis on focused literacy and numeracy sessions is undoubtedly going to squeeze IT time in the short term. However, the targets for pupils' ICT use, especially for e-mail and WWW, means it will have considerable emphasis too. (In England and Wales, IT is also still in OFSTED's gaze!)

- **Use ICT resources as much as you can.** What you can achieve with ICT will depend upon how often, and for how long, pupils in your class have access to the technology. The more equipment or computers pupils have access to, the more they'll use them and the more they'll be able to achieve.

- **Use computers to teach and demonstrate.** It can be difficult to organize a classroom so that large groups of pupils can see the computer. However, it's efficient to introduce a new program to the whole class rather than repeating the introduction lots of times. Some ideas can be more easily demonstrated that explained. When using a word-processor for demonstrations, try increasing the font size or the magnification (usually 'view per cent' for example), explain 'copy' and 'paste', or demonstrate sentence-level work.

- **Be critical.** Just because it's on the computer does not necessarily mean it's a good idea. Check that the software or particular activity is actually helping the pupils achieve the learning outcome you want. Pupils quickly learn how to operate a program and may avoid reading any text on screen, for example, unless they actually need to read it to progress to the next part of the program. Similarly, in maths drill and practice programs, many of them have an automated feedback prompt, or move pupils on after two or three incorrect responses. Some pupils quickly learn that they can move on without doing much, so their apparent progress through a program may not indicate their real learning.

- **Be flexible about borrowing and lending equipment.** To make the most of the equipment you have in school, share things round and organize your equipment to get the best from it. If a task really requires all of the floor robots or half a dozen computers, plan to borrow equipment from others and be prepared to lend whatever usually resides in your room!

- **Decide the best place for the equipment.** In practice you'll probably have little choice, but it's worth considering your options. Could you have a computer in the school's TV room? You could then demonstrate programs to a whole class. A cable to connect a computer to a TV or video monitor (called a display converter) is relatively cheap and might allow you to organize a whole-class teaching session once a week. Pupils could even present their work this way – the impact for them of seeing their work on a large TV screen is considerable.

- **Maximize the time that computers are in use.** Resources are expensive and it's difficult to plan for ICT equipment to be in use all the time. Can you provide access at break times or lunch times? What about before and after school? Are there other adults or older children you could get to help out? Can you use Mrs Cummerbund's computer while her class is doing PE?

- **What about the summer term?** Could you reorganize the resources for the summer term so that classes that are not delighting in national assessment tests could get best use of the equipment in school?

- **Involve the children in the management of the computers.** You could train pupils to be responsible for switching on and shutting down at the beginning or end of the day whenever possible – even the youngest children are easily able to do this! Pupils usually take this sort of responsibility very seriously.

■ **Limit your objectives to what is achievable.** Try setting up a record of who used which program on which day, so that the record is completed by the pupils themselves. You can then concentrate on assessing and recording their IT capability.

■ **Don't show your frustration when the equipment goes wrong.** Some pupils will assume that you're cross with them, particularly young children. If a computer doesn't do what you expect, either someone has made a mistake, or it's faulty. Pupils, particularly young children, very rarely make deliberate mistakes. If it is faulty, it's not your or the child's fault.

3. Developing self-supporting activities

You need time to teach a group effectively, and therefore you need to ensure you're not always leaping across the classroom to sort out problems on the computer. However, you also need to make sure that the pupils do not teach each other incorrectly – pupil-to-pupil instructions can all too easily become a cascade of misleading whispers!

■ **Keep it simple.** It's easy to make a supposedly self-supporting activity too complicated by bombarding the pupils with information. Plan for one step at a time!

■ **Keep in step.** If your school has a detailed scheme of work for IT, make sure that what you do follows on from what the children should have done last year, and leads nicely in to what they'll be doing next year. The easiest way to make sure children can work independently is to make sure they are working at an appropriate level.

■ **Introduce the activity to the whole class.** If this isn't feasible, then at least introduce it to a large group, with a demonstration at the computer. It may be possible to organize a demonstration at the end of the morning by getting pupils to help move furniture so that they can all see. A bribe of 'only *sensible* children will be helping me to demonstrate what to do' usually works!

■ **Use support cards.** Try using information cards, prompts, wall charts, step-by-step instructions and so on. Don't forget to prepare these on a computer, and keep a copy on disk, so that they're easier to replace when they become too chewed, glued or printed over by mistake. Older pupils can even help to write them as they become more familiar with the software. The language coordinator will love this idea!

■ **Teach others to give support**. This can include other pupils in the class, older pupils, as well as adult helpers. It takes longer in the beginning but pays off in the long run. Some primary schools have a coordinated programme of teaching adult volunteers, who have their voluntary work accredited to lead on to further training for them.

- **Train pupils in a system.** For example, plan for pupils to have the responsibility to go and get the person whose turn it is next. This might be by using a list of names as a sign-up sheet, or allowing a set time with a kitchen timer, or a set number of problems on screen, and making them responsible for helping the next pupil or pair of pupils. Don't forget that such systems need monitoring, as 'Oh, Miss, I was just helping like you asked!' can seem an excellent work-avoidance strategy!

- **Give the pupils time to play.** When we learn something new we all need time to explore and find out what it can do. You might consider letting pupils have a go at break or lunch time to play with new software before setting them tasks to do. They may even learn things you don't know about!

- **Change the groupings of the pupils at the computer.** Have more experienced pupils work with less experienced pupils, but make sure they understand *how* to take turns or share the work in the particular context of the program they are using. For example, prescribe a set number of screens per pupil, or make one child responsible for putting full stops in a piece of writing correctly.

- **Make sure no one dominates.** It's worth making sure that a range of pupils become the 'experts' and that your experts know how to *explain* what to do, rather than just do it for others. 'Helen, fold your arms and *tell* them what to do' helps the others to learn, and Helen herself to learn even more than if she just does something she already knows how to do.

- **Make sure the pupils are clear about *what* they've got to do and *why* they're doing it.** Ask them now and again why they're doing things, and what exactly they're trying to do. When pupils know what they're supposed to be learning from a task, and why, they're much more likely to learn effectively and productively.

- **Be explicit about where pupils are to get support from.** Explain to them when they are *intended* to use prompt cards, other (specified) pupils, or an adult, or you.

- **Review each activity with the whole class.** Preferably do this at the computer. Review what some successful pupils have done, to give others a clear picture of what they have to try to do when it's their turn.

4. Effective use of support materials

Pupils will learn how to get support from the easiest source possible. If you always leap across and sort the computer out they'll always nag you to help. But, if their turn with the machine ends when they get stuck, it can be a great incentive for them to learn how to do it correctly! The following suggestions may help you to make your pupils more self-sufficient in their usage of computers:

- **Tell them *when* they get it right.** Make sure pupils use the support which is available and praise them publicly when they do. There is a tendency in education (and in life in general) to be quick to tell people when they've got something wrong, and not to mention everything that they've got right.

- **Tell them *why* they got it right.** Pupils learn much more quickly when they understand why they did something well. Other pupils also pick up what it is you're looking for.

- **Make sure the easiest way to get support is the way you want them to get it.** Make it easier for them to use the support you provide than to simply ask you (unless you're supporting a particular activity). If you usually leap enthusiastically across the classroom to show them how to do something they'll continue to pester you. Pupils will always take the easiest option – don't always be it!

- **Use prompt cards and help sheets.** Especially use those that the children have helped to write or refine. Simple cards with 'save' or 'print' instructions can help remind pupils of what to do when they get stuck. Laminating cards and sheets can increase their life, and can protect them from being written upon. Clear plastic envelopes are almost as good.

- **Keep written instructions brief and use pictures if possible.** Many manuals (if you've got one!) or guides have illustrations you could photocopy. It's also relatively easy on most computers to take a snapshot of the screen and clip out the relevant tool bar, window, or menu. Sometimes you can print out a screen dump, and cut and paste sections of this into instruction sheets.

- **Train pupils to use on-screen help where it's available.** Decide first whether the on-screen help is useful. Try to use it yourself first, then point the children in the right direction. Text-to-speech can make writing easier to read by providing prompts. Many CD-ROMs and word-processors have this facility.

- **Use support materials provided by the program.** Many have step-by-step instructions, along the lines 'Getting Going' or 'Quick Setup', as provided by the manufacturer. Most of these are easily simplified! Some can even be used by pupils directly. This may be something to consider when buying new programs.

- **Support computer tasks with other activities that can be done away from the computer.** This way some of the motivation and enthusiasm spills over into other tasks, and it can be a good way of linking ideas and skills, so pupils practice them in another situation.

- **Share your support materials.** Other teachers will be more likely to swap theirs too! It can be useful to have several different kinds of support materials, and to find which works best for different pupils, and maybe to differentiate the level of support to match pupils' abilities to use it.

■ **Keep copies of everything you do.** Whether hard or soft copy, it won't last forever. It's quicker to photocopy a master kept in a plastic wallet than print out a new one from a file. If you think you might want to change it however, an electronic copy is also essential.

5. Planning appropriate activities for ICT

Don't reinvent the wheel! There's a lot of published material available about planning for IT, in the UK not least the QCA schemes of work, which clearly detail what 'they' think of as good practice. Since these schemes are not compulsory you may need to look to other sources: your Local Education Authority should have resources to share. Other teachers in your school and beyond will have prepared and planned activities too. The following suggestions could help you to learn from others' experience:

■ **Use the National Curriculum IT program of study and your school's scheme of work (if available).** If you're lucky, you might have access to suggested programs and examples of planning from previous years. The QCA has published a scheme of work for IT in Key Stages 1 and 2, offering some good examples of how to cover the National Curriculum effectively.

■ **Find out what other teachers use working with the same age pupils, and similar machines.** Sharing ideas and practical suggestions from other teachers is an excellent starting point. Find out what worked well, and ask where the problems were found to be.

■ **Get support from the LEA IT Centre or advice from an IT adviser.** They may already have teachers' and pupils' guides for the software you're using. The Centre or adviser may be able to arrange visits to schools with similar resources to see what they do; they may even tailor training programmes to help!

■ **Get materials from the National Grid for Learning.** In the UK, BECTa (http://becta.org.uk) (formerly the National Council for Educational Technology, NCET) produces suggestions, materials and ideas for the national grid for learning at (www.ngfl.gov.uk) and at the Virtual Teacher Centre (www.vtc.ngfl.gov.uk).

■ **Find out what programs the pupils have used before.** It's always best to start out with activities the pupils are familiar with at the beginning of the year, while you're establishing new routines and becoming familiar with the class.

■ **Plan a range of activities over the course of the year.** This might be with a specific focus for each half term. For example it could be along the lines of: Half term 1: Word-processing; Half term 2: Graphics or drawing package (Christmas/Festivals artwork); Half term 3: Maths number; Half term 4: Maths shape and space or data handling; Half term 5: Combining pictures and text; Half term 6: Control/IT implications.

■ **Integrate the IT components into your main teaching aims.** This could be for a block of work where possible. Examples could include using a Roamer for work on estimation in maths by setting the scale to appropriate units for your pupils, or planning a redrafting activity on the computer to support the sentence or text level work you're doing in English.

■ **Use the computer for direct teaching too.** Often a computer activity can be completed by pupils alongside class work. Could you use the computer with a group where you redraft some prepared writing as an introduction for them to complete a paper-and-pencil exercise?

■ **Don't get pupils to copy-type finished work into a neat version.** It's a waste of the computer's time. It's also a waste of the pupils' time. It's much more valuable for pupils to use the computer to redraft and make changes to their work than laboriously key in their hand-written story, particularly for children who are struggling with keyboard skills anyway. If typing skills are the issue, set up a lunchtime club with a typing tutor program.

■ **Be realistic about how long activities will take.** If everyone is to get a 'turn' doing the same thing it will take a *long* time for a class of 30 pupils. Consider whether they could do variations on a task which focuses on the same skills, and which can be made into a class book, for example.

IT AS A DISCRETE SUBJECT

Despite the fact that England and Wales National Curriculum takes great pains to stress the cross-curricular nature of IT, it's important to think of IT as a subject in its own right too. (This is clearly demonstrated by the fact that the QCA has produced a very detailed scheme of work for IT but has also gone to great lengths to exemplify how ICT can be used across the curriculum by including it in its schemes for other subjects.) If not, it becomes extremely difficult to ensure that children make progress in IT and it becomes almost impossible to focus on what IT skills you're trying to teach. In this situation progress in IT may still happen, but which skills are developed and how far those skills are stretched is simply left to chance – a situation OFSTED inspectors could get their teeth into!

In this section we'll consider the sorts of IT-related skills teachers might be looking to develop, and the sorts of activities they might use to try to develop them. These ideas will be focused particularly on the needs of the class teacher, whereas the section on 'Managing ICT in primary schools' covers some similar ideas but is focused more on the needs of the IT coordinators and school's management.

6. Why consider ICT as a discrete subject?

Language skills are applicable across subject areas. We often think of the sorts of language we might develop in maths, science, humanities and so on. Some ICT skills are applicable across subject areas too, but those skills may need to be identified in terms of the IT curriculum. Here are some reasons why you might want to consider ICT and IT separately:

■ **Because you have to.** It's a statutory part of the curriculum and will be inspected. Formal assessment of IT capabilities is firmly on the agenda, and with the government committing so much money to the development of ICT in education, it'll want proof that our money has not been wasted.

■ **Because you need to teach IT actively.** It's no good expecting children just to acquire skills. As long as they have access to resources they'll acquire skills, and probably almost as quickly as they might if you were teaching them. But you need to raise their awareness of what ICT can do, you need to extend their technological vocabulary in order to ensure they can be taught in the future, and you need to help them to put their skills in context. With the onset of the 'digital revolution', talk is going to be even more important, because the personal computer is still a very long way from being able to enter in to any kind of meaningful dialogue.

■ **Because you have to try to ensure continuity.** Especially if your school has quite a detailed scheme of work, you need to make sure that you have fulfilled your side of the bargain.

■ **Because you have to ensure progression.** If you don't teach it, how can you be sure that it'll get any better? If it's not formally on the agenda, it could remain as an optional extra in people's vision.

■ **Because OFSTED will expect to see it.** The recent revision in the inspection framework has increased OFSTED's beady glare in this area. They'll want to see evidence that IT skills are being taught, not simply absorbed by osmosis.

■ **Because it's a national priority.** A lot of money is being spent on ICT and you need to make sure that your pupils and your school don't miss out.

■ **Because pupils are motivated by ICT.** The majority of pupils enjoy using ICT, particularly computers, and are therefore keen to engage in the learning tasks that computers offer.

■ **Because ICT is effective.** Identifying where ICT has the potential to make a significant difference to pupils' learning is therefore vital.

■ **Because ICT is useful.** ICT has had a tremendous impact on the world outside school. Many pupils will continue to use ICT well beyond their schooldays. There are ways it can be beneficial in school too!

- **Because you can have the computer in use all day every day and still not be doing IT.** IT in the National Curriculum is about the pupils *themselves* using ICT in their learning. Try working out where a spelling-practice program fits in to the programme of study!

- **Because if you think of IT just as a subject, you won't do it justice!** IT is primarily a tool for teaching and learning across the curriculum. Although there are specific skills in ICT, they need to be delivered through some content. It makes sense to ensure that the content is linked to other work the pupils are doing.

7. What should I teach in IT?

What you need to teach will usually depend upon the age of the pupils, their previous computer experience, the appropriate part of the programmes of study in the National Curriculum for IT, your school's scheme of work for IT and the particular focus of work in your classroom at the time. The following suggestions may trigger your own thoughts on how and when to teach using IT:

- **Teach skills that can be used across the curriculum.** Many aspects of the ICT skills that pupils learn should have a more general application. It's pointless teaching them how to use a complex package that is difficult to use, no matter how much of a computer wizard *you* are. It's very likely that an easier one will soon be available.

- **Teach basic word-processing skills.** Pupils need to be taught about things like word-wrap (when the computer moves a word onto the following line automatically), the return key, when to use the shift and not the Caps Lock keys, and similar everyday word-processing skills. Bad habits may not make much difference in the early days, but they can make a huge difference by the time the children are reaching the end of their primary education.

- **Progress to more complex skills.** Pupils need to be taught both *how* and *when* to use cut and paste, for example. It would be silly to try to teach them these skills while they are still struggling to build simple sentences.

- **Consider getting a typing tutor program to develop keyboard skills.** This could be for regular, brief practice at the beginning of a longer IT session, if you have lots of computers or as part of a lunch-time club. Though you might believe that typing may be set to become a thing of the past, with voice input on its way, don't bank on it! Voice recognition software has now been available (and working) for a long time, but more and more people still need to use keyboards.

- **Combining words and pictures is a good place to begin.** This could be basic, factual writing with some clip art. From here, the pupils can easily progress to creating their own pictures and deciding on fonts and layout in an integrated or desktop publishing package.

- **Teach pupils how to use a toolbox or palette program.** Most drawing and painting programs use this approach. A window or bar contains tools like a pencil or circle shape for pupils to choose to make a drawing. It's essential that you teach pupils how to select and alter the tools they choose for drawing and painting. Using a rectangle tool to draw a house outline is more efficient (and pleasing) than using a freehand tool or building it up with a series of straight lines. A whole-class demo is an efficient way of showing pupils the advantages of the appropriate tools.

- **A calculator is a good way to explain a spreadsheet.** The formula you put in a cell is the same as a series of key presses on the computer. Spreadsheets can therefore be seen as a whole series of linked calculators. Unless pupils understand the different ways in which a cell can be used, they'll not appreciate the possibilities in a spreadsheet. They'll simply use it as a grid and not see it as hundreds of little calculator boxes.

- **Teach pupils, at least once, about a database that is *not* on the computer.** It can be difficult for pupils to get a picture of what a database is and how it works. Children will have no experience of a card-index system, and they should be given an opportunity to develop their understanding of a database at some point. This does not have to be before they use a database on a computer, but could usefully be done at the same time. This way they can also consider the advantages and disadvantages of using the computer as a tool in this context.

- **Teach analysis and interrogation of databases and charts too.** Children often enter data and create graphs and charts, though they are rarely taught how to ask appropriate questions and how to find answers from them. In later life, they're likely to spend more time working with existing databases than on creating new ones.

- **Remember to review ICT work with the children.** It's often revealing to ask children questions about what they've learnt, or to get them to ask questions of each other. You should discover all too accurately what they understand, and what has not yet clicked! Reviewing ICT work is often ignored at the end of a lesson, because the whole activity can continue for a number of days.

8. Covering the IT National Curriculum

The National Curriculum requirements for IT are demanding in themselves, even without adding the capital C for Communications and considering e-mail and the WWW. The following suggestions may remind you of some of the main things to be covered. Once again, the QCA scheme of work for ICT may offer more useful suggestions:

- **Remember that IT is a tool for pupils to use.** IT in the National Curriculum is about exploring and problem solving across the curriculum and about helping children to understand how IT can be used to create, explore and solve problems.

■ **Remember to make IT relevant.** IT in the National Curriculum is about relating it to their own lives. However it's difficult to predict how we'll be using ICT in five years' time when some of the Year 6 children will be leaving school, let alone in more than 10 years' time when this year's reception class will finish compulsory schooling.

■ **Remember that ICT is a powerful *communications* tool.** Communicating and handling information – text, graphs, pictures and sound – is a major strand of the National Curriculum and emphasizes IT as a tool for pupils.

■ **Combining text and pictures for a specific audience can be as easy as designing and making a card or a poster.** You would also need to get the pupils to evaluate the effectiveness or appropriateness of what they had done to achieve the learning objectives.

■ **The problem with using pie charts is that pupils think it's just a piece of cake!** Plotting graphs and adding text is easy with current programs. Interpreting this information and analysing it is not so straightforward. When the construction of graphs and charts is easy, the teaching emphasis needs to be on interpreting and making connections to other areas of maths, particularly number. This way, visual information will reinforce and develop pupils' understanding of number.

■ **Analysing information is often missed out.** Pupils don't always need to go through the complete cycle (identify the problem, pose a question, evidence, data, evaluate, check solution). Pupils are not expected to organize a database from scratch until Level 5.

■ **Identify a purpose for finding information.** Database and CD-ROM work is not just about printing vast sections of text and pretty pictures. Emphasize the value of information retrieval skills, and making searches purposeful and efficient.

■ **It's not as hard as you think.** Controlling, monitoring and modelling work needs good resources. If it's currently unmanageable you might need to reconsider your equipment or what you're trying to achieve. Helping children to learn to use a tape recorder, or to set the timer on a video player, or to program a microwave oven, are all examples of control. Control work with Roamer, Pip or Pixie is hugely versatile, getting young children in Key Stage 1 to get it to draw a square, or use it for non-standard measure can be absorbing and valuable, yet Year 6 pupils can become just as absorbed planning escape routes involving measurement in centimetres and degrees using the same piece of equipment.

■ **Remember your targets.** Your target is that by the end of the primary school all pupils can:

use and combine different forms of information, and show an awareness of audience. They add to, amend and interrogate information that has been stored. They understand the need for care in framing questions when collecting, accessing and interrogating information. Pupils interpret their findings, question plausibility and recognize that poor quality information yields unreliable results. Pupils use IT systems to control events in a predetermined manner, to sense physical data and to display it. They use IT based models and simulations to explore patterns and relationships, and make simple predictions about the consequences of their decision making. They compare their use of IT with other methods. (Level 4 level description)

■ **Get real!** The target quoted above means that pupils have to be able to achieve it in *real* situations. By the end of Year 6 your pupils should be using IT in the process of working on an open-ended task. This could be searching for information on a CD-ROM or on the WWW and then presenting what they find with a desktop publishing package as part of a project (maybe producing a leaflet or poster). They should use databases as a starting point when looking for possible answers to questions in history, say, 'Why did the Spanish Armada set sail?' They should be able to cross-reference and compare what they find on a CD-ROM with what they find in a book. They should be able to enter data from a survey into a database or spreadsheet with care, compare results with others and look for reasons why their answers don't quite match. They should be able to make the decision to use a spreadsheet to record various measurements, for example plotting distance against time, in a scientific investigation. A scheme of work for IT should not only give children a range of experiences showing what IT can do, it should also help them to develop the necessary skills to decide when and how to use it in their work.

9. Integrating IT with the curriculum

IT is only a tool. The content can be as varied as you need. It's therefore essential to consider how you can integrate it into your teaching so it's effective both in developing pupils' IT capability and their skills, knowledge and understanding in different areas of the curriculum. Already we have stressed the need to make usage of IT real and meaningful for pupils. The following suggestions may give you further ideas for integrating IT:

■ **Use IT to support other areas of your teaching.** It can help in finding and compiling resources for your teaching sessions. These can be ideas and activities for pupils to use away from the computer.

■ **Use whole-class demonstrations to start pupils thinking.** A CD-ROM entry or talking story book page can be used as a discussion point with the whole class and can be an excellent starting point for further activities away from the computer.

■ **Use IT to support pupils' learning.** This is particularly relevant when working on group activities based around the computer. The computer can be used as a resource initially using a CD-ROM, and then as a focus for the presentation of the work using a word-processor or desktop publishing package. Planning a timeline of the Victorians in history, with pairs of pupils writing or illustrating a particular date, or an annotated map in geography with individual pupils covering different aspects of a country, can both follow this type of organization.

■ | **Combine the work different pupils do.** Unless you're very well supplied with computers, the amount of work pupils will be able to complete using a computer will be limited. However, assembling work into a collection (such as a class book on the various aspects of their study of the Egyptians or a guide to using a computer-based simulation) enables IT work to be used as a resource by everyone while still producing a significant piece of work that everyone feels part of.

■ | **Get the pupils to use slide shows and presentations.** They are easier than you might think and are appropriate across the curriculum as a summary of a theme or unit of work. The slide show module on KidPix, for example, is remarkably easy to use and even Claris Works or PowerPoint are usable by older children.

■ | **Short regular sessions are best for practising skills on the computer.** This is true for IT skills, as well as drill and practice programmes in other areas like maths or spelling.

■ | **Try the Internet.** Almost everything on the WWW seems to be copyright-free, so use it for finding relevant pictures and information for pupils to include in desktop publishing that is related to a topic or theme. Do check each site before you start downloading, just in case.

■ | **Think of other aspects of ICT.** Try tape recording, faxing and video. Annoy some education ministers and use calculators! They're all relatively accessible these days and can generate valuable discussion of IT experiences and applications.

■ | **See that IT is mentioned in every other subject's planning.** Every subject coordinator should be looking for opportunities to use IT in their subject areas, and if they aren't, get them to (or at least raise the idea)!

■ | **Make it fun!** Using the computer creatively in music and art can be motivating and rewarding for a range of pupils. Indeed, it can be the best way to cover certain aspects of the National Curriculum for IT, for instance, modelling can be a difficult strand to cover. Getting children to use a simple musical composition program can provide excellent opportunities for modelling. Just changing an instrument in an existing composition to see what it sounds like is modelling! If you can get them to compose their own stuff and they adapt, speed up, slow down, changing instruments, etc then that is even better. Similarly, using different effects in a painting program on the same picture can be a great way to discuss pattern, texture, colour, line, tone, shape, form and space in art, and to use IT to explore these aspects into the bargain.

10. Planning for continuity in IT

This is really an issue for the whole school and you should not be tackling it on your own. Most schools will have procedures for handing on records but you may still need to make sure you're not just repeating skills and using programs the pupils have used before. The following suggestions may help you to get started on this:

- **Know what is expected of you.** This should be in the school policy and scheme of work but if you aren't quite sure, check with a senior manager or the IT coordinator before planning your own work in any depth.

- **Find out what pupils have already done.** There should be some records from last year, either directly indicating what pupils have done in IT, or indirectly if there are copies of word-processing or pictures in children's records.

- **Know how the previous teacher organized access to the computer.** You may want to alter how you manage it, but at least you might start with a system that the pupils are familiar with.

- **Find out what your pupils do at home.** Some pupils will have wider experience of ICT at home. It can be useful to train these pupils as experts or helpers to get peer support established. Be careful, however, to avoid pupils without ICT opportunities at home feeling disadvantaged.

- **Get your own routines established.** For instance, if you want your pupils to get the next pupil when they have finished with a machine, and to record what they have done, get a system going early on in the year. Like most things, it's hard going to start with but pays dividends in the long run.

- **Have a clear idea of where you're trying to get to.** If you know what sort of things you want them to be able to do in word-processing or painting using a toolbox program, you stand more chance of developing the relevant skills to the right level.

- **Use a tick list to keep track.** Simple, easy to interpret records of what pupils have done is the first step. They'll help you keep track of what the children have done and help ensure equality of access. Such records will provide useful evidence for the next teacher, and will be valuable when inspections are due. Reviewing the list can then lead on to effective assessment.

- **Concentrate on transferable skills.** Learning the intricacies of a complex program that the children will never see again is inefficient. Identifying skills in word-processing, like 'cut and paste', is more likely to ensure a progression in skills. You wouldn't expect all children to pick up new mathematical skills the first time. You would usually cover a basic concept several times, perhaps in different ways, before moving on. Good practice in ICT is just the same.

- **Agree which programs different year groups will use.** There's no point in each year group using different word-processors for example. There should be overlap from year to year, maybe even throughout a Key Stage so that skills and familiarity can be built upon and extended.

■ **Be creative too!** Can you think of a *different* activity for developing word-processing skills this year? Just because you've done it one way before doesn't mean it's the only way. So long as you cover the necessary skills or learning outcomes, a new approach is worth a try. It also stops *you* from becoming set in your ways, and allows you to discover new and better tricks.

IT AS A CROSS-CURRICULAR SUBJECT

IT can find its inspiration and context within the rest of the curriculum. It can support, enhance and extend learning in many other subject areas. It can also be an excellent source of inspiration and motivation, but often ICT is used primarily as a source of 'drill and practice' (sometimes referred to as 'drill and kill') activities. This situation can cause stagnation and does not promote IT or ICT skills in any useful way.

In this section we focus on how ICT can be used primarily to support other areas of the curriculum but with the caveat that all such work can be valuable to both. While we would not like to suggest that you should be putting everything discussed here into practice immediately, being aware of the potential and the possibilities may help you both to plan and to implement the use of ICT more effectively into your classrooms and into your teaching style.

11. Organizing IT work in other curriculum areas

The following four sections discuss in some detail the variety of ways in which ICT can be used and developed throughout the curriculum. However, many of the ideas should probably be viewed in light of the possibilities there may be for how you can organize access to ICT equipment and resources. This can vary widely from school to school and from one education authority to another, but consider the possibilities before you write off an activity as being totally impracticable. The famous phrase from Health and Safety legislation, 'so far as is reasonably practicable', can be applied to organizing IT:

■ **Be prepared to be flexible.** It you genuinely want to get the best out of the opportunities presented by ICT, you have to be prepared to consider changes, even quite radical changes to the way you work and the way you organize your classroom and resources.

■ **Try to consider possibilities, rather than put up road-blocks.** Everyone has, at one time or another, opted out of doing something because it seemed impracticable. Before you do, try to consider what the best possible scenario for a task or experience might be. Then consider how close you could get to that with the resources available in your school. Consider whether other schools in your area, especially your feeder and transfer schools, may be able to help. Consider whether other local institutions, such as colleges, universities or libraries, may be able to help. If it's a worthwhile experience, the extra effort may be time well spent. Of course, you'll need to ask your headteacher, but you can still start the ball rolling.

- **Be prepared for a bit of upheaval.** Because ICT can be used throughout the curriculum, it may be appropriate to move resources around, especially if you have a classroom organized into learning areas. There is little point in having a computer stuck in the language area while it's being used in a science investigation. Here, it needs to be seen as a piece of scientific equipment. So, if possible, try to use it as such.

- **Consider the needs of the activity.** For some tasks, managing with one computer and spreading the work over a fair time is not only reasonable, it can be the most effective method. But for other tasks a greater level of access may be essential. Consider the options. Just borrowing two or three extra machines from other classes for a morning could considerably enhance an activity. Ideally, your school might set up a dedicated resource room but where this is not practical, possible or available, try other methods. Furthermore, a dedicated resource room has its own drawbacks, not least the risk of sidelining computer equipment rather than mainstreaming it.

- **Consider whether the children need to have access to resources to learn.** There is no reason why children need to have access to ICT resources in order to benefit from them. You could use a floor robot to demonstrate an idea, and the children could then work on a task using pencil and paper. They could compare solutions and try out ideas by pretending to be robots. Of course, it would be a shame if they never got to try their ideas out for real, but the other options may make group work far more effective.

- **Why not use technology as a teaching aid?** There is no reason to assume that children need to be sitting at the computer to make use of it. As long as your class or group are where they can see it, you could use the computer to demonstrate ideas, a bit like a blackboard. You may have gathered some data in science work. You may want to discuss which would be the best sort of chart to use to present your information. If the data is put into a spreadsheet, you can produce several possibilities and discuss their merits before the children go off and produce their own charts with pencil and paper.

- **Try to get others involved.** More often than not, it isn't practical or desirable for you to be directing and supporting the IT work in your classroom. There may be students, auxiliaries, parents or governors who would be willing to help out. An extra pair of hands can take away the need for reorganization, as the extra support will help to keep the children focused and on task.

- **Consider whether you can use other spaces within school.** When working with floor robots it may be appropriate to use the playground or corridors adjoining your classroom. When using sensors, control boxes and so on, having a computer on a trolley so that it can be moved around easily can be a real help.

■ **Get hold of a set of headphones.** There is no doubt that computers can interfere with the general peace and harmony of the classroom, and vice versa, especially with software that insists on playing mind-numbingly repetitive tunes all day. Many computers can have headphones fitted, and with an adapter can even take more than one set, turning your computer area into a quiet one and avoiding some of the distractions a computer can cause. This won't always be appropriate, but when practicable can make life much more pleasant.

■ **Finally, ask for it!** In our experience, IT coordinators can feel very isolated when it comes to steering their curriculum area. Many would be only too delighted to have someone else making a few suggestions. If you feel you're missing an opportunity, why not ask to have a look through the huge pile of free catalogues your coordinator is bound to have stashed away. (It might be wise, however, to check that you aren't about to try to spend a budget that has already been spoken for.)

12. ICT in language

ICT can be used to support the development of language skills throughout a child's schooling. It can also be used to provide contexts and opportunities for the use of language that would be hard to achieve otherwise. While ICT is specified for use in certain parts of the literacy framework, it can be used to support this framework in many other ways. This can include everything from a precise and concise message for use in electronic mail to reading and making sense of information from teletext, or from a recording of a radio news bulletin to developing pencil control using a special 'mouse pen' on the computer. What follows are some ideas that might help you make the most of these opportunities:

■ **Find out what sort of additional hardware you have available.** Your IT coordinator should be able to tell you whether you have additional hardware, such as concept keyboards, touch screens or 'mouse pens' (great for practising pencil or brush control with basic software such as paint programs). Also, tape recorders, videos, TVs with teletext, CD-ROMs, Internet access and the like can all provide good opportunities for language work.

■ **Find out what sort of additional software you have available.** There is certainly plenty! Talking books are widely acknowledged as being excellent for developing early reading skills, with the additional bonus that they are basically self-supporting once the pupils have the idea of the intuitive controls. You'll need software to drive concept keyboards, you can get programs that are designed to help with letter formation; copy and match programs often have activities that develop a range of early literacy skills. There is a huge range of multimedia CD-ROMs that are fairly self-supporting once the basics have been mastered. Your IT coordinator should be able to provide you with further information on software that will support your language teaching.

- **Try to identify a couple of programs that best suit your needs.** It's unrealistic and possibly counter-productive to try to use too many different programs. To get the best from them, you need to put in time and effort (not necessarily your own time and effort!). Give your class time to get to grips with programs, making sure everyone has a go. Then try to make it available so that the pupils get the chance to extend and consolidate what they have learnt. They can't do this if there are too many programs to choose from.

- **Try to get the best out of what you've got.** Concept keyboards, for instance, are incredibly versatile. They can be used for very early literacy skills in nursery and reception classes where simple sentences can be built up using sight vocabulary and picture clues. They can provide sources of information in, say, history work, where pressing a picture of an artefact presents information about that artefact on the screen. They can be a way of communicating information where the children design overlays and program the computer to present their ideas to others.

- **Use word-processors to their full potential.** Obviously word-processors are useful for presenting written work neatly but, if used well, can do a lot more besides. Pages can be set up that act as a stimulus for written work. A piece of clip art or decorative border that may help inspire creative writing can be prepared in advance. They are perfect for drafting, editing and redrafting work because making alterations is so easy. They often contain spell checkers and the clarity of the text can make identifying errors much easier. Activities that you prepare using a word-processor and then print out for use on paper can often be adapted easily for use on screen. They are too expensive to be used just as typewriters, so try to use their potential!

- **Use technology as a source of inspiration for language work.** Taped interviews with important people, news reports, teletext and so on can be great sources of inspiration for research and creative writing activities with older and more able pupils.

- **Use technology to record ideas for written work.** Clearly, word-processors are great for recording ideas once keyboard skills have been acquired and access is available, but other forms of technology can be great for assisting with language work. Get those children who find it difficult to maintain direction in their work, perhaps due to slow or illegible handwriting, to record stories or ideas onto audiotape. Listening to what they recorded, they can then copy out a piece at a time, helping to keep them focused on the task.

- **Use technology for recording ideas for speaking and listening.** Consider tasks such as preparing a news bulletin or a play pupils have written for recording on video or audiotape, or enhancing role-play activities with an old telephone or old radio, or retelling familiar stories for others to listen to. Technology provides some of the best opportunities and motivation to talk *and* to listen.

- **Try not to be afraid of apparently complex computer activities.** If the thought of letting your class have a go at multimedia authoring rather chills your blood, don't let it. It's amazing how much children can achieve with even just a little nudge in the right direction. If you learn the very basics to get them started, they'll probably discover a surprising amount for themselves, then they'll teach you. (Could this be online INSET?)

■ **If you have access to the Internet, use it.** For developing higher order reading skills such as reference and research work, what could be better than access to the largest, continuously growing body of information ever collected? There are security issues, but software that provides some protection is freely available. You could even download whole sites for use off-line; this way you get to vet the sites' content.

13. ICT in maths

ICT is specified for use in the numeracy framework but it can offer a range of contexts and opportunities for developing and extending mathematical work at any stage far beyond the opportunities outlined in the numeracy strategy. Often without even realizing it, children can be acquiring and consolidating mathematical skills as they work. So look out for the possibilities. Here are some to start with:

■ **Find out what sorts of additional hardware you have available.** Ask your IT coordinator about floor robots, remote controlled toys, and resources that will help you use them effectively. You'll need to see your maths coordinator about calculators and support materials for using them.

■ **Find out what sorts of additional software you have available.** As with packages for language work, there are many pieces of software that can be used as drill and practice for basic number skills. Everything from early number recognition to number bonds to times tables to simulated adventures involving mathematical problem solving can be useful. Your long-suffering IT coordinator should be able to make a few appropriate suggestions!

■ **Remember that floor robots can be used even with very young children.** The controls on many of the more popular floor robots are very clear and they often use non-standard units of measurement, allowing for comparative measurement, estimation, investigation and discussion with small groups of Early Years children.

■ **Remember that floor robots can be used even with older children.** The beauty of controlling floor robots is that the work children do is as hard as the problems they are set. These robots can often be used with standard units of measure and degrees of turn. They can hold complex sequences of instructions to solve problems that may require investigation, measurement, calculation, recording, teamwork and experimentation to get right.

■ **Try to get one generic maths program that may be used throughout the year.** You'll probably need a package that allows you to work on data handling and perhaps spreadsheet work, and a LOGO package can be very useful. As with all generic programs, try to get one that suits your age group and stick to it. As the children's familiarity with the program develops, so does their ability to use it independently. If possible, try to get one that is used throughout your Key Stage to promote this aim.

- **Keep the number of drill and practice programs to a minimum.** To get the best out of a program it's usually better to keep it around for a while. If you organize it so that each child has a go and then never sees it again, you're missing out on one of the best motivational factors – trying to get a higher score than last time! Watch children (and adults!) using computer games to remind yourself how addictive this factor can be.

- **Try to get hold of drill and practice programs that are flexible.** See your IT coordinator about drill and practice or simulated adventure software that the children will not have seen in previous year groups. Most programs will have some degree of control over the complexity of the problems built in, often found under the 'teacher controls' menu. Try to set it so that the program challenges the children, but not so high that they rely heavily on your assistance.

- **Consider how you're going to ensure that everyone has the same opportunities.** If you're not going to have the use of these sorts of programs as planned activities, recorded by you, the chances are that some children will dominate the use of them. You could try getting them to record when they have used the program, even to record how far they got. At least you'll know who to encourage and who to point in different directions!

- **Look out for effective support packs.** Many simulated adventures come with resource or activity packs, collections of worksheets that go along with a piece of software. Sometimes they provide good support materials, work that you can do away from the computer, but often they are to be used alongside the computer. If you only have one machine in your classroom, using these materials can become a logistical nightmare.

- **Don't underestimate the power of peer tutoring.** Children working in pairs on mathematical tasks teach each other very effectively. Just try sitting and listening to the quality of the discussions and cooperation going on between two children trying to solve a mathematical problem using a floor robot, if you want proof! Often, when using ICT-based resources, less (of you) is more! Sometimes, very little teacher input is required. Also the 'expert/apprentice' model of working for disseminating knowledge, understanding and strategies, can work very well in these contexts.

14. ICT in science

ICT fits into the science curriculum in a variety of ways. It can be used as an experimental tool, for gathering and exploring data, for recording information and presenting ideas, and even for consolidating basic concepts. What you can achieve is limited largely by what you have access to, but with even quite limited resources, you can provide effective support for your science work using IT:

- **Find out what sort of additional hardware you have available.** Another visit to your IT coordinator should give you an idea or the sorts of hardware you have available. Ask about sensors or data logging equipment for measuring work. Ask about control boxes that can be used to explore electrical circuits and conductors, as well as actually controlling powered apparatus.

- **Find out what sort of additional software you have available.** While you're there, ask about simple spreadsheets and database software. Ask about any simulated adventures that might cover relevant scientific concepts and about the software that you should use alongside the available hardware. Ask about CD-ROMs if appropriate: many are geared specifically to scientific concepts.

- **Don't expect to be able to do it all at once.** If your school is well resourced, the possibilities and the opportunities you'll be able to offer may be very different. It takes a lot of time and effort both to get to grips with new resources and to integrate them into your teaching. Over time you'll be able to incorporate more and more in to your work, but don't try to do it all at once.

- **Try to take it one step at a time.** If you want to get the children in your class to use spreadsheets to record results of tests, they'll need to do a bit of work first. Playing simple number function games in maths, taking some prepared data and drawing different charts and graphs, even just using it as if it were a glorified calculator will help them to become familiar with what a spreadsheet can do. This understanding is very important if they are to get any benefit from using spreadsheets in scientific investigations.

- **Remember that databases can be an excellent place to start investigating.** There are many aspects of science work that do not lend themselves to practical investigations, but databases on CD-ROM can still offer potential for exploration. For instance, if you were to discuss the differences between amphibians and reptiles, searching a database and noting the characteristics of each could provide a stimulus for a great deal of debate and further investigation.

- **Remember that computers are great for sorting and classifying.** Even in the Early Years computers can be used for basic scientific work. If children can 'point and click', they can pick up and sort information on a computer screen. Try the various 'My Worlds' screens for instance, or a picture-based concept keyboard overlay for recording what they did.

- **Try using data logging equipment in group work.** Giving every child the opportunity to set up and carry out an experiment using sensors and so on would probably take a very long time! However, setting up an experiment with a group of 10 or so is far more realistic. As long as each can see the computer screen then each can participate equally in the investigation.

■ **Try using technology to take the drudgery out of recording.** Children sometimes find it tough to investigate and to record at the same time. The use of the school's video camera or an audiotape machine may provide a more reliable system for recording. It may also provide one of the best sources of motivation and discussion you could hope for. Photographs are a lot more accessible and easier to manage, and they can also be extremely effective.

■ **Try using technology to take the drudgery out of reporting too.** Children can often find reporting scientific investigations a long and boring process. Could they present their ideas on video? Could they make a picture of the investigation using a digital camera, and then talk about it? Perhaps a computer-generated chart as the centre piece for a presentation to the rest of the class would provide much interest.

■ **Remember that modelling can be a valuable but complex process.** In theory, computers are perfect for modelling events and trying out possibilities. In practice this is true, but they neglect to tell you that setting up reasonable models, and making it clear what these models are supposed to represent, can be really tough. You'll find that it's much easier to stick to published software, unless you're a bit of a whiz!

15. ICT in foundation subjects

While the current trend is away from foundation subjects and towards the 'basics', there is still a clear need and a legal requirement to develop children's understanding of life beyond English, maths and science. Once again, technology has a valid role to play, particularly in those areas of the curriculum where 'hands-on' experience is not easy. Here are some ideas to get you thinking of better ones!

■ **You need to be aware of what's available.** Perhaps by this time, if not done already, your IT coordinator will have decided to put together a list of what's available. Better still, such information will be included on core planning sheets, where resources may be listed and possibilities briefly described.

■ **Research sources of information and data.** Prepared data, such as well-presented information on CDs and so on can give a really good focus to study in geography, to history, to art, music and even technology as well.

■ **Identify simple sources of information.** The talking storybook idea has been extended and adapted and now there are talking non-fiction books too. With a little support and some purposeful structure to their work, even quite young children can start to carry out research work.

■ **Find resources that enable comparisons.** Many educational software developers have been putting together collections of photographic evidence, and occasionally video footage, together with a few notes and a searchable index to allow children to draw comparisons between, say, physical features of the local landscape and other, more varied, land forms, or their own and other's customs and practices.

■ **Get a couple of historical simulations.** There are quite a few of these around. They get the children involved in the subject they are studying at a more personal level, where the children are making discoveries and establishing links for themselves.

■ **Look out for simple-to-use databases.** If you want to get children into research and reference work, try making a class database, a place to collect the information you have gathered about a topic from various sources. This can provide a good purpose to a task and will teach them a great deal about how information can be stored, sorted and classified.

■ **Get a good, easy-to-use paint program.** A good paint package can be worth its storage space in gold. While it can allow children to put together illustrations for desktop publishing activities and so on, it can also be used to work in a way that can be too frustrating when done traditionally. While many simple paint packages are a bit crude, they do allow children to experiment. This allows you to claim with justice that you're using computers to model situations. Illustrating work in different curriculum areas with the same program will develop key ICT skills and support different subjects.

■ **Consider simple drawing and design programs.** These are especially useful in technology where a design can be repeated and altered fairly subtly several times without the need to start again. There are a few programs designed specifically for this purpose that are extremely easy to use. With some, you can even test out your design on the computer to see if it works!

■ **Find suitable sites on the Web.** If you have access to it, it's amazing how many libraries and museums have Web sites. Just looking at one with a small group of children could open up many new avenues of study. Not only will it give access to new and previously unobtainable sources of information, but it'll give children new ideas about how they might organize and present their own work in future.

■ **Make collections of clip art.** While it might seem like a bit of a cop-out, clip art provides instantly effective results which children love. They can provide a stimulus for written work, for example pupils can write explanations of what a Victorian woman is wearing or how a steam engine worked and so on.

■ **Look out for freebies.** More and more institutions and companies are putting together CD-ROMs that promote their interests but that educate too. Obviously, the World Wide Web is a good source of freebies as well. You may not like the idea of using the Internet in class, but there is no reason why it shouldn't provide you with the information you need to help you to teach!

■ **Use desktop publishing.** Possibilities include creating a history timeline, or an annotated map for geography, a design for technology, or a portfolio of pictures in art.

SUPPORTING SPECIAL EDUCATIONAL NEEDS WITH IT

ICT is an excellent tool to support children with special educational needs (SEN). It can give them access to an appropriate curriculum. However, the wide range of special needs to be catered for, and the range of contexts in which such work might be undertaken, means that this is not a straight-forward process. Individual children will need individual educational programmes, different support systems and activities, and access to different hardware and software. All of this needs to be managed by the individual class teacher, perhaps in consultation with senior management, and people in roles such as the special educational needs coordinator (SENCO) and the IT coordinator.

A lack of knowledge about what is achievable in such cases is perhaps the greatest obstacle to getting the very best out of what's available. In this section we'll discuss what's possible and how to exploit its potential. Computers have the potential to extend the learning of *all* pupils and that is precisely the challenge.

We would like to stress that our tips in this section are general suggestions, intended to help the non-specialist class teacher or SENCO. For a wider range of further suggestions on helping pupils with SEN, not restricted to their usage of computers, we suggest that you look at Part 4 of this book.

16. Deciding on appropriate input devices

Though there are a great many additional pieces of hardware you can strap on or plug in to your ICT equipment to make it more appropriate for children with specific needs, there are also a few things to consider about the sort of hardware you should get in the first place. We share below a few ideas to take into consideration:

■ **Try alternatives to mice.** If children find it difficult to use a mouse because of coordination problems or because they simply can't hold a mouse, there are several other devices that might help. Some of these are described below.

■ **A track ball.** A very simple alternative that is basically an upside-down mouse. Instead of moving the mouse so that the ball underneath rolls along the table top, you roll the ball with your fingers. Children using this sort of device will need reasonable hand–eye coordination but it does make clicking the mouse button in the right place much easier. The larger the ball, the easier it is to control.

- **Joystick.** This is a fairly straightforward alternative to the mouse. It still needs a reasonable degree of hand–eye coordination but it can be used with parts of the body other than hands. Many children (not to mention adults!) develop a good degree of control of joysticks through playing with computer-based games.

- **A touch screen.** This is the most expensive of these devices but the easiest and most intuitive to use. There are various types, but basically they all work by putting a touch-sensitive, see-through screen in front of the computer monitor. Children can then select and move objects on the monitor just by touching the appropriate points on the screen.

- **Concept keyboards.** Concept keyboards are great for all manner of ICT-based activity. They can be designed to handle everything from simple text input to reference and research work. Many can also be used to guide an on-screen pointer, though if a program to make this work is not included with the keyboard driver software, you may need to find someone who has had a lot of experience with programming concept keyboards.

- **Headphones.** Almost all computers will have a jack socket for speakers. In classrooms speakers give general sound and may add significantly to background noise. Working in these conditions is distracting and could well be impossible for children with mild hearing difficulties. You can almost always plug headphones into the speaker sockets, though do be aware that sometimes a comfortable volume setting for external speakers can be very loud when using headphones. A splitter plug to run two sets of headphones from one socket costs less than £2 from electrical chain stores.

- **Alternative keyboards.** Some educational suppliers have been marketing adaptable and adapted keyboards. There are large, clear keyboards with keys shaped like lower case letters, ones that have letters set out in alphabetical order, ones that use picture inputs, ones that can be split and angled to meet the users' hands more easily. You'll need to check that the keyboards you might want will work with your computers, but these sort of adaptations may well help to improve access for children with poor visual discrimination or coordination problems. Remember, however, that you may well want your special needs pupils to progress towards becoming able to work with the sorts of keyboard in everyday usage, and using an alphabetical one could mean them having to re-learn the position of keys when moving to the endemic 'qwerty' keyboard.

- **Identify key keys.** As a cheaper alternative to buying an adapted keyboard, suppliers also offer products that adapt keyboards cheaply and easily. Coloured stickers that you stick on the keys of your keyboard (eg, delete, tab and return – if they are not already labelled) or guards that hide unnecessary keys, can be useful.

- **Switches and pads.** The most basic input devices are simple switches that allow for very basic control of the computer or other devices. They are appropriate for those with fairly severe physical difficulties but are also great for use with control boxes and so on.

■ **Remember that if it's good practice for SEN, it's good practice.** The kinds of adaptations and supports that you may want to build in to support those with special needs will almost certainly provide useful support to those who don't have such needs. So spending money to support one child will probably be beneficial for a great many more – it may help justify the investment!

17. Adapting computer interfaces

A great deal can be achieved in adapting your computer to fit the needs of pupils with special requirements. Often such changes can be achieved very simply, and sometimes simple and relatively cheap pieces of software can make a considerable difference. The following suggestions might trigger your imagination about where to start:

■ **Start somewhere easy.** Many computers and operating systems come with simple tools that allow you to adapt the way information is displayed on the screen. All modern computers have ways of adapting screen resolutions, background colours, menu and dialogue fonts and so on.

■ **Consider whether changing the screen resolution might help.** This is just a way of determining how many parts what is displayed on the screen is split in to. The lower the resolution, the bigger the things on the screen appear to be. To help a child who is mildly visually impaired or has trouble with visual discrimination, turn the screen resolution down (how this is done varies widely; if unsure, ask your IT coordinator or see the handbook).

■ **Find out if your computer has an adaptable interface.** For instance, an Apple Mac will have a thing called the Launcher. Launcher is just an alternative way of getting to files and to programs. It's adaptable so you can restrict certain children's access to certain programs and files. It can even be adapted for individual pupils – and it's free!

■ **Put folders and programs where pupils can get at them.** Most computers now have Graphical User Interfaces – basically the pictures that represent files and folders that you see on the screen. These interfaces are usually fairly adaptable. Try setting up short cuts (since Windows 95) or aliases (Apple Mac) so that the icon for a program or a folder for work is the first thing a child can see on the screen. This way they don't have to remember complex journeys through files and folders to find what they want. They're also less likely to stray into areas you don't want them to find.

■ **Try changing background colours.** Modern computers can have the patterns and colours that cover the screen changed and adapted. Children who have problems with visual discrimination may find certain background colours much easier to work with.

■ | **Adapt pointing devices.** Most modern computers have some kind of input device to control an on-screen pointer. Sometimes this pointer can be very difficult to see, but many of these on-screen pointers can be adapted to make them larger and clearer, or to make them appear in brighter colours, or to give them a three-dimensional appearance. Your IT coordinator or ICT centre should be able to help. If not, try ringing your local educational ICT software supplier.

■ | **Try third-party solutions.** Some software developers have tried to tackle the problem of boring interfaces, which were, after all, designed for adults to use. There are a few programs that will adapt the desktop of your computer and make it more child-friendly. One turns programs into items on a child's desk and files into books or folders on a shelf, almost as if everything were stored in a child's bedroom or study. Ring your supplier or ICT centre for advice.

■ | **Look out for 'short cuts' palettes.** Most generic programs, word-processors, databases, spreadsheets and art packages have buttons around the screen that help users to control what goes on on the screen. Some also have the option to add more buttons using a short cuts palette. Buttons, with helpful icons, such as print, save, new folder, speak, page setup and so on can sit discretely in the top right-hand corner of the screen, so that children don't need to remember which menu to go to. Once more, see your coordinator or the manual!

■ | **You may want to consider voice navigation.** This is where, in theory at least, a computer can respond to voice commands using a small microphone on a stand. This technology is still relatively new and some problems have been reported, but technology marches on so quickly that it would definitely be worth investigating as a way to support children who cannot control other input devices at all. Anticipate, however, that voice navigation may not have the desired effects if the machine is sited in a noisy classroom.

■ | **On-screen concept keyboards might be worth a look.** Programs such as Clicker, which works with Acorn, Mac and Windows, work just like a concept keyboard but are actually displayed on the screen and work with almost any word-processing package. These can be very motivating and a flexible source of support; children can simply take it or leave it!

■ | **Look in catalogues and leaflets.** The range of devices and software for supporting access to IT for children with special needs grows and changes rapidly. It'll always be worth checking through up-to-date catalogues to see if there are solutions that might help you with a specific educational special need in your classroom.

18. Developing activities

It often seems that, given the time and money, you could use ICT to totally transform the way you work with children with SEN. However, finding the time and money to develop all the activities you can think of is almost certainly impossible. A little planning and the repetition of some simple concepts may help you to decide where to start:

- **Before starting to develop activities for specific individuals, look at their statements or IEPs.** These documents will help you identify specific needs and, therefore, the sorts of activities that might be appropriate.

- **First of all, consider what minor adjustments could be made to existing activities.** Obviously it's going to be easier and quicker to adapt activities that you're already using. Can you, for example, take a word-processing activity set up for more able children, and put together a concept keyboard overlay that will support those with special needs? (Bear in mind the other adaptations suggested in the previous section, too.)

- **Look at commercial solutions.** One of the major problems with supporting special needs with IT is that no two special needs are exactly alike. Sometimes commercially produced solutions to learning difficulties such as dyslexia can be a good starting point. Consider whether such software can be adapted to support individual circumstances and ring suppliers to see if you can arrange a free trial of the software before you buy it.

- **Go for adaptable software.** There is an increasing number of programs that act as a framework to support a wide variety of 'add-on' software. Programs such as 'My World' and 'My World II' for Acorn and PC have a vast number of add-on activities that cater for a wide range of abilities and that can be used in a wide variety of contexts. If you can't buy the activity you want, perhaps you can adapt others or just be very fussy as to which add-ons you use.

- **Try to make the most of what you've got.** One thing that inhibits the efficient use of ICT equipment is a lack of knowledge about what's achievable. Knowing the extent to which some of the software and hardware you have in school can be stretched means that you can get the best out of it. Many manuals now contain an overview near the front. It may be worth having a look before you go out and try to get to grips with something entirely new and expensive!

- **For tackling problems with literacy, try talking word-processors.** Many schools will have access to a simple talking word-processor. These programs can 'read' the children's work, either word by word or sentence by sentence. Studies have shown that talking word-processors are not only motivating, but they also help children correct work independently, help with phonemic awareness and can considerably enhance reading and spelling skills.

- **You could try talking books too.** There is a significant amount of research that suggests that talking books can have considerable impact on the performance of both beginning and struggling readers, especially in Key Stage 1 and early Key Stage 2. However, the activities can be a bit limited and short-lived. Try using the images from the books to make overlays for concept keyboards for story structure or sequencing activities. You could use pictures of characters as a stimulus for further work with talking word-processors. You could focus on key words within the books, counting how many times they occur, for example. The possibilities are extensive!

- **Don't be frightened of what sounds very complex.** Multimedia authoring sounds difficult, primarily because the multimedia software we see is complex, but multimedia simply allows you to add a bit of sound to text and to pictures. With a microphone and a simple multimedia authoring program you can develop basic activities with vocal prompts at complex points or in response to their input. Even voice prompts at the level of 'try again' and 'well done' can guide children through simple tasks on a computer and will help enhance independent work.

- **See if software has built-in differentiation.** If you're using software to develop or consolidate knowledge in other curriculum areas, see if the level at which it operates can be altered to meet the requirements of lower attaining pupils.

- **Don't underestimate the 'motivation factor'.** It's often very surprising how much apparently less able pupils can do on computers. There are many ideas about why this is, including suggestions that pupils look more closely when they are motivated so mistakes are easier to see, and the fact that errors are easy to change means that mistakes are less frustrating. But perhaps it's simply that children find computers, and what they can achieve when using them, exciting and interesting so they try that bit harder. Nothing succeeds like success.

19. Developing support for children with SEN

Clearly, you're not going to be able to support children with special needs in the way you might like to every time you would like to. Sometimes, using computers can actually save you time in class, but often additional support *will* need to be provided. Managing and organizing such support to get the best from it is essential:

- **Do your best to rope in other people.** This can include parents, governors, volunteers, grandparents and Uncle Tom Cobbley to help out in the classroom. It will also be worth asking an educational psychologist or the educational support services, who should be able to offer advice or even provide direct help in supporting children with special needs with ICT.

- **Do your best to rope in people in the know.** People who have some familiarity with the children involved or the sorts of ICT work you want to undertake, or preferably both, will be able to support children with special needs on computer-based activities with relatively little input from you.

- **Consider the use of peer tutoring.** Children often seem to be able to explain things to one another more effectively and succinctly than any teacher can. Someone who has just learnt something can remember *how* the light dawned, and this makes it easier to help someone else to learn it. They can often be relied upon to support their peers with a good deal of understanding and sensitivity too.

- **If the opportunity arises, try to train a parent or two.** If you work in a school that encourages parents to work in classrooms and support all aspects of school life, see if you can track down a parent with some ICT experience early on. They could become an invaluable source of support for you and the children who most need it.

- **Use printouts to help with the sequence of events.** In a specific activity there may be several steps. If you print out an example of each step along the way, you can then use them as teaching aids, and as aides-memoire. This small additional support can guide those who have trouble remembering sequences of instructions or who lack confidence, allowing them to work through the task unsupported.

- **Try making step-by-step cards.** As an adaptation of the idea above, writing or printing simple prompts on to a series of cards and fastening them together in the appropriate order might be all that is required to guide less able children through more complex tasks. If these can be picture clues, then the range of abilities you can support can grow even further. Look out for clip art collections aimed at education.

- **Consider whether it's appropriate to get an auxiliary or support teacher trained.** Where specific needs have been identified and one-to-one support is recommended, see if you can either find the time to (or ask your ICT coordinator to) train support staff in the use of appropriate software and hardware. You may be able to negotiate additional time for more worthy cases, such as during assemblies, break times of even lunch breaks.

- **Ask about enlisting help from older children.** Recent reports suggest that mentoring, when an older child helps a younger child with a specific sort of task on a regular basis, is at least as beneficial for the helper as it is for the learner. Older children often accept responsibilities such as these extremely well and can be trained, to a certain extent, in what is and what is not appropriate when working with younger children who may be struggling a little.

- **Never forget the value of experimentation.** Children with special needs know how to play with computers. It's perfectly possible that they learn just as much, if not more, when they're allowed to work with computers without any overt goal. Free experimentation can have a significant impact on the quality of more structured work later.

- **Remember that ICT has a lot of pulling power.** If you're seeking additional support or funding to help a child with special needs in school, and you can make a strong case that an increased ICT provision would help, you stand a good chance of attracting attention. Because ICT is the 'new' educational idea there is a good deal of desire to promote its use; you might as well try to get something for your trouble!

20. Stretching more able children

Many very able pupils find ICT a very motivating way to work. Don't forget that highly gifted children have their own kinds of special educational needs, and need to be kept interested and appropriately challenged. Besides, if they're not duly stretched, they can become disruptive or lose motivation. Giving them opportunities to work with technology and ways to stretch their abilities and skills is a path worth taking:

- **Use the never-ending activity.** Work with computers, floor robots, calculators and so on is perfect for more able children, mostly because the possibilities are endless and each new thing learnt opens up new possibilities, keeping those children who always finish everything in half the time you want, engaged in their work.

- **Use ICT to provide contexts for open-ended investigation.** Some teachers find the idea of programming a computer daunting. But LOGO is a simple programming language, the basics of which can be learnt quickly, and which is well supported across the age range. Even better, some of the more creative LOGO programs or activities provide wonderful opportunities for open-ended investigation, problem solving, planning and communication, as well as developing useful mathematical skills. Even better, you don't need to know much to get them going – just the first few, obvious commands and some children will get the idea quickly.

- **Set them a challenge.** If you have drill and practice software that is adaptable, crank the level up a bit and set your more able children a challenge. You could even run a competition on the quiet!

- **Remember, pupils can often teach themselves better than you can.** Given a purpose and a starting point; all children, but especially able children, test the boundaries of what is possible far more quickly than adults tend to do. Teachers should not be frightened of this but should use it to their advantage. After all, there's no reason why they shouldn't teach you, is there?

- **Keep the handbook handy.** When bright pupils get stuck using technology and want an answer that you don't have, give them the handbook. It's an excellent context for non-fiction reading and a good way of giving them control of how far they go! This tactic depends, of course, on your view of the truthfulness as well as usefulness of manuals.

- **Try to keep reference and research material available too.** If you can have a CD-ROM encyclopaedia handy, or perhaps a spreadsheet program for maths investigation, or even access to the Internet or a topic-related database, you'll always have somewhere to go with children who learn quickly. All the better if you can have each of these at the same time. If you can direct able pupils to such resources, they'll be positively engaged and you'll be able to get on!

- **Don't worry about blind alleys.** Just 'cos they're clever, doesn't mean they'll always get it right. It's often tempting to guide children towards the 'correct' answer, but mistakes are valuable learning experiences and it doesn't hurt to get things wrong once in a while. This is most especially true with ICT, because you have to learn how to get out of trouble too! It can be damaging to protect pupils from ever making mistakes with technology.

■ **Let them teach.** As long as the children are fairly social creatures, quick learners can support others by acting as experts in peer-tutoring situations. Clearly, you need to be careful, but evidence suggests that the expert will learn as well as the learner!

■ **Let them plan, or at least negotiate, what they might try.** Because they are bound to have their own ideas about what they want to do, you might like to encourage this. It's useful in such a situation to have a model or plan they can follow. Ideas for starting points can be found in books or from organizations like the National Association for Able Children. A good multimedia package like 'HyperStudio' (Roger Wagner, multi platform) has limitless possibilities.

■ **Try developing logic and critical thinking.** Some programs like 'The Logical Journey of the Zoombinis' (Brøderbund, Mac and PC) can be used by able 5-year-olds but will tax Oxbridge graduates! The only issue is: can you cope with your pupils solving logical problems that you can't?

RESOURCES FOR TEACHING IT AND ICT

Clearly, resourcing issues for ICT are relevant to the class teacher but often remain the headache of the IT coordinator and senior management. But there are two sides to the problem of developing resources for the teaching of IT. This section is concerned with the sorts of resources that a teacher may use to support children during classroom work. We offer suggestions on resources such as work cards, effective starting points, targeting the use of the Internet, as well as how to get the best out of software such as talking books and CD-ROM materials.

21. What can your equipment do?

It's amazing what some computers and software programs can do. It's worth spending time learning about some aspects in detail. The following suggestions are things for you to do before getting your pupils to use computer-based resources:

- **Use a computer yourself.** The very best way of finding out what a piece of software can do is by using it in real contexts. If you have a word-processor that can create tables or a desktop publishing package in school, why not see if you can do your planning on it? Make sure you always word-process letters to parents and so on; ask whether end-of-year reports can be done on the computer. In the long run it *will* save you time!

- **Sit and play.** The best bet is little and often (this applies to your learning as readily as to that of your pupils!). Learning all about all of the programs you have in a marathon session is impractical. You'll learn more effectively if you can use the programs you've played with. If you want to use a new piece of software, don't play with it weeks in advance! Almost certainly, you'll find that you've forgotten much of what you learnt within a week or so!

- **Use what you've got.** ICT involves computers, calculators, programmable robots and a whole host of other electronic devices. Some aspects of the National Curriculum require you to consider wider uses and applications of ICT. Find out what you've actually got access to, and make your way through it a little at a time.

- **Put yourself in your pupils' shoes.** Make sure you've worked through a program in the way you think your pupils might. It's amazing where clicking little fingers can end up! If you've been right through the activity that you want your pupils to do, you'll have a real working knowledge and a fair idea of some of the problems that might crop up!

- **Know your computer.** Different operating systems have different features and may let you do more than you think. For instance, most have ways of letting you take a snapshot of the screen for making instruction cards. Can you cut and paste between applications? Can you drag and drop files to the printer to make them print?

- **Use a simple program to the full.** Learning how to use one program well is more important that knowing a little about a lot of programs. A simpler program is also easier to teach the pupils to use.

- **Use what programs are good at.** For instance, a painting package may let you do what you want, then you can copy or import what you need into a presentation or publishing program. There are a few different approaches to this, but most types of painting file can be used in desktop publishing packages, though may need a little trial and error to find the easiest way to do it.

- **Identify what you want to achieve and then see if the program will do it.** It's easy to be seduced by fancy features, so it's important to keep your eye on what it is you want the pupils to learn.

- **Let the pupils find out more for you.** You won't have the time to exhaust all the possibilities in complex programs. A CD-ROM will have thousands of entries. Let the pupils play and explore, perhaps outside of lesson times too, and then try to review their work with them, getting them to explain or show you bits that you didn't know about. Asking a couple of pupils to review a new CD-ROM over a couple of lunch times and then reporting to the class what they found out is good for them, and can be a practical way for you to become more familiar with the software too!

- **Plan to develop pupils' skills.** Perhaps set a task to learn to use a new tool in a painting package or a new font in word-processing and then get them to write a report or make a few suggestions about how and when they might use what they've learnt in the future.

- **Get the pupils to share ideas.** This could be in the introductory and plenary sections of lessons. Otherwise encourage sharing during group work either at or away from the computer. You'll probably find that they'll tend to share ideas almost without you even noticing, but it's such a valuable opportunity that it should not be left to chance.

22. Starting points... for teachers

Often it's just a question of getting going. Once you've started, ideas will frequently lead to other ideas. The hard part is just getting started! It's worth having a look at the Internet resources, particularly the National Grid for Learning:

- **You've made a start if you're reading this!** There are other books, newspapers and magazines which all have useful ideas you can use as a starting point, but the will to do it is nine-tenths of the battle.

- **Start with something that catches your attention.** You're more likely to have success with something you feel enthusiastic about. This in turn may lead on to other ideas. Try a drawing or painting program to recreate painting styles of the old masters – spray-can tools are great for the impressionists! Or how about a book of your children's book reviews? Or a slide show of pupils' work to run on a loop for a parent's evening?

- **Team up with a colleague.** Working with someone teaching the same age group and swapping resources is a good way to develop your ideas. If you're in a small school and are the only one teaching that age group, you may have a colleague in a neighbouring school you could collaborate with.

- **Employ the best method for disseminating information – a cup of coffee!** Try discussing ideas, desires, aspirations, and queries about what it is you think you should be able to do, in the staff room. Your colleagues may not thank you for bringing up taboo subjects during break, but if you can get them to talk, you may well find there is a lot more understanding of ICT than you think. Also try more formal occasions, staff and key stage meetings, and planning sessions.

- **Try the National Grid for Learning (www.ngfl.gov.uk).** It's designed to support practising teachers and has a wealth of information, ideas and resources for all areas of teaching, particularly literacy and numeracy. Most of (former) NCET or (present) BECTa's site is easy to access, too.

■ **Other Web sites are also expanding rapidly – try visiting them!** It's worth developing your own favourite bookmarks of places to visit. Your LEA may well have an intranet or Web site that lists sites that they have helped to set up or support. These should provide links to sites whose content has already been checked, so are safe to use with children!

■ **The Internet has a vast source of free and shareware programs.** Some of them are not so good; many are valuable. They are usually organized by operating systems (eg, PC, Mac, Acorn) and there'll be different areas containing system, utilities and educational programs. A good place to start might be a Web site by the mining company, www.miningco.com or Tucows at www.mirror.ac.uk/sites/ftp.tucows.com/.

■ **Read magazines and software catalogues.** They'll often give you a good overview of what's available and what you can do. The advantage of software suppliers' catalogues is that once you're on the mailing list you can sit back and wait for them to flood in (which they'll do with startling regularity).

■ **Ask local resource centres.** They'll sometimes have exhibitions and open days in addition to courses. These can be good opportunities to try out new stuff and to talk to people who have much more time to find out about and keep up to date with software and hardware developments.

■ **Visit other schools that may have exhibitions or displays.** These will give you ideas, even if the focus of the display is not ICT.

23. Starting points... for pupils

A range of ideas for getting going in the classroom can be helpful. The computer or other ICT resources can be used in a variety of ways, as either the main focus of a lesson, or as supplementary parts of computer activities, or simply available for pupils to use:

■ **Start activities away from the computer.** There are many occasions where the pupils don't need to begin an activity at the computer. If you're introducing the idea of a database, for instance, see if you can get hold of a real card index to show the concept behind a digital database.

■ **Try problem-solving activities that can use the computer in a variety of ways.** The computer can be used as a log or diary by a group. A Newsroom simulation uses the computer to deliver the latest news to pupils at determined intervals. Computer sensors can help collect information when tackling a scientific problem, or a control box can give a high degree of control in a technology activity.

- **Use task cards to get pupils to develop search skills.** Simply setting an open-ended task involving some form of investigation may lead children to use a CD-ROM encyclopaedia, the Internet and so on. This way of working, where ICT is a part of a process rather than an end in itself, will lead to increased use of equipment as a tool to assist pupils in their learning.

- **Use the computer as a resource for a group.** For instance, when researching information for a writing task, a small group can share information they find in books, from CD-ROMs or from the Internet to help one another. You may have to limit how long each group gets to consult it. Deciding who in a group gets to use the computer will always be tough!

- **Competition will motivate pupils.** Setting up a 'design an advert' competition for a local shop or company may help community links, but it'll certainly get the best out of the children. It will most likely get them to delve more deeply into the potential of the software you're using. If you agree to give only technical support (no assistance with the content at all) it will also provide good opportunities for problem solving and assessment.

- **Try timed races to inject new fervour into familiar programs.** This need not just be in skill and practice programs. You could have a 10-minute writing or painting task to develop pupils' pace of work on the computer.

- **Combine tasks.** A newspaper day (or maybe week?) or producing a brochure or class book can involve all pupils in using the computer at different times and in different ways. They can use it for research, art work, layout and so on.

- **Science or other curriculum areas may give you a starting point.** Here you may be able to use real data in an investigation or experiment. In art, try using a spray-can tool in a painting program to develop understanding of Monet's paintings, for instance.

- **Pupils don't need to start activities from scratch.** Investigating a pre-prepared database is much more efficient when the focus is on asking questions and using evidence rather than collecting and entering the data. Finishing a story or picture, or editing a text with lots of examples of errors you want pupils to identify, may be a better way to use the computer to achieve your specific learning objectives.

- **Show Web sites of other pupils' work.** If you're going to get them to design and put together their own Web site, or maybe present a project in hypertext, pupils will need to see examples of how it works! You can always download a few examples in advance of the lesson, so you can guarantee they'll appear when you summon them.

- **Publish information on the WWW or send an e-mail summary to another school.** You may agree to do a joint project with another school, say a local study. Your children can collect information and resources to prepare and send to the other school. This may give you a focus for a great deal of work away from the computer, which is only used in the final stages of compilation or exchange.

24. Building in support for activities

Newer computers and software have of a lot of built-in help features, and many older programs will have help sheets or cards written for them. It can be a real benefit to work out how to use these efficiently and effectively so that you can use your time with other pupils:

- **Train the pupils to use the support.** Pupils will choose the easiest way to get help. Make sure that this isn't you, or you'll always be on call. Training pupils to use on-line help is hard. There can be a lot of reading involved and it can be quite hard to know where to start. You could pick out key features, copy and print them to make support materials that are easier to use.

- **Use on-line help where it's available, and at a suitable level.** You'll often get help or instructions as part of the program. Sometimes you can turn this feature on or off as required: only turn it off if you're supporting the children in a different way.

- **Try 'tutorials' and 'wizards'.** They'll often demonstrate how to use basic features of the program you want pupils to use. Sometimes they can be amazingly informative, but be warned, sometimes they can also be irritatingly unhelpful!

- **Look for programs with good interactive help.** Not all programs have good help features, so it's worth making sure new and complex programs have help features that pupils can use. If you want help features that are aimed at children, you need to go for educational software. Commercial software may have help built in, but it's usually at an inappropriate level for use in school.

- **Help sheets and cards are worth your time and effort.** To begin with it's worth developing cards and notes for the most commonly used activities such as saving and printing. Using screen shots and pictures is invaluable, and when you have made them, you may find staff use them just as much as the children. Try swapping these with other members of staff, and other schools. You can get more, and distribute yours even further afield, by visiting edit at www.editsite.demon.co.uk.

- **Get the pupils to write a guide.** You can then get another group to test it out and improve it! This way you can really push the use of a piece of software forwards and produce differentiated help sheets into the bargain.

■ **Use speech or sound features of a program.** Many word-processors have speech built in, so having instructions the computer can read out can offer support to pupils who need it. Sometimes you can record your voice and add instructions yourself.

■ **Use a cassette recorder to tape instructions on what to do.** As long as you have a couple of sets of headphones, step-by-step instructions can be followed. At the same time you're developing children's use of control by getting them to use the controls on a tape recorder to their full potential.

■ **Structure a series of tasks so pupils' skills are developed.** Have a series of specific questions for pupils to find the answers to on a CD-ROM. Start with easy, specific questions, then some that are more open. This is far better than a general instruction to 'see what you can find out about the Egyptians', for instance.

■ **Deliberately get things wrong when *you* try out a program.** It'll help you design better instructions and support cards!

25. Targeting IT use

Schools can plan both how hardware and software are used over the course of the year as part of a programme, and also how specific groups of pupils can be targeted to support their learning. The following suggestions may help you to fix your sights appropriately:

■ **Pupils don't all need to do the same thing.** So long as all pupils get a chance to develop their IT skills, they don't all need to do the same activities on the computer.

■ **Identify specific opportunities for SEN pupils.** Practising particular skills frequently for short periods of time (15 minutes, three or four times a week) is likely to be beneficial. Don't just give them routine tasks though!

■ **Identify specific opportunities for higher attaining pupils.** Investigating a database or spreadsheet with more complex questions might be a good starting point. They need to be given different challenges to develop their thinking skills at an appropriate level rather that just kept busy with more of the same work on the computer.

■ **Train pupils to work to a deadline.** This will improve overall pace. Pupils *enjoy* using the computer, yet the reward they usually get for finishing a task is stopping work on the computer! You'll need ways to keep up the pace of their work.

■ **Build in *lots and lots* of time for activities you want everyone to do.** A task that takes one pupil 30 minutes will take more than a fortnight if you only have one computer available!

■ **Be ruthless and give pupils who'll get the most from an activity the most time.** You may want to make sure that over the term or the year that this balances out. There is no point in giving them all equal access if they won't all benefit equally!

■ **Try to revisit skills over the course of the year.** It's probably better to ensure pupils have mastered a relatively small range of core skills in word-processing, drawing, painting and data handling, rather than simply having had a go at a large number of programs.

■ **Timetable scarce resources.** If you have a small number of floor robots or just one colour printer, decide how the equipment will best be used.

■ **Use scarce resources.** It follows on from the previous point that if it's your turn for the robot or colour printer, use it. Have something planned for when your turn comes up, so you don't waste your valuable time thinking about what to do.

■ **If you can't use it, pass it on to someone else.** Where resources are limited you may decide you can't use what you've got, or on some occasions when it's your turn you may not be able to make the best use of it. Someone else may be waiting for the chance to try out an idea with the equipment.

■ **If an activity works, tell someone.** Sharing ideas with colleagues about what you've found to work well is the best way for you in turn to get information from them about what works well for them.

26. Maximizing potential

Schools cannot only plan how hardware and software are to be used over the course of the year as part of a programme, but also how specific groups of pupils can be targeted to support their learning. You'll never have enough equipment to meet all your pupils' needs, so setting your priorities is essential:

■ **Pupils don't all need to do the same thing.** We've said this before, but we think it's worth repeating! So long as you have an idea of what skills the pupils are developing, they don't need to do identical tasks.

■ **Target groups of pupils to support specific skills.** You might have a group of pupils who could do with more work on punctuation. Set them a word-processing task where they know that is the focus and it'll help them. Another group might do a similar task but with an emphasis on using more descriptive words.

■ **Be clear about what you want pupils to learn.** If you aren't sure what it is you want the pupils to get out of an ICT activity, you won't know if it was successful. It's best when you can tell your pupils exactly what you're intending them to get out of an activity.

- **Share the learning objectives with them.** Pupils will attend better to the relevant aspects of the task if you let them know why you want them to use the computer.

- **Review the learning objectives with them.** If they know what they were supposed to be learning, whether it was spelling, or how to cut and paste, they should be able to tell you if they think it worked.

- **Little and often is usually better that lots but infrequently.** This is particularly true for developing skills. However, that doesn't necessarily mean it needs to be drill and practice. Pupils could do a timed 'look, cover, write, check' spelling task on the computer which will also develop keyboard skills. They could also print out what they'd done for homework!

- **Find more time for pupils to use the equipment.** With whole-class introductions and plenaries in literacy and numeracy sessions, it's no longer possible to have the computers used all the time. Before school, break, lunch time, and after school may all be possible if you can crack the problem of appropriate supervision and support.

- **Get support.** Who can help you? The IT coordinator? A colleague, student, parent, or older pupil? When you want to get something new off the ground you may find an extra pair of hands helpful. With ICT you may expect it'll be more difficult to get help. You may be surprised if you ask.

- **Get things finished.** ICT tasks often take longer that planned. Anticipate this and have strategies to get things completed. You'll feel better about ICT if you accomplish your goals.

- **Look back!** Every now and then, think back to which ICT tasks and activities turned out to have high learning payoff for pupils, and which were interesting for you to set up and to support. Build on your successes. Also look for which tasks didn't work out in practice. Work out why. Was it the software, or was it the equipment, or was it the way the tasks were set up? How could you have another go with these tasks, this time making them work better?

RESOURCES FOR THE IMPLEMENTATION OF ICT

Getting hold of the resources to facilitate the effective teaching of IT is far from an easy task. Tight budgets, rapidly changing needs and possibilities, and the terrifying rate of perceived obsolescence make keeping pace and getting the best from the equipment you have, quite a juggling act. Add to this the fact that many schools operate a variety of different hardware, operating systems and, therefore, software and it becomes clear that where resources are sited and how they are used is an issue that'll continually plague any ICT coordinator.

In this section we offer advice on the sorts of issues that need to be addressed, and some practical tips on how these issues can be tackled.

27. Access to equipment (for children)

It's good practice in any curriculum area to make sure that children have access to the equipment they need and to the routines associated with the use of that equipment. A disproportionate amount of money is spent on ICT hardware and software in any school where provision is reasonable, and therefore it's important to try to get the best out of what you have:

■ **Be creative in the management and organization of resources.** For instance, there may be situations or activities in your classroom that realistically require access to more than one computer. Could you arrange to use another class's machine while they're in PE, and can they use yours when you're out of the room?

■ **Consider establishing a cluster.** By arranging some computers and other hardware in one area you might be able to provide better access for everyone in the long run. You'll probably need to draw up a timetable so that people can plan what to do, and know when they're going to be able to do it. It also pays to have times when no one class has priority, and the equipment can be used on an ad hoc basis.

■ **Can you implement an open access policy?** Consider whether it would be possible to provide access to ICT equipment during break times and so on. If you run activities such as curriculum-based projects, making a school newspaper or magazine, setting up a Web site with older children, where access to equipment is either highly beneficial or essential, open access is the only way to ensure success. Plus, it's worth loads of OFSTED brownie points!

■ **Ensure children have appropriate physical access.** It may sound obvious, but is surprisingly often ignored, that the heights of chairs and computer trolleys should match each other and the children using them. There is much debate about the ergonomics of computer equipment within the private sector, and with good reason. Just tilting the screen to a better angle can help!

■ **Keep monitors and keyboards close together.** There is some evidence to suggest that the physical relationship between a computer keyboard and its monitor has a significant effect on both the speed and accuracy of pupils' work. Basically, the further children have to switch their gaze between keyboard and screen, the slower and less accurate their work tends to be. Perhaps lap tops and palm tops may be better for young children after all!

■ **Maximize!** If opportunities to purchase new equipment come along, think carefully about what will provide the best value for money. Palm top computers are becoming increasingly sophisticated and easier to use, and you can buy five of them for the same price as a new desktop machine. There is plenty that they can't do, but consider the possibilities before committing hard-won funding.

■ **Consider whether access to the Internet is really worthwhile.** Establishing new links to the Internet can be an expensive business. It's important to consider whether one new line can really have an impact. Even with cheap local calls, you aren't going to want to have a computer hooked up permanently to the WWW, and without that level of access it might not be worthwhile. There are ways of using Internet services without actually being connected all the time. These include e-mail, offline browsing, printouts of information, and others such as video conferencing that require relatively short periods of time on-line. The message is, don't bother arranging access to something you won't be able to use efficiently.

■ **Maintain easy access to software.** If you can manage to set up every computer so that it has access to the same software (either stored on hard disk or with a standard collection of floppy disks) you can maintain equality of access and…

■ **Remember that floppy disks give universal access.** You may be able to make more efficient use of the computer equipment you have by using floppy disks to store children's work. If children have their own disks, with copies of all their own work, provided each computer has appropriate software they may be able to go and work on someone else's machine. Of course, if you have a network, this problem disappears altogether.

■ **Consider how much access is really necessary.** Some ICT activities require sustained access over a long period of time, say when children are using computers to collect, store and interrogate information for a science investigation. Other activities really need short but frequent periods of access, say for improving keyboard skills or mental agility using a drill and practice program. Keep this in mind when you're trying to set up systems to provide appropriate access.

28. Organization of resources

Where resources are stored and how they are organized will have a significant impact on how they're used. It'll be up to the coordinator to establish and maintain routines and procedures for the use and organization of equipment:

■ **Keep organization as simple as possible.** For your own sake, as well as that of your colleagues, try to keep organizational procedures as simple as possible. For one thing, simple ideas tend to work the best, and for two thing, if they're too complex, people will simply ignore them and do it the easy way anyway!

■ **Organize your equipment to maximize its potential.** Putting the majority of your computer hardware into one, dedicated resource centre may be the best way of using it to its full potential. Alternatively, perhaps a more flexible approach will suit your school better. One thing is for sure: if you have one computer in one classroom, especially if it's shared with other classes on a rotational basis, the chance of that computer being used to its full potential is low.

■ **Organize less fundamental resources centrally.** Equipment such as floor robots, sensing equipment, control boxes and so on should be held in a single, central area if possible. Choose an area where everyone knows what's available, and where it is. You may need to circulate information about these resources, and a gentle reminder and update every year or so won't go amiss.

■ **Target software.** Partly due to the higher costs of site licences and partly due to the need to ensure progression, it's a good idea to target software to appropriate age groups and teachers. A few good programs, well placed within the curriculum and in relation to individual teachers' skills and experience, tends to be far more productive than simply providing a wide range of software in the hope that the children will learn through bombardment.

■ **Old equipment may still be useful.** Just because a piece of equipment is old, it doesn't mean that it can't enhance the ICT curriculum. Even if an old computer is only used for keyboard skills or developing redrafting, number crunching, even role play, if there's room for it, it's worth keeping.

■ **Give teachers access to consumable resources.** Dishing out new ink cartridges or replacing floppy disks is unnecessarily time-consuming for an ICT coordinator. Try to set up a system that gives teachers access to these resources but makes them responsible for preserving stocks too. Just signing out new stock can add the required measure of guilt that ensures people don't take advantage. Remember, it's not your job!

■ **Provide staff with as much information as possible.** The more information they have about what's available and where it is, the less they'll have to bother you about it. Of course, there's also the old adage to consider: 'You can lead a horse to water, but you can't make it drink.' Don't expect everyone to use the systems you set up, and try not to condemn them for it either!

■ **Consider what others can do to help.** Try to keep resources accessible to both teachers and pupils. Label everything and encourage the use of whatever systems you feel necessary. You may well find that the children are a lot better at sticking to the procedures than your colleagues are!

■ **Provide 'hands-on' access.** As a general rule, what people have to go and look for won't get used! If possible, try to make sure that the resources that each year group *really* needs are to hand. Where certain resources have to be passed round, try to arrange for these resources to be delivered to the people who should need them next. If nothing else, this will provide a gentle reminder.

■ **Communicate!** This means communicate in both directions – talk and listen. Keep your colleagues informed about what's where, but also try to set up procedures that allow them to pass on information about problems, or ideas to make life easier for them too. If you have a cluster of machines, it's a good idea to keep a log of what goes wrong so that busy teachers can pass on relevant information without having to spend hours tracking down the coordinator!

29. Effective continuity and progression

In ICT, time is short and ensuring effective continuity and progression will be another important factor in maximizing the impact that ICT can have on your schools curriculum. Here are some starters for continuity and progression:

- **Put skills first.** If you look at all ICT work from the point of view of developing ICT-specific skills (and hopefully supporting various other skills from across the whole curriculum into the bargain) it's easier to ensure that what you teach in each year group will build upon work done in the previous year. Map out what ICT skills you think should be developed and when, and use this as the basis for all your school's ICT planning.

- **Make sure that statements of intent are clear and concise.** If you've mapped skills across your school, try to make sure that the statements you use are clear and unambiguous. Don't be afraid of making it sound like an idiot's guide: the clearer such descriptions are the less likely repetition and misinterpretation become, and that means that time is spent constructively.

- **Target the use of content-free or generic software.** It's tempting to try out lots of different word-processing or desktop publishing packages because they all promise so much in their advertising. But if every year group has a new package to get to grips with, it can slow their learning down. With a bit of research and discussion you should be able to get just two packages that will do the job – one for Early Years and Key Stage 1 and possibly another for Key Stage 2.

- **Disseminate information.** It's important to make sure that everyone knows, in broad terms, what everyone else is doing. Your scheme of work should map what happens, and where, in reasonable detail. Use this as a focus for introducing ICT across the school and across the curriculum. The more others know about what's going on, the less likely you are to come across repeated activities or to miss out important concepts.

- **Assess to ensure continuity and progression.** Though formal assessment of ICT is not statutory at the moment, it most likely will be before long. But whether it is or it isn't, assessing abilities has many advantages for ICT. It should be kept simple but formal, and will indicate whether skills are being developed at appropriate levels (is your scheme of work realistic?) and whether activities are developing relevant skills.

- **Make sure records are passed on.** If you have formal planning and assessment procedures in place in your school it might be a good idea to ask if you can collect the ICT-relevant paperwork and pass it on to the next teacher. This will also give you an opportunity to develop a better overview of what is (and what is not) working out.

- **Encourage displays of ICT work.** If the work that is done in each year group is regularly displayed, other teachers will have clear ideas of what's going on. This should give a good indication of the level they should probably be working at too. You can then use some of it to…

- **Compile a portfolio of work.** As with displays, this can provide a good indication of what can be achieved and where. It will also help disseminate good ideas and effective practice. This work may not need to be assessed, but should include a brief description of the purpose of the task and the level of support offered to put the work into context anyway.

- **Get staff to share their successes and failures.** More than likely, staff in your school will already spend more than enough time in meetings and you don't want to make this situation worse, but it may be a good idea to encourage, where appropriate, the sharing of good ideas and of heroic failures, a kind of 'show and tell' for ICT.

- **Take colleagues' concerns seriously.** You may face quite a few road-blocks to your plans. These road-blocks are usually put up because activities make unrealistic expectations of your colleagues' own skills, or present real classroom management issues. There's no point just hoping to avoid these issues. And if work isn't being undertaken, then continuity and progression don't really have a chance.

30. Helping to ensure compatibility and consistency

ICT coordinators might find themselves faced with a range of different hardware, operating systems and software that they have to maintain, support and weave into a coherent and effective scheme of work. Without detailed knowledge of each different platform this can be very difficult, though many basic ideas are transferable. If you already have that detailed working knowledge, you'll manage, but if not, there are plenty of people who should be able to help:

- **Unless you know – ask.** There are a great many people who have it in their best interests to keep you informed, particularly service agents and suppliers who want you to be happy with what they do and to have little if any reason to come back and complain. So, don't be afraid to ask for their help and advice.

- **Hold suppliers to their advice.** When ordering new hardware or software, explain in some detail what you want to do and how you want to do it. Make sure you get them to confirm that what you want to do is achievable with the product they're offering to supply, and hold them to their promises if it doesn't, or if it doesn't do it very well.

- **Get help from your local ICT centre.** That's what they're there for, to give you help and advice and to ensure that what you want to do is achievable and that it's achievable with the hardware and software you have access to.

- **Remember that this is one of the things the WWW does best.** Virtually every ICT supplier or manufacturer has a Web site these days. If you have access to the Internet, visit relevant sites, which often have highly detailed product specifications that run to several printed pages.

The down side is that these are usually written in Martian, or at least Modern Geek. Nevertheless, it's useful to have these details to hand so that you can check your approximate translation with a supplier or help-line assistant, by old fashioned methods of communication such as the telephone and voice.

- **Get in touch with suppliers' teacher support services.** Once more, that is what they're there for, and if they can't answer specific queries they'll know where to look. Sometimes this will be a matter of giving you a useful phone number, other times they'll get back to you with the information you need.

- **Get together with other ICT coordinators in your area.** Meetings of such people are bound to happen once in a while, so try to go along. It's quite amazing how many irritating problems (ICT-related, naturally) you'll have in common, but also how many simple solutions you'll come away with. Only other ICT coordinators know how it feels – these situations are definitely the most productive, even if they only confirm that you're not alone!

- **Get on to feeder schools.** Secondary or high schools tend to have access to staff who specialize in ICT and it's in their interests to help you out because, in their heart of hearts, they know where the *real* ICT teaching goes on and they don't want to do it if they can get you to do it first.

- **Contact your local college or university.** They'll certainly have someone with technical expertise, particularly with e-mail and the Web. They may even be happy to 'adopt' you.

- **Ask to see new hardware and software working.** Before splashing out on new hardware or expensive software, ask for a free trial. Many software developers and suppliers now do this as a matter of course; hardware is a different ball game. As likely as not, the onus will be on you to go and see it working. If this is impossible, make sure you have some sort of comeback if what you order doesn't do what you stipulated. (And don't get complacent – we all get caught out by this one from time to time.)

- **Don't just accept one point of view.** It's always worth double checking information with different suppliers. It's amazing how often you'll get conflicting information and advice, so it's sometimes necessary to talk to the 'technical department' too.

- **Accept that it's a battle you can't win.** No matter how hard you work at it, technology marches on too quickly and, more often than not, is irritatingly unconcerned with backwards compatibility (Geek for 'No of course your old program/machine won't run (on) our wonderful new program/machine' accompanied or preceded by a slow sucking in of breath over teeth). Some manufacturers are a lot better than others (notably Apple, believe it or not. A 6-year-old Mac will still run most modern software, given enough RAM and a bit more waiting around!).

31. Offering INSET

All primary school teachers are now expected not only to be teachers but also to be trainers for their colleagues. As the 'ICT expert' you'll probably find yourself in the position of offering training more often than most, both formally and informally. Even if you feel far from qualified it will still be your responsibility. Here are some short cuts:

■ **Identify training needs.** You can do this yourself, based on how you feel things are going in ICT or through a curriculum audit, but probably the best and least threatening way is through the School Improvement Plan. If your school has one that's readable, get hold of it and see if your curriculum area is, or contains an area that is, in need of attention. When helping to put together new improvement plans, try to identify a realistic number of such areas in need of attention.

■ **Don't rush in!** Once you think you've established a training need, it might be tempting to go ahead and organize some INSET, but it might be worth taking a step back and considering why this need has arisen. It could be that a lack of resources is more to blame, or it could be that there is a lack of progression and problems are being experienced because the groundwork is not being done effectively. Changes in staffing, sickness, unfamiliarity with resources, inconsistent interpretation of attainment targets and so on, could all be sources of the problem, and so training needs could require careful consideration.

■ **Do you have to do it yourself?** If the problem seems to be limited to a small number of staff or a single, isolated problem, you might be able to tackle it effectively by yourself, but if it's a more complex issue, why not ask if you can invite your LEA adviser in, to see if he or she can offer a fresh perspective?

■ **If you think you can do it yourself, try not to get carried away.** Set yourself very specific and achievable targets. How much work you do to support staff in attaining those targets is up to you, but write a specific brief and tell the staff exactly what you intend to offer them before you start. This will help to keep everything clearly focused.

■ **If you're approached to offer training, make sure you're set specific targets.** If your head wants you to run a training day, make sure he or she gives you a clear brief about what to do. Once the head has set those targets it may be worth discussing the feasibility of the targets and how you might go about tackling them.

■ **Then, ask for time to get ready.** Arranging whole-staff INSET is a very time-consuming job and many school managers would try to give their staff time to arrange it. However, if the offer isn't forthcoming, set out what you think you'll have to do and approach your headteacher with your proposals. Once they see what is involved they may be even more sympathetic.

- **Most of the INSET you offer will be one-to-one.** Simply because most ICT-related training is about specific problems that arise during the normal teaching day, colleagues are bound to approach you for a quick fix! Keep a note of what you do as a demonstration of what you've done in your curriculum area.

- **Ask if you can tackle recurring issues with the whole staff.** If the same problems arise regularly, it might be worth considering a whole-staff training event. At least it'll help you avoid repeating yourself too often.

- **Don't try to tell people too much at once.** This is especially true at the end of the day, so try to provide notes and visual prompts on what you're talking about. Many are happy if they just have something to take away with them that looks nice and acts as a memory jogger.

- **Make it practical.** Listening to one person for an hour or so gets boring. Practical activities are easier to remember and often make more sense. They tend to be more fun and people get to do exactly what they would try to do in the classroom.

32. Disseminating information

In the interests of promoting debate and good ideas, it's important to try to share as much information as possible. How you go about this will have a significant impact on how useful this information will be to your colleagues and, ultimately, the children. Here are some principles for productive dissemination:

- **Be brief.** Information needs to be useful and accessible, otherwise colleagues probably won't have the time to go through it all. Brevity is certainly an art!

- **Disseminate information about courses yourself.** Even if you don't go on the course, it's important that you get feedback from the person who did, and then pass that information on to colleagues yourself. This way you can put what was discussed into an appropriate form for use in your school.

- **Keep colleagues up to date.** This is especially important when you manage to get hold of new resources. A brief description of new hardware and software is useful to allow others to make informed decisions about what they want to have a look at. One easy way of doing this is to cut out or copy product descriptions from catalogues.

- **Grab time where you can.** Taking five minutes at the end of a staff meeting (or preferably at the beginning of a staff meeting) to go through new information, is far more effective than distributing a couple of pages of notes and expecting your colleagues to get around to reading them, let alone making sense of them.

■ **Set up a 'show and tell' session of your own.** For those who are interested to see first-hand what the list of apparently unconnected statements on a handout are really all about, offer a time, probably after school, to do a quick demonstration.

■ **Target your audience.** If a new resource or idea for effective teaching strategies, activities and so on, is not appropriate for everyone, try to target your audience. Attending Key Stage or departmental meetings may be an effective way of doing this.

■ **Get parents and governors involved.** See if you can get members of the school community to contribute by bringing in ideas from home. Find out what the children do at home and see if it can be woven into school work.

■ **Shout about your successes.** Encourage everyone to share the good experiences. If they let you know, it might be possible for you to build these ideas into your training, or to introduce the ideas at staff meetings and get the teacher concerned to describe what went on.

■ **Share ideas with the whole education community.** Organizations such as MAPE, magazines such as *Child Education* or less ambitiously, your ICT centre's newsletter are all places where you can share your ideas and get others' ideas about good practice.

■ **Get connected to an appropriate e-mail bulletin board.** If you have Internet access, try to get on to an education bulletin board once in a while. This is a way of sharing your ideas and receiving others in return. The SENCO forum for special needs is particularly good.

TROUBLE-SHOOTING, TOP GOOD HABITS, AND HOME–SCHOOL LINKS

In this final section, we offer just a few of our best ideas for some areas not covered in the preceding sections. These are about solving common technical problems and some suggestions for teaching in the classroom and developing links with children's experience at home.

33. If it doesn't work...

The most efficient way of trouble-shooting is to promote awareness and understanding amongst all staff and pupils. If they're aware of what can go wrong, and have a few ideas about how to put it right, then one of the major stumbling blocks for the implementation of ICT in schools can be reduced a little, hopefully! Try copying these suggestions, and offer them to each member of staff before calling out the emergency services! If it doesn't work…

- **Is it plugged in?** And don't just check the electrical sockets, check that you know where the mouse, keyboard, monitor, disk drive and printer should be plugged in and then make sure they are. Make sure they're all switched on too.

- **Look for a light to see if power is getting through.** If there's no power light on, could the electrical connection have failed? It may just need a new fuse!

- **Check all fuses.** There may be a number of fuses in any electrical chain – one in the plug, one in the extension socket, one in each of the plugs that go in to that – and any or many could have failed.

- **Are the brightness and contrast buttons turned up?** Check because we have all fallen for this one at one time or another. One of us remembers spending a very sad day thinking he had broken his new computer, not realizing he had knocked the brightness control right down!

- **Check the leads.** Are they damaged in any way?

- **Look for option switches.** Check for things that could inadvertently have been set incorrectly, everything from the 40/80 track switch on an old BBC to the SCSI ID switch on a CD drive.

- **What has changed since last time?** If it worked before, something must have been altered since last time. If you can work out what, you'll have solved your problem.

- **How did you fix it last time?** If you've seen the problem before, do what you did last time (as long as it worked).

- **Are the batteries fully charged?** If there's a spare set, try them to see if you get any joy.

- **Is it correctly formatted?** It may be that the floppy disk you're about to use isn't compatible with the machine you're trying to use it in!

- **Is it locked?** Files and applications can be electronically locked to stop them from being tampered with. Check to see if any protection is installed on your computer.

- **Is it full?** If the disk is full, either delete something or get a new disk.

- **Does it have enough memory?** It's easy to leave applications running on more modern computers, and they can take up large amounts of memory. This may cause a memory shortage that can cause all sorts of weird problems. Quit anything that's not actually being used.

- **Do you have the right driver?** Many peripheral devices require special bits of software to make them work. Is the software you have the right sort?

■ **Is it going already?** You might have launched an application already and that's why its icon looks strange and it doesn't seem to do what it normally does!

■ **Is a button jammed down?** A button on the keyboard or a volume control that's stuck in can cause all sorts of problems. Unstick them and try to clean them with an appropriate cleaner.

■ **Can you make it happen again?** Sometimes problems are just one-offs. If you can't repeat the problem, it's probably safe to ignore it! Are you running a new piece of software that might have caused a conflict? If you are, try removing it and starting again.

■ **Try to remember to run diagnostic software if you have it.** Every time your computer hangs or crashes you're supposed to run some sort of fault diagnosis software. In reality, few people have the time, but try to do it once in a while as a precautionary measure.

■ **Keep a record of error messages.** You may not know what they mean, but someone, somewhere might.
      Use the fault sheet before asking for help. (For obvious reasons!)

34. The top 12 good habits to teach

These are the sorts of things that staff and pupils need to get in to the habit of doing: they'll save them and you a lot of grief in the long run!

■ **Save before you print!** The number of times things go wrong at the moment when you try to print is incredible. If you save your file *before* printing, you won't lose it, and you could also save yourself a lot of additional work!

■ **Check spelling before you print.** There's nothing worse than wasted ink when running a spell checker could so easily have corrected errors first!

■ **Give files sensible names.** Calling your file 'hello' or 'myName' or 'new' or 'today' isn't likely to give you much of a clue as to what it is or what it's about. It'll not help anyone else work out what to do with it either!

■ **Save it in the proper place.** If you have set up a folder or area of the disk for work to be saved in, put it there; it'll make finding it later so much easier!

■ **If you can't find it later, try 'Find File' or 'Browse'.** Both functions let you search for missing files as long as you know roughly what its name is, or when it was created.

■ **Print once.** And if it doesn't work, don't just print again, try to find out why it didn't work the first time. Many an additional copy has mysteriously appeared out of the printer when the real problem has been cured! Phil's First Law of Printing states that, 'A printer *knows* when some- thing is really urgent, and likes to establish its control over you by choosing such times to run out of ink, jam paper, and decide that you really wanted to print landscape rather than portrait.

- **Type first, present later.** Messing around with layout, sizes and fonts before work is completed is just an excuse not to think about what you're supposed to be doing.

- **The space bar is not for spacing!** Well actually it is, but if you want to put a bit of text in the centre of the page or indent paragraphs, the tab button or the alignment buttons are much better. If you use the space bar, when you change font sizes, the spaces change too so you're back to square one!

- **Don't forget to exit or quit!** This is not the same as *closing* a window. Closing leaves the application still running in the background where it takes up memory, and could cause problems.

- **Read – and think about – error messages *before* clicking 'OK'.** First, if you don't you might lose all your work. Secondly, it will probably help whoever has to fix it if they know what the computer's final words were before passing away.

- **Hitting it harder won't make it work any faster or better!** Like as not it will have the reverse effect. It may make you feel good in the short term, but do try not to!

- **And finally, one for the pupils: 'Don't do as the teacher does, do as the teacher says!'** And we all know why, don't we?

35. Developing home–school links

Schools need to keep parents up to date with what is going on at school, and ICT is one area which most parents now expect schools to be working on. There are a variety of ways home–school links can be developed. Here are some ideas to start with:

- **Tell home about what you're doing in school.** This might be on a notice board, in a letter, with an exhibition, through the local press, a Web page, in the annual report or any of the many ways schools communicate with parents and carers.

- **Include pupils' ICT work in newsletters.** Why not get children to design a cover or section, or get them to produce the programme for the summer performance? It may take longer but it's a really practical and public way to get children's work seen.

- **Focus on the learning benefits.** Some parents and carers may be sceptical of the benefits of using ICT, particularly with young children. If you can show them examples of how ICT helps children to learn, they'll be easier to convince.

- **Suggest activities for children to do at home.** Children who use computers at home tend to make more progress with IT at school. A leaflet or parents' workshop, with some ideas for home use, will be welcomed. You may even want to recommend some software for different types of computers.

- **Develop a progression of home activities.** If you start with one year group you could extend your leaflet into a booklet over the next couple of years.

- **Show them what pupils do at school.** Most parents will not have seen programmable robots or control technology. Organizing a session for them will help them to see the educational benefits, and may recruit you a few classroom volunteers too.

- **Have an ICT exhibition.** This will not only get parents in, particularly if you have children demonstrating, but will also emphasize the importance of ICT at school.

- **Reassure them about the Internet.** Many parents have anxieties about the sort of material that's available on the Web. A letter, or better still an open-evening demonstrating how the Internet will be used, and the safeguards you have in place, will help to put their minds at ease.

- **Find out what children do at home with computers.** Asking them and their parents separately may well be revealing! This will also give you an idea of the areas you can complement and compensate for at school.

- **Send portable or pocket-book computers home.** Experience in the inner city suggests that the equipment will be well used and well looked after. It may even be worth considering investing in some pocket books or cheap portables for basic writing and keyboard skills. If this is done at home you can concentrate on developing the content of the writing at school.

- **Be careful not to disadvantage any children.** It's not their fault if they can't have access to their own machine at home, or if there's no interest in their ICT work there. Try to make it up to them, by arranging for their access at school to be easier or more extended.

36. Jargon-busting ICT terms for education, or 'It's all geek to me!'

Most computing terms are deliberately chosen so as to be confusing to the uninitiated. Either their normal everyday meaning refers to something else entirely, or a deliberately archaic word is used in a new and still more unusual way. It's all part of the 'geek-speak' of the computer world. Learning all of these nerd words is clearly neither necessary nor helpful, unless you particularly wish to develop some anorak camouflage. The words and terms below are current educational technology jargon. We have offered what we hope is a helpful definition. Most of them are serious. Words in *italics* are mostly defined in the relevant alphabetical place in the list.

address	The identification of a specific physical or *virtual* place in a network. On the Internet, this address is called a *URL* (Universal Resource Locator). For instance: http://www.ncl.ac.uk is the address for Newcastle University. An e-mail address contains the '@' symbol, eg, s.e.higgins@ncl.ac.uk is the address of one of the authors.
adventure program	A program which usually puts the player or *user* in an imaginary situation. The player is required to take decisions to control the way the adventure progresses. One of the early educational adventure programs was 'Granny's Garden' (produced by 4mation); a current example would be the 'Logical Journey of the Zoombinis' (Brøderbund).
application	A computer program specifically designed for a particular purpose (eg, a word processor is an application that handles text).
ASCII	American Standard Code for Information Interchange. This is an agreed standard code for letters, numbers and control codes; it is understood by most computers in the same way that American English is understood by other English speakers – or English English is understood by Americans, only imperfectly!
AUP	Acceptable Use Policy. An agreement that explains the rules of Internet use for an institution. Schools will need such an agreement, both to have clear guidelines for pupils to use and so that parents and governors understand how access to the Internet is managed.
bandwidth	A nerd-word used to describe how much data you can send through a connection to the Net. The greater the bandwidth, the faster the rate of transmission. You can think of it as the information-carrying capacity of a connection.
baud rate	Geek-speak for the speed of a *modem* (measured in bits per second). It's interesting that the computer world is as obsessed by capacity and speed as car fanatics or trainspotters. 56Kbps (kilobits/sec) is currently a fast speed.
bit	An abbreviation for BInary digiT. It's the basic unit of information in the computer world. A bit is binary number and has one of two values, 0 or 1. Computers can only count to one as they have no fingers.
browser	Software that allows people to access and navigate the *World Wide Web*. Most Web browsers, such as Mosaic, *Netscape* or Internet Explorer, are graphical and use text and pictures (and even sound or video). A few are only text-based, such as Lynx. As with most things in the computer world you never have the latest version that lets you hear the latest whistles and bells.

bug	An error in a computer program that may cause the computer to 'crash' or behave in an otherwise inexplicable manner. Of course if the computer's behaviour is usually inexplicable it can be difficult to tell.
byte	A single computer character, generally eight *bits*. Each letter displayed on a computer screen occupies one byte of computer memory: 1000 bytes, 1 kilobyte (k), 1000 k = 1 megabyte (Mb), 1000 Mb = 1 gigabyte (Gb).
CAI	Computer Aided (or Assisted) Instruction.
CAL	Computer Aided (or Assisted) Learning.
CBL	Computer-based Learning. All of these neat acronyms obscure the fact that the computer is only a tool or a medium to present learning material, albeit in a sophisticated way. Teaching, however, is not the same as learning, a fact all teachers know well. You can lead a pupil to computer aided learning…
CD-ROM drive	A form of disk drive that stores information on optical or compact disks. A *CD-ROM* drive is used for getting the information from the disk but cannot usually be used for writing or storing information (though now recordable CDs are becoming available too).
CD-ROM	Compact Disc-Read Only Memory: A record-like storage medium that uses digital and optical laser technology to store up to about 600 Mb of text, pictures and sound on a single disk. With newer versions (CD-ROMXA, CDTV, CD-i) animation and video clips can be stored on the disks.
clip art	A file of pictures specifically prepared for use in other files. Clip-art files contain graphic images (geek-speak for pictures).
commercial online services	A company that charges people to dial in via modem to get access to its information and services, which can include the Internet. See also *Internet Service Provider*.
concept keyboard	An input device (geek-alert!) comprising a tablet (A4- or A3-sized) connected to the computer on which overlays can be placed. By pressing different areas of the tablet, actions can be made to happen on the computer (sounds; letters, words, phrases of text; pictures; animations; the control of output devices such as a turtle or robot).
content-free software	Open-ended programs which permit more control of the computer by the user. A word processor, database and spreadsheet are all 'content-free' in that the person using them decides what the content of the file will be. By contrast a 'drill and practice' program has predetermined content.
control	A computer can be made to control a device to which it is connected, such as a disk drive, a printer, a model or robot. The means by which a computer directs a device is often called control technology.
copy	An editing term: the duplication of an item (text, image, sound) to be subsequently *pasted* elsewhere in the same document or transferred to another file.

cursor	The flashing mark that appears on the screen to show where text will appear when a key is pressed on the keyboard. A cursor's shape can be changed. Depending on its shape, a cursor is also called an I bar, a caret, an insertion point, or a mouse pointer! If all else fails try cursing the cursor… it's guaranteed not to work but may make you feel better.
cut	Another editing term: to remove an item (text, image, sound) which can then be *pasted* elsewhere in the same document or file or transferred to another file.
data	The 'raw' information which a computer handles. Data can take the form of text, numbers or pictures. If your first thought was Commander Data, from Star Trek NG, award yourself two extra nerd points.
data logging	A means by which a computer monitors and records events. For example, a computer can be set up to record the temperature in a room at hourly intervals and then 'log' the data over a period of a week. Sorry, no lumberjacks, OK?
database	A computer application enabling information to be stored, retrieved and manipulated. The most common form of database is the 'flat file', which is like a card index system in structure. There are also many information databases available now on the Internet for searching.
desktop publishing	An application for designing and producing documents that may include text, borders, headings and pictures.
dialogue box	A window that appears on screen giving information that requires a response. In fact no dialogue is possible. You're usually forced to do what the computer requires, a bit like a consultation document in the education world.
Dialup Internet connection	Lets a user dial into an Internet service provider using a modem and telephone line to access the Internet. (See also *SLIP* or PPP connections.)
digital camera	A camera that captures an image and stores it in electronic form which can be downloaded directly into a computer without the need for film. Despite the derivation this has nothing to do with fingers.
digitizer	Geek-alert! A piece of software that transforms a video signal into a digital signal which can be manipulated by the computer. A nerd-word.
dip switch	A small switch (usually in a bank of eight or more) usually found on a printer. Setting the dip switches to different positions controls the way the printer behaves. So called because when nimble little fingers change the position of the switches it makes the printer (and often the teacher) dippier than before.
directory	A collection of files is stored in a directory. A directory is usually given a name to help identify the files it contains, eg, 'My files' for your files. Online directories are lists of files or other directories on a computer at an Internet site.
disk drive	A device used for storing computer information on magnetic or optical disks. Schools make use of floppy, hard and optical (CD-ROM) disk drives, some may even have zip and Jaz drives.

domain name	The part of the Internet address that specifies your computer's location in the world. The address is written as a series of names separated by full stops. The most common top level domains are: .ac academic (UK higher education) .edu education (US) .com commercial (US) .co company (UK) .gov governmental or public .mil military .net network resource So http://www.ncl.ac.uk/ is a Web site (http://www) for Newcastle (ncl) University (ac) in the UK.
download	The term describing the transfer of information from one computer to another (such as through a modem or from an Internet site). To upload is to send a file to another computer.
drill and practice	Low-level educational programs designed to provide instruction or practice with specific skills (eg, spelling, addition).
e-mail	A means of sending (usually) plain text messages between two computers connected via a network.
emoticons	'Smileys' used in e-mail messages to add emotional emphasis – :) for happy ;) for a (knowing) wink :(for sad – turn the page sideways if you don't see why these symbols are used. Part of the geek language.
error message	A message the computer sends you to inform to you that there's a problem, often caused by a *bug* and displayed immediately prior to a system *crash*. However it is usually *not* you who has made the mistake. These are almost always bad news!
export	To transfer information from one application to another. Typically if you export something you will probably not use a *port*. Please remember if an export fails try a Newcastle Brown instead. (A local tip, for inhabitants of North East England.)
FAQ	Frequently Asked Questions. Files on the Net that store the answers to common questions. If you're stuck, check the FAQs first, before you ask your own question. The following ftp site is useful and holds most FAQ on the Net: Ftp to: rtfm.mit.edu. Go to the sub-directory pub/usenet/news.answers.
file	Information that is stored, usually in a *folder* or *directory* on a disk. A file is usually given a name to help identify it. Most pupils build up a collection of files either called by their name Steve1, Steve2, Steve3, or 'untitled'. These names are therefore almost completely indistinguishable and it means much time can be fruitlessly spent in locating previously saved work.
filter	Hardware or software designed to restrict access to certain areas on the Internet.

flame	To send a sharp, critical or downright rude e-mail message to another person.
floppy disk	A form of disk used for storing information in electronic form. The plastic case contains a disk of magnetic material, similar to that used in audio and video recorders. Floppy disks store a maximum of 1.6 kilobytes of information. Cunningly a floppy disk has a hard, rectangular plastic cover so that it appears neither floppy nor disk shaped.
FTP	Geek-alert! File Transfer Protocol. An application program that uses TCP/IP protocol to allow you to move files from a distant computer to a local computer using a network like the Internet. Non-geeks use sensible computers and programs, which means they can avoid the technical details.
function key	A key (usually labelled F0, Fl, F2, etc) which is used by an application to perform a particular task (eg, printing or saving a document). However, in most programs they serve no function or you can't remember which action they're supposed to perform.
gigabyte	See *byte*, or if you don't want the detail, it's bigger than a megabyte, a thousand megabytes in fact.
graphics program	An application that enables the user to create or manipulate images on screen. However sophisticated it is, it will *not* draw graphs.
GUI	Graphical User Interface. Software designed to allow the user to execute commands by pointing and clicking on icons or text. It is nerdily pronounced 'Gooey'. See also WIMP.
hard disk	Most modern computers have internal hard disk drives. Like a floppy disk; a hard disk just holds larger amounts of information.
hardware	Computer devices such as the computer itself, the printer, the monitor, the keyboard and mouse – the 'kit'.
highlight	Marking an area of the screen, usually for editing. Most applications show highlighted areas in reverse colours (eg, white on black rather than black on white).
homepage	The first page you see when visiting a World Wide Web site.
HTML	Hypertext Mark-up Language. The programming language of the World Wide Web, HTML software turns a document into a hyper-linked World Wide Web page.
HTTP	Hypertext Transfer Protocol: The protocol used to provide hypertext links between pages. It's the standard way of transferring HTML documents between Web servers and browsers. Hence why most Web addresses start http://.
Hypertext/ hyperlink	A highlighted word or graphic in a document which, when clicked upon, enables you to see the related piece of information from elsewhere on the Internet.

icon	A small picture (or graphic) that can be selected with the mouse pointer and which visually represents a program or file. Most computers now use icons as part of the way you interact with it. (See also WIMP.)
ICT	Information and Communications Technologies. Used to be just IT (*information technology*).
ILS	Integrated Learning Systems. Complex (and expensive) programs offering sophisticated drill and practice for pupils and detailed feedback for teachers.
import	See *export*.
Infobot (or mailbot)	An e-mail address that automatically returns information requested by the user.
Information Superhighway	Originally an American idea, the official US government name for the Internet and other computer networks was the National Information Infrastructure but it's more commonly known as the Information Superhighway.
information technology	Electronic means for storing, changing and transmitting infor- mation.
input device	A piece of equipment for entering information into a computer. A keyboard is an input device for entering text into the computer. Nerd word.
interface	A device for connecting equipment to a computer. A modem is a form of interface, as it connects the computer to a telephone line.
Internet	No, not World Cup '98 or '02 but the global network linking millions of computers around the world. These computers are called hosts, which our dictionary defines as 'an organism on which another lives as a parasite'. Geek-speak would probably define it more as a sort of virtual space in which users can send and receive e-mail, log in to remote computers (telnet), browse databases of information in text or hypertext format (gopher, World Wide Web, WAIS) and send and receive programs (ftp) contained on these computers.
Internet account	Purchased through an Internet service provider, the account assigns a password and e-mail address to an individual or group.
Internet server	A computer that stores data that can be accessed via the Internet.
Internet Service Provider (ISP)	Any organization that provides access to the Internet. Many ISPs also offer technical assistance to schools looking to become Internet information providers by placing their school's information on-line. They also help schools get connected to the Net.
Internet site	A computer connected to the Internet containing information that can be accessed using an Internet navigation tool such as ftp, telnet, gopher, or a Web browser.
intranet	A local network, for example, within a school or cluster of schools.
IP address	Every computer on the Internet has a unique numerical IP address, which will look something like 123.45.678.9.

IRC	Internet Relay Chat. Interactive, real-time discussions between people using text messages. People log into designated Net computers and join discussions already in progress. Some IRC channels even discuss nice things!
joystick	An input device that allows control of objects or images on the screen through the movement of a lever, most often used for computer 'arcade' games.
justification	The manipulation of text on a line in a word processor. 'Right justify' aligns all lines to end against the right margin, 'Left justify' aligns the beginning of lines to the left of the screen and 'Fully justified' inserts additional gaps between words so that each line aligns with both margins.
keyword	A word or words that can be searched for in documents or menus.
kilobyte (k)	See *byte*.
LAN	Local Area Network: A restricted network that connects computers within a building or among buildings for the purpose of sharing voice, data, fax and/or video. In some parts of the country schools and LEAs are creating LANs.
laptop computer	See *portable computer*.
LCD screen	Liquid Crystal Display screen: a thin form of monitor screen (about the thickness of two pieces of glass). Electrical charges cause different areas of the screen to change colour. Most calculators use LCD display to show the numbers.
load	To transfer information from a storage device (such as a disk drive) into the computer's memory.
LOGO	A computer programming language whereby instructions are written to control the actions of the computer. LOGO was written by Seymour Papert (among others) to provide a 'low floor, high ceiling' approach to programming – easy enough for infants to use, potentially complex enough to challenge graduates. Professor Seymour Papert now, confusingly, holds the Lego chair!
log on	To sign on to a computer system.
mailing lists (or mailbases)	There are more than 4000 topic-related, e-mail-based message bases that can be read and posted to. People subscribe to the lists they want to read and receive messages from via e-mail. Mailing lists are operated using automatic mailbase (or listserv in the US) software. Thus, many users call mailing lists 'mailbases'. There are two types of lists: moderated and unmoderated. Moderated lists are screened by a person before messages are posted to subscribers. Messages to unmoderated lists are automatically forwarded to subscribers. 'UK-schools' and 'SENCO forum' are examples of mailing lists for teachers.
megabyte (Mb)	See *byte*.

menu	A list of options that can be revealed and then selected by the mouse. Like most menus, they never quite seem to have what you want.
menu bar	A section of the screen (across the top with PC and Macintosh computers, across the bottom of the screen with Acorn computers) on which menus or the icons of applications are placed. None so far serves alcohol.
merge	To bring two different pieces of information together in the same document or file. For example, addresses from a database can be merged with a letter in some word processors to personalize a mailing: hence 'mail-merge'. Geek-speak.
MIDI	Musical Instrument Digital Interface – a system (set of agreed guidelines to ensure conformity) for connecting musical instruments to computers. Quite why trumpets might want to browse the Internet we have not yet discovered.
model	A representation of a situation which enables predictions to be made. Mathematics is used to model reality (eg, when three objects are placed with four objects, there will be seven objects all together; the model for this is 3+4=7). A computer uses mathematical patterns and algorithms to model quite complex situations (eg, global weather patterns) and gets these wrong too.
modem	An electronic device that connects a computer to a telephone line enabling information to be transferred between computers. A modem is required for connection to the Internet. Fax modems enable faxes to be sent and received by a computer. It is an unhelpful abbreviation for MOdulate DEModulate. Modems are available for any computer, can be internal or external, and come in several speeds, known as the *baud* rate. The higher the baud rate, the faster the modem.
monitor	Just another word for the thing with the screen showing you what the computer is doing: an output device.
mouse	A small plastic box that sits on the table beside a computer and is connected to it or the keyboard by a wire 'tail'. By moving the mouse and pressing its one, two or three buttons, the computer can be controlled. You can now also get tail-less mice which use infrared to send signals to the computer. On laptops a variety of trackball, trackpads and what look like little bits of chewing gum are all designed to confuse the uninitiated. Geek-speak plural: 'mouses'. Anorak definition: a computer input device.
mouse pointer	See *cursor*.
multimedia	An application that makes use of more than one medium eg, words, pictures and noise. Easier than it sounds.
net surfer	Someone who browses the Internet with no definite destination. Now widely regarded as ancient geek.

netiquette	A geek dialect. The rules of conduct for Internet users. Violating netiquette may result in *flaming* or removal from a *mailing* list. Some service providers (*ISPs*) will even cancel a user's Internet account, thus denying him or her access to the Net, if the violation is severe enough. A fitting punishment indeed!
Netscape	Internet navigation software that allows users to access information through a graphical, point-and-click interface rather than text-only screens or menus. Netscape is known as a Web *browser* because it accesses World Wide Web information formatted into special home pages using hypertext. It's free to educational users. Other graphical Web browsers include Microsoft's Internet Explorer, Mosaic, and Opera.
network	A system linking computers. A local network links computers on the same site (eg, within a school, see LAN). The Internet is a global network.
OILS	Open Integrated Learning Systems: Even more complex (and still more expensive) programs than *ILS* offering still further sophisticated drill and practice for pupils, and detailed feedback for teachers, with more flexibility than basic ILS.
online/offline	When you're logged onto a computer through your modem or a via a network, you are said to be online. When you're using your computer but are not connected to a computer through your modem, you're said to be working offline. When teaching with WWW materials you might want to *download* them so pupils can use them *offline*.
operating system	The internal software that controls the way a computer operates. No matter how new your computer is, you never have the latest version. Technical helplines always ask you which version you have and will reply, with the customary sucking in of breath over the teeth, 'Well, if you'd upgraded to version 9.7.1 you wouldn't have had this problem.'
output device	A piece of hardware that enables the computer to represent data for users. A printer is an example of an output device.
palmtop computer	See *portable computer*.
paste	An editing term meaning to place a previously *copied* or *cut* item in a file or document. An unusually appropriate term as many children can get into as much of a mess with cut and paste on a computer as with scissors and glue. Of course it's harder for them to damage and daub glue on their clothes when cutting and pasting on a computer. Also fewer parents are likely to claim for damage to clothes.
peripheral	A piece of equipment connected to the computer by a cable or wire. Most printers are peripheral devices; they are separately plugged into the computer. A scanner or external hard drive are also types of peripherals. (It's tempting to call them 'ephemerals' because they only work properly when you don't need them to work urgently, and you can never pin down why.)

photo CD	A CD on which photographic images are stored. An ordinary colour film can be processed by most high street chemists into a photo CD (for a small extra charge) enabling photographs to be *imported* directly into the computer.
pirate software	Software that has been illegally copied and used on a computer. Tempting and easy to do in most cases, but illegal. Make sure you have the appropriate licence for the software you use.
pocket computer	See *portable computer*.
podule	An electronic circuit board that is plugged inside a computer to extend its capabilities. Geek-speak.
pointer	See *cursor*.
port	A socket on a computer to plug something into.
portable computer	A small computer. A laptop computer is about the size of a small attaché case. A palmtop or pocket computer is about the size of an adult's hand.
posts	E-mail messages sent to a mailing list or Usenet newsgroup to be read by subscribers or others on the Internet. Nerd word.
printer	Dot matrix printers are cheap but are noisy and produce a poor image; ink-jets and bubble-jets are relatively cheap, but use water-based inks; laser jets provide high-quality images but are more expensive.
program	A list of instructions to control the operation of a computer. The term is also used as a verb, 'to program' meaning to create, such as a list of instructions.
programmable turtle	A device that children can program to move by carrying out a series of instructions, this could be either just on the screen, or making a robot to move across the floor.
programming language	A particular vocabulary and syntax of instructions that can be used give instructions to a computer.
RAM	Random Access Memory: part of a computer's memory used for storing loaded programs and files. The easiest analogy is that it's the computer's working, thinking or operating memory.
ROM	Read Only Memory: part of the computer's memory that contains fixed information such as the computer's operating system. Also used for a CD-ROM as the disk can only be read and not written to.
save	To transfer information from the computer's operating memory to a storage device such as a disk drive.
scanner	A flatbed scanner looks like a photocopier. It takes a picture of what's being scanned and turns it into digital information so that it can appear and be used by a computer. A hand-held scanner is a smaller device that performs the same function but it's 'swiped' across a piece of paper-based information.

sensor	A device that a computer can use to monitor external events such as temperature or light levels.
shareware	Software that doesn't have to be paid for until it's used. Shareware can be downloaded from the Internet. Most shareware authors deny that they ever receive *any* money. This is either because anorakish users are too mean to pay for something someone was foolish enough to make available free, or it's a good tax dodge. Most shareware programs are excellent, some may have unexpected results like a *virus*.
signature file	Return address information such as name, telephone number, and e-mail address that is automatically put at the bottom of e-mail messages to save retyping basic information.
simulation	A computer model of a situation: the user can enter information into the simulation and the computer will respond with an appropriate outcome. Simulations make it possible to model parts of expensive, difficult, complex, hazardous or impossible situations. However, like most complex things that are simulated, there is always something missing.
SLIP or PPP	Serial Line Internet Protocol (SLIP) or Point to Point Protocol (PPP) Internet connections. Both allow a computer to connect to the Internet using a modem and telephone line. Users then navigate the Internet using software on their own computer. This is in contrast to using a Dialup Internet Connection, where a user has to navigate the Net using a text-based set of menus.
software	The programs (or procedures) used to instruct the computer.
sort	To put items into order (alphabetical or numerical). This process is often used by databases and spreadsheets. Some word processors allow paragraphs and lists to be sorted alphabetically.
spam	Slang for posting the same message to multiple newsgroups – frowned on by most people on the Internet.
speech	See *voice synthesis*.
spreadsheet	A computer application that resembles a large grid of cells. Each cell can be linked to any other by a formula. If information is changed in one cell, all other interlinked cells are changed according to the linking formulae. As might be predicted, you can't spread it straight from the fridge but it will print out on lots of sheets of paper.
stress sensor	All modern technical equipment has a hidden stress sensor. The more stressed you are or the more anxious you become the more likely the stress sensor will leap into action. On a computer this means that it will perform mundane tasks in a new and creative way, wiping half of your word-processing file as you print it out, for example. Every school's office photocopier has one attached to the green 'start' button which ensures a major breakdown the day before all the school's paperwork has to be sent to OFSTED.
system software	See *operating system*.

Telnet	Allows people to access computers and their data at thousands of places around the world, most often at libraries, universities, and government agencies. Text based, but relatively fast.
trackerball	An input device that controls the mouse pointer by means of a large ball mounted in a cradle – similar in action to an upturned (or dead) mouse. Can be particularly useful for pupils with limited fine-motor skills.
turtle	See *programmable turtle*.
upload	To send information to another computer or network.
Usenet newsgroups	More than 17,000 topic-oriented message bases that can be read and posted to. Also called newsgroups.
user	One who uses a computer. However, to most normal people the word clearly has anorakish and addictive connotations.
user group	A group of like-minded people who have a similar interest. User groups communicate by e-mail. See also *user*.
VDU	Visual Display Unit – see *monitor*.
VGA	Video Graphics Array – a standard that specifies the way computers communicate with monitors to ensure conformity.
virtual	A much over-used term implying something is not quite real. A computer-generated environment.
virus	A computer virus is a cunning and occasionally malicious little program which 'infects' a computer's files or operating system. Some viruses can damage a computer by, for example, altering or deleting the contents of files. Viruses are often transferred from one computer to another by floppy disks or over the Internet. All hard-drive-based machines should have some virus protection software installed. It's depressing to consider that they have been created by talented individuals with nothing better to offer the computing community than a widget which weasels its way into your computer and damages it.
voice input	Some computers can be controlled by voice. There are also several software programs that can learn to recognize an individual's voice so you can dictate and have your words appear on screen.
voice synthesis	A software application which almost, but not quite, unsuccessfully simulates the sound of the human voice. It usually comprises a series of phonemes (phonetic sounds) which are strung together by the computer to form sounds which are almost, but not quite, unlike words. A more accurate description would be a synthetic voice, perhaps polyester or rayon.
WIMP	*Window*s, Icons, Menus, Pointers – the environment that is used to interact with most mouse-controlled computers. You move the mouse and point and click. A *GUI interface* is operated through a WIMP environment. There! You can now read geek!

window	A framed area of the computer screen. Several windows can be displayed on the screen. Usually only one window is 'active' at any one time and is able to be used. So called because you can't see through them. They rarely shed any light on the situation and the one you actually want to see is hidden by all the others.
word processor	An *application* for displaying and manipulating text. Unfortunately computers are not yet able to produce appropriate words to process.
World Wide Web (WWW)	Part of the Internet that communicates information in text, images, sounds and animation using 'hypertext'. By moving the mouse over parts of a World Wide Web page and clicking a button, you're given more information or are transferred to other Web sites. Also know as the 'World Wide Wait' because of long download times over telephone lines.
zoom	To magnify part of an image for more detailed work, or to reduce the size of an image to see more of it on screen. Often shown as a percentage of the full size. Zooming to 200 per cent increases the area to four times the original (2 x 2). When interviewed, most teachers claimed to prefer Strawberry Mivvis.

37. Some British educational acronyms and abbreviations ('ed' speak?)

Frequently in this book we refer to documents, procedures, governmental organizations and various kinds of personnel by their acronyms or abbreviated versions of their proper titles. Readers who are teachers based in England and Wales will be familiar (maybe all too familiar!) with this terminology. Even as close as Scotland and Northern Ireland there are significant differences, and for readers in different parts of the world some of the jargon could be impenetrable without some help (even though there are likely to be similar systems and terms under different names). For anyone to whom these terms are not clear, and for those who might enjoy a wry smile at the expense of some familiar friends, we offer a brief and perhaps only slightly jaundiced 'translation' of them below.

| Attainment Targets, or Ats | Statements that describe where every child should be in terms of their educational development by the end of each Key Stage. |
| Department for Education and Employment, or DfEE | The closest thing there is to an educational deity in England and Wales. Many teachers are beginning to wonder whether burnt offerings or sacrifices are required to appease the great DfEE spirit to help it to stop changing its mind all the time. |

Grant Maintained	A system introduced under the Conservative government 1993–97 whereby a school had all of its budget handed over to use however it saw fit (previously a significant proportion of each school's budget had been controlled by its Education Authority). Suspicions about this apparently rather sensible notion were raised simply because the government of the day seemed to think it was *such* a good idea.
Individual Education Programme, or IEP	Many children identified as having special educational needs have an education programme written from them, setting out how identified issues will be tackled. Often these are agreed between the class teacher, the special needs coordinator and the child's parents.
In-Service Training or INSET	The process by which qualified teachers have their skills updated and enhanced by highly trained educators, coordinators or advisers, theoretically! In practice, a bit of a lottery really.
Key Stages, or KS	In England and Wales, children who have not yet reached compulsory school age (the term in which they turn 5) but are attending mainstream school are considered to be in the 'Early Years'. Children in mainstream school between the ages of 5 and the year in which they turn 7 are in Key Stage 1 (usually from reception to Year 2) and those between 7 and 11 are in Key Stage 2 (usually Year 3 to Year 6). It's amazing how many complications such an apparently simple system can produce, though the children seem to tune in to it without much difficulty!
Local Education Authority, or LEA	Basically just the section of the local council that is responsible for all public sector educational establishments that have avoided Grant Maintained status.
Office for Standards in Education, or OFSTED	The second closest thing there is to an educational deity in England and Wales. OFSTED is responsible for inspecting schools and advising them on how to improve standards and efficiency. Many teachers are beginning to wonder whether it's the OFSTED inspectors who should become the burnt offerings sent to the DfEE spirit!
Programme of Study, or position	Set out in the National Curriculum, and often rewritten in greater detail for use in individual schools. Simply, it sets out what sorts of skills and knowledge should be acquired, and the sorts of experiences and activities the children should have, and roughly when they should have achieved them.
Scheme of Work, or SOW	A more detailed plan that puts flesh on the bones of a Programme of Study.
School Improvement Plan, or SIP; School Development Plan, or SDP	It would be thought that these terms are fairly self-explanatory but surprisingly, the plans themselves are used with highly varying degrees of success. A plan sets out a school's goals and how it intends to meet these goals, usually over a three-year period – during which time the National Curriculum will be updated, OFSTED's criteria will have been improved twice, three government initiatives will come and go, and the office that deals with assessment and curriculum will have been merged, scaled up, scaled down and renamed. We can't understand why Improvement Plans seem so difficult to manage.

Special Educational Needs, or SEN	Receiving much more attention now than in the past. The term is used to cover everything from a pupil experiencing a brief period of difficulty in a single, specific area of learning, to extreme learning difficulties. SEN is subject to strict guidelines.
Special Needs Coordinator, or SENCO	The only teacher in school with a job that is even more impossible than the ICT coordinator's! We know of one poor soul who has the dubious honour of holding both posts at once, but who still manages to stay relatively sane.
Standard Attainment Test, or SAT	Compulsory, national tests, currently in English, maths and science, that are supposed to assess attainment at the end of each Key Stage. Recently, pilot tests have been used at more frequent intervals, giving a fair indication as to the direction that formal testing is heading in UK schools!
The Qualifications and Curriculum Agency, or QCA	The bit of government that puts the DfEE's desires into practice. It's responsible for producing assessment materials and processes. It disseminates information about the curriculum and how it should be tackled. Kind of like an enforcer!
The Teacher Training Agency, or TTA	A government organization that generates research and papers on the state of the British education system at a mind-boggling pace. Its apparent objective is to try to ensure that all teachers have access to the 'right' kinds of training and the 'right' kinds of resources to help them improve their teaching. What 'right' actually constitutes is still under debate but that fact doesn't seem to dampen the TTA's spirits much.

Part 4

Special educational needs

Strategies for enhancing learning by children with special needs

Improving unacceptable behaviour

Pupils with special needs are not a coherent group, although in the past they were sometimes treated as if they were. The special needs dimension transcends the boundaries between primary and secondary education, and justifies a short detailed part in this book, even though some of the issues have been touched upon already in the preceding parts. This part aims to provide pragmatic advice from experienced practitioners for teachers who work with pupils with special needs, whether they have a designated role specifically for this purpose or whether, as classroom teachers, they want advice on how best to support the pupils in their classes. This part, as with the whole of this compendium, is not designed to be read through from start to finish, but to be dipped into as need and interest suggest. More detailed advice on special needs teaching is avaible in *500 Tips for Working with Children with Special Needs*.

In the past, young people with special needs were often taught exclusively or mainly in special classes or special schools, but over the years it has become *de riguer,* following the UK Children Act and Government Green Paper, to teach them with their peers in mainstream classes.

The specialists who work with children with special needs undertake focused and specific training for their work, which this part of the book is designed to enhance rather than replace. However, we hope that you will find the tips and wrinkles we provide to be useful, thought provoking and practical. As such, this part may well be especially helpful to teachers in training and at an early stage in their working lives, although we hope experienced staff will find something of value here too. Certainly we wish we had had access to this much accumulated wisdom much earlier in our careers.

This part of the book comprises tips arranged in two sections.

The first section, 'Strategies for enhancing learning by pupils with special needs', contains a range of suggestions to help teachers make the most of each pupil's ability to develop and learn effectively. The second section, 'Improving unacceptable behaviour', tackles some of the thorny issues that surround some of the problematic ways that some pupils with special needs interact with teachers and each other, and gives pragmatic advice based on long years of experience.

STRATEGIES FOR ENHANCING LEARNING BY CHILDREN WITH SPECIAL NEEDS

The tips in this section include a whole range of strategies for use in the classroom to help to improve the confidence and capabilities of pupils with special needs.

1. Strategies for effective communication and problem solving using good listening skills

Often when a pupil has a problem the need for change has to come from the pupil. As a teacher you can aid this process, but there are pitfalls. Sometimes it's easier to ask leading questions, offer sympathy or suggest solutions than to take the long and arduous route which active listening entails. The following suggestions may help you to be an effective listener:

- **Adopt an attentive posture.** Remember that we communicate with our whole bodies. Be aware that the way you sit or stand will speak as loudly as the voice. Make good eye contact. You could also adopt a relaxed body posture and lean slightly towards your pupil in an encouraging way.

- **Be aware of the importance of silence to good listening.** You can learn to cultivate an awareness of when to keep quiet. The pupil may need a patient listener to wait as long as is necessary to hear the problem. You can also ensure that the listening environment is quiet and private.

- **Once the pupil has begun to talk, you can give encouragement to continue.** For example, you can let the speaker know you are listening by making small tokens of acknowledgement. You can say 'Hmmmm', 'Yes… I see'. You can also echo the pupil's words by saying something like, 'You're saying you think nobody likes you.'

■ **Give further encouragement to continue by giving an open invitation to say more.** You can say something like 'Keep going… tell me a bit more about that.' Or you could say, 'Would you like to talk about that?'

■ **Try to achieve active listening.** That is, you allow the pupil to lead the way in how the problem is discussed. This could entail feeding back your understanding of the pupil's story or how you think the pupil is feeling. You could also keep checking to see if there is mutual understanding of the problem. In this way you as the listener can take an active but not a dominant role.

■ **Be aware that you can hinder good listening by over-direction or moralizing.** If a pupil is trying to tell you of worries concerning workload a response such as, 'You've got to make more effort', or 'Stop complaining and finish that piece of work' may prevent an airing of the real problem and the working out of a realistic solution.

■ **Try to avoid judging or criticizing.** You may be justified in saying, 'You're just too lazy to make the effort', but it will not inspire your pupil to greater heights. Even giving a perfectly logical argument such as, 'It's quite obvious that the only way to get this done is to stay in for the entire half-term holiday' may prevent you listening to the pupil's real concerns.

■ **Ensure that you don't fall into the trap of labelling your pupil.** For example, if you say something like, 'You're behaving like a pupil from the Lower School, not someone in Year 11', or 'I've never known you to get coursework to me on time', it closes up the possibilities of useful discussion and positive solutions by your insistence on having the final word.

■ **Guard against interpreting the pupil's motives or feelings.** This will prevent the pupil looking deeper into the problem. For example, if you say, 'I think you're just trying to find ways of not doing this work', your analysis may be accepted and the real reason may be disregarded. Even sympathizing by saying something like, 'You're not the only one who has found this work hard' may prevent examination of the issue.

■ **Avoid withdrawing from the problem.** Try not to be sarcastic by saying something like, 'Someone got out of bed the wrong side this morning' or, 'Life's too short to argue about this.' If you divert attention from a problem by declining to listen, it may come back to haunt you and your pupils at a later date.

2. Suggestions for teachers of mathematics on how to support pupils with SEN

These tips are designed for special needs teachers who don't have specialist training in maths, but who nevertheless are called on to support pupils' needs in this area. Make use of these suggestions to boost your confidence and to enable you to provide real help to the pupils you're working with:

■ **Make mathematics fun.** This may be considered by some to be comparatively easy in the primary school, but it can be more difficult in mixed-ability classes in the secondary school. You could build up a store of games to reinforce basic concepts and you could devise tasks that result in the creation of colourful display work and models for the classroom.

■ **A stimulating equipment box is an essential aid.** This could contain toy money, counters, clocks with moveable hands, connecting cubes, peg-boards, measuring tapes, coloured sticky paper, and all the usual equipment required for the teaching of mathematics.

■ **Try to make sure that you relate mathematics to the everyday experiences and lives of your pupils.** For example, you could devise shopping tasks with discounts for sales or you could plan journeys using maps and bus timetables. Don't forget that in a multicultural society, lifestyles and interests will have a wide diversity. Perhaps you could teach graph skills using the climates, rainfall and so on of countries where some of your pupils were born.

■ **Remember to reinforce basic skills on a regular basis.** As children progress through school, it's easy to think that tables and basic mathematical concepts have already been learnt. For some pupils this is far from the case. There are readily available a number of tapes and computer games for the learning of tables. Test regularly, perhaps at the beginning or end of a lesson. You can turn this into a game and give out merits or awards for good achievement.

■ **Produce material at an appropriate level.** It may be that your school uses the SMILE resources and the necessity for differentiation will not be so pressing, although there are always some pupils who are still working below appropriate Key Stage levels and who will need further differentiated material. It might be simpler to visit your local primary school to borrow resources or to ask for ideas to make your own resources for your most needy pupils.

■ **Encourage keyboard and computer skills.** There are many good commercial packages that are suitable for the teaching and reinforcing of basic number work. Many of them are good fun too and can be offered as an incentive for slow learners.

■ **Teach proficiency and familiarity with calculators by use of the SMILE calculator activity book.** Some of these activities require pupils to key in certain sums whose answers, when turned upside down, spell out words. For example, 'Mystery 3751' reads 'Mystery Isle' when held upside down, and leads the pupils on a mathematical treasure hunt. Pupils can also work in pairs devising sums and questions which will give the answer to say, 663, which reads 'egg' upside down. For example, 'I had 329+334 for my breakfast today.' There are many variations on this game.

■ **Remember to teach the vocabulary of mathematics.** Pupils who have difficulty remembering key words can be set homework on this theme and also be given vocabulary books to write down words new to them. You can also make good displays for the wall with key words and pictures. If you work in a multicultural classroom, you can produce key words in appropriate languages. For some of your bilingual pupils, the acquisition of a mathematical vocabulary may be their only need. Their mathematical skills may already be excellent.

■ **Help pupils to practise the skills of mental arithmetic on a regular basis.** Don't assume that this is too difficult for slow learners. Just be sure to start from an appropriate level. You may have noticed that pupils who have learning difficulties are often very competent when working out what their pocket money will buy. This is because they first of all have an interest and secondly they get plenty of practice. These are good starting points for mathematics in the classroom.

■ **Make sure that all pupils have regular homework at the right level.** Many pupils with learning difficulties actually love their maths homework. It is a subject that is highly structured and, like training for athletics, it improves with constant practice and repetition. You can give rewards and lots of encouragement for completed homework and you can record progress publicly on classroom wallcharts.

■ **Encourage pupils to become independent of their memory.** In pupils with learning difficulties, this can be a big problem. Rather, concentrate on encouraging pupils to work their own way through problems. For instance, the pupil who cannot remember 6×5, may write down 6 five times and add up the numbers. You can also reduce on the photocopier, tables or number squares to a size that will fit pockets or pencil cases.

■ **If you have a number of pupils with learning difficulties, try to obtain extra help in the classroom.** This can be sought from the school's support department, the peripatetic learning support teachers or from classroom helpers. This greatly reduces the waiting time of pupils with basic queries and frees you as the expert to attend to more pressing needs.

3. Strategies to support pupils who are school or classroom refusers

This problem is more common than many people realize, and teachers need to use all their powers of tact, persuasion and strategic thinking to help pupils overcome this particular hurdle. These tips are designed to help pupils (and their parents) to overcome difficulties and move towards resuming more normal attendance patterns:

■ **If a pupil has been identified as suffering from school phobia or selective classroom refusal, it helps if you can find a pattern of absence.** For example, the absence may be affected by the time of day, the subject, or the teacher of the lesson. You can assist in identification by keeping scrupulous records of non-attendance. You can also check with colleagues on their perceptions of the problem.

■ **When your pupil is present, be welcoming and friendly.** Try not to be judgmental about past absence. You can show your pleasure at their return. Be sensitive to the difficulty of this situation for your pupil and don't create extra stress such as battling over the removal of coats or insisting that they sit where you decree. Small and routine issues like this can provide the flash point for another departure.

- **Discuss the situation with the pupil as soon as possible.** You can suggest ways in which the school can help. For instance, it may be possible to arrange a staggered return to normality by excusal from lessons that the pupil finds it too difficult to attend. The pupil can be invited to agree to a voluntary imposition of an internal attendance report. This will at the very least provide the school with knowledge of where the main difficulties lie.

- **Try to avoid being manipulated into agreeing to unworkable conditions.** These might include the pupil agreeing to work only outside the classroom or to complete only selected tasks. This may seem to be a step in the right direction, but is more likely to be a way of diverting attention from the problem.

- **Lend a sympathetic ear when listening to the problem.** You may need professional expertise from other sources to provide effective counselling, but you may be the recipient of some revealing information that you can pass on to others. Very often the pupil will explain classroom refusal on quite trivial grounds such as, 'I haven't done my homework' or, 'I don't like History.' You could suggest to the pupil that you think something else might be worrying them and then offer to help to sort out the problem or find someone else who can.

- **Enlist the help of sympathetic pupils where possible to facilitate a return to the classroom.** You could perhaps let these pupils know that their fellow pupil is in need of some support and a warm welcome back. Perhaps you should warn your pupils that their kindness may be rejected and provide them with some strategies to cope with that.

- **Remember that the role of the parents and carers in this problem is crucial.** If it is at all possible, try to enlist their help and support in getting their child to school. You may, of course, discover that the home situation is actually contributing to the problem, in which case this is much more the province of other professionals in outside agencies. Some parents, however, may be glad to be telephoned whenever their child fails to get to school and may have some strategies to help.

- **Seek the help and advice of pastoral staff in the school.** A problem of this severity is obviously their responsibility, but they may be glad of your interest and may know best how to use your offers of help. Your records, at the very least, will help to provide a full picture of the problem.

- **Make it as easy as possible for pupils to make up lost time.** Your pupil will naturally have missed a good deal of the work of your class, so you could provide potted versions of essential information or you could make it possible for resources to be taken home for private study. Be aware of the possibility that such materials may not be returned to you and don't lend anything irreplaceable. However, your actions may just provide a continuing link with school or establish for the pupil that they are of concern to the teacher.

■ **Encourage the pupil to seek out sanctuaries at difficult times such as breaks and lunch times.** This may involve use of the school library or attendance at homework or activity clubs. The relaxed and informal atmosphere may well be therapeutic and may encourage the pupil to open up to staff about his or her problems.

4. Helping pupils who have English as a second language

Increasingly teachers are likely to find that they have pupils in their classes who are fluent in one or more languages, but whose first language is not English. This set of tips is designed to enable you to help pupils make the transition into fluency in English, which may be their principal or only special need:

■ **Create a welcoming environment.** Check that you know how to pronounce your pupil's name. Introduce the pupil to the class. You could practise a few phrases in each other's language. Perhaps you could find an opportunity to use the globe to find the country the pupil comes from. Make sure you reassure the pupil (through an interpreter if necessary) that many other pupils have been in the same situation.

■ **Respect the pupil's space.** Give your pupil time to settle in. A silent or receptive period is quite normal in the first stage of acquiring a second language. Be aware of the educational value of focusing on the mother tongue and do not advocate the use of English only at school or home.

■ **Think carefully about where you will place your pupil in the class.** Pair the pupil with a responsive, caring pupil who can act as a good role model, explain procedures and guide the pupil around the school. Place the pupil in close proximity to others who share the same language but be careful not to create closed community groups.

■ **Make good use of visual materials.** You could perhaps label everyday objects in the classroom using bilingual labels if possible. You could also put up posters and artefacts from various cultures. Make sure you change visual displays to coincide with class subjects and topics or festivals.

■ **Where possible, provide reading materials in dual languages and mother tongue.** If you can, ensure that they are amply illustrated. You could also make sure that your pupil has access to dictionaries. These may be available in many schools from bilingual support staff. Perhaps you could also get hold of some dual language tapes from school library services.

■ **Prepare differentiated materials for use in class.** You can identify and present key words in a box at the top of worksheets, on the board, on a poster or underlined in text. Make sure you draw attention to them and build them into testing. Familiarize yourself with the wide range of differentiated activities, which could include Cloze work, guided sentence paragraph writing, sequencing, ranking, circling, highlighting, underlining, diagram completion, true/false statements and many more.

- **Liaise regularly with bilingual support teachers.** You can ask for advice and suggestions for work activities. They are sure to be able to help with the loan of materials. It might also be possible to ask such teachers to take your class on occasions, so that you can work individually with a particular pupil.

- **Look out for opportunities to widen your pupil's learning experience.** For instance, if you're asked to help with a spelling, there might be an opportunity to explain a general rule such as, 'i before e except after c,' or that in English, u always follows q. Another aid to building up vocabulary is to get the pupil to keep a vocabulary notebook of newly learnt words and to check regularly for recall and comprehension.

- **Encourage active participation and collaboration.** One way to do this is to set up small-group task-oriented situations where pupils of varying language abilities interact with each other and can 'talk while doing'. You can also make sure that bilingual pupils are involved in routine responsibilities such as collecting the register, giving out books or taking messages.

- **Be aware of the range of ability amongst bilingual pupils.** Having English as a second language is not in itself a learning difficulty and many pupils will have reached high standards of education in their own countries. You can ensure that pupils know that their bilingualism is valued as a special achievement. Let your pupils know how much you respect their efforts to achieve fluency.

5. Facilitating the completion of examination coursework

Overseeing examination coursework for pupils with special needs offers teachers a particular set of challenges that these tips aim to address. Coursework tends to demand planning ahead, regular inputs of activity over a period of time and good time-management skills, and these are often particularly difficult for students with erratic attendance or difficulties in organizing their studies:

- **Provide models of good coursework.** Show pupils what they are expected to achieve. You can do this by arranging a lead lesson that can be shared with other groups. You might have samples of past work from a range of grades that you can use to demonstrate what is required. Or perhaps you can introduce some ideas and strategies for their own projects.

- **Inform pupils of deadlines well in advance.** Display these dates clearly in the classroom, perhaps using a weekly countdown device. You could also make a large and eye-catching chart containing pupils' names and the titles of each piece of coursework. Provide coloured stickers to indicate completion. Follow up tardy pupils regularly.

■ **Ensure the safekeeping of completed work.** Work should be kept in a very secure place and preferably not in the classroom. If students have to take an unfinished piece of work away for completion, photocopy it if at all possible. Never assume that because a piece of work has been painfully and slowly produced it will necessarily be kept safe.

■ **Avoid setting coursework as ongoing homework.** This may work satisfactorily with able and well-motivated pupils, but for those with learning difficulties it may be disastrous. It enables lengthy postponement and the giving of false assurances that they are on schedule. You could set aside a weekly spot in lessons for checking, recording and advising on coursework.

■ **Develop strategies to facilitate coursework.** For example, if your student has to compare two characters in a play or novel, you could provide lists of suggestions for them to tick if relevant. You could also use Cloze-type frameworks to provide information to begin, say, a consideration of the possible causes of World War II. If your pupil is going to use a questionnaire to gather information, you could provide a working model and advise on possible pitfalls.

■ **Encourage the use of computing facilities to aid good presentation.** However, you should first check against the possibility that coursework has to be hand-written. You could, perhaps, book several lessons in the computing room for this purpose. Be careful, however, about allowing pupils to spend too long on presentation at the expense of content.

■ **Involve parents in the completion of coursework.** Of course this doesn't mean that parents should help in the production of the work, but they should be informed about deadlines and asked for their cooperation in urging pupils to complete. Possibly they can impose effective sanctions.

■ **Set up regular coursework 'surgeries' during lunch times or after school.** You could establish a rota system with other colleagues, which would minimize your time commitment. Make sure that these times are well advertised in assemblies, registration and tutorial periods and on classroom walls.

■ **Liaise with SEN and support staff.** Keep specialist staff, who may have good relationships with your pupils, well informed about their coursework demands. It may be possible for this work to be supported during individual withdrawal lessons. Inform staff as to how much support is acceptable.

■ **Be aware of coursework fatigue.** Although your main priority is for completion of coursework on schedule, there may be times when everybody needs a break. Try to make your class lessons at these times especially stimulating or take the opportunity to show an appropriate video. If it can be made relevant to the coursework in hand, so much the better. Offer some incentives for a class celebration of an end to coursework within your restrictions of time and expense.

6. Supporting pupils with a hearing impairment

Pupils who can't hear well in class are sometimes seen as difficult, inattentive or even outright disobedient. Problems particularly arise when teachers don't know about hearing problems, or forget that this might be the cause of a pupil failing to respond to a question or instruction. Loss of hearing is not an absolute matter either, and you may well have pupils who have intermittent hearing loss due to glue ear, asthma, allergies and other, sometimes hidden, ailments. These tips are designed to help you to recognize the issues and do what you can to assist pupils with hearing impairments to participate fully in class work:

- **Consult Individual Education Plans when you know or suspect hearing loss.** This is your starting point for information; it will describe the level of hearing loss where identified and should include advice to teachers and targets for pupils. It may also give you a contact number for the specialist teacher who is responsible for this aspect of your pupil's school life.

- **Ensure that pupils who find it difficult to hear sit in good listening positions.** This may not necessarily mean under your nose at the front of the class. Make sure your pupil has good eye contact with you and has good sight lines to the blackboard. The pupil should sit in an individually appropriate hearing range. You should soon become aware if this is not adequate.

- **Be sensitive to the noise level in the classroom.** Pupils who wear hearing aids may suffer discomfort if the noise level is too high. Instructions and information may be missed or distorted in a noisy classroom. Check if your pupil is happy with the general level of background noise and take action if it's causing undue problems.

- **Check that your pupil always wears his or her hearing aid.** Make sure you do this in a sensitive manner. Some pupils, particularly in adolescence, may refuse to wear their aids. Try to reassure the pupil and stress the benefits. If you're not successful, let your SENCO know about the problem. Perhaps parents or specialist staff should be informed.

- **Pay good attention to your own diction and classroom delivery.** You don't need to shout but can help hearing-impaired pupils greatly by articulating distinctly. Enunciate clearly and make sure your pupil can see your lips. Don't speak while you are writing on the board unless you're writing what you're saying. If you read from text, hold the book away from your face.

- **Be aware that you may need to wear a connecting aid to your pupil.** Make sure that you know how to use this equipment in advance. Remind your pupil to give you your part on arrival at your lesson. Warning: do not visit the toilet while wearing your microphone unless you wish to entertain your student with the sound effects or your conversation!

- **Make good use of visual aids in the classroom.** Keep an up-to-date vocabulary list for each new topic. You can also supply your pupils with small vocabulary notebooks. Use pictures and diagrams to illustrate subject material.

- **Check on literacy and oral skills.** Having a hearing impairment does not affect one's intelligence but it may have led to delays in learning and difficulties with speech. Encourage oral participation in class. If necessary, provide structured literacy work. Hearing-impaired pupils often require practice with blends such as spl, spr, tw, tr, ch, sh, and so on. It may also give you clues to hearing loss.

- **Be aware of your pupil's need to read aloud.** Encourage shy pupils to participate in this activity. One way to get this started is to get your pupil to practise with you in the knowledge that you will ask them to read from this known text during a mutually agreed lesson. You can also ensure that the listening skills of the other pupils are employed to help and not hinder this pupil.

- **Use your pupil's skills and knowledge to increase self-confidence.** For example, in a science lesson on the subject of sound, your pupil may know a great deal about the working of the ear and can offer insights and knowledge to the group on the subject of sound. Think of other ways in which you can boost self-esteem and self-confidence.

7. The use of writing frames to assist pupils in non-fiction writing

Writing frames are invaluable aids to help pupils to develop confidence in their writing abilities and to ensure that they all achieve some success in writing. By providing a skeleton outline on which pupils can build, using key words and phrases, you can help them to concentrate on communicating what they want to say, rather than getting lost in the format:

- **Understand the aims and use of writing frames.** You can use these devices for pupils who are not yet able to produce independent non-fiction writing. The aim is for the pupil to outgrow this useful prop and move step by step to independent writing. Once pupils have grasped the format they can add to or reject parts of the frames that are intended as flexible aids and not rigid structures.

- **Be aware how writing frames can aid writing.** You can offer pupils a structure that gives them a sense of what they are writing. You can teach pupils to use personal pronouns thus encouraging identification with their work. You can avoid presenting pupils with a blank piece of paper for a starting point.

■ **Familiarize yourself with resources that have already been produced.** The EXEL Writing Frames booklet is an excellent resource, which comes with photocopiable sheets. When you have absorbed the techniques, you can devise frames to suit your own individual needs in your unique subject area.

■ **Teach your pupils how to write by your own good practice.** First you will have to guide the pupil in the use of writing frames by discussion and example. Some pupils may need many pre-liminary oral sessions and you may have to act as a scribe until they're ready to attempt their own work.

■ **Be careful to integrate the use of writing frames into topic-based lessons.** The frame is merely a guide and is never a purpose for writing. Do not teach this strategy in study skills les-sons. You might initially need to produce large size versions of frames for use in the demon-stration stage.

■ **Use frames to enable pupils to recount events.** This type of writing is meant to inform and entertain. It's usually written in the past tense, in chronological order and focuses mainly on 'doing' clauses. A very simple frame could begin, 'I enjoyed our visit to… I learnt that… I also found out… Another thing I discovered was… The thing I enjoyed most was…'.

■ **Devise frames for use in reporting or describing the way things are.** Often pupils are asked to compare and contrast. As a preliminary aid you could devise charts with two columns in which characteristics could be compared. A good example would be 'My Life' and 'A Roman's Life'. Now you can continue with frames such as, 'Although… and… are not the same they are alike in some ways. For instance… has… whilst… has… They are also different in that… Another difference is… Finally…'.

■ **Teach pupils how to explain processes in a series of logical steps using causal conjunc-tions such as because, therefore.** A frame could go like this: 'There are several reasons for… One explanation is… The evidence for this is… A further explanation is… The most likely one is…'.

■ **Use frames to assist pupils to describe procedures.** These are written in the present tense in a series of sequenced steps using imperatives (do this, do that). A frame could be devised like this: 'How to… You will need… First you… Then you… Next… Finally…'.

■ **Use frames to assist writing that is designed to discuss and persuade.** As with comparisons, you might start with columns of, say, 'Arguments for' and 'Arguments against'. A frame could now proceed: 'The issue we are discussing is… The arguments for are… The arguments against are… After looking at all the arguments I think… because…'. More sophisticated frames can be produced when appropriate.

8. Supporting refugee pupils in the classroom

Some schools are unlikely ever to accommodate refugee pupils in their classes, while in others, the presence of refugees is a daily fact of life. This set of tips is designed to give some guidance on how best to induct, welcome and support pupils who may be seriously traumatized and certainly will need extra help to make sense of a very different world from that which they've left behind:

- **Carry out welcome procedures.** Check that your pupil has received a simple plan of the school, knows the name of the class teacher and has a copy of the timetable. Introduce the pupil to your class. Make sure you can say the pupil's name correctly. Check that your pupil can pronounce your name too. Write it down in your pupil's book.

- **Be sensitive to the placing of the pupil in your class.** Try to seat your pupil next to a sympathetic friend and preferably one who speaks the same language. If your school has a 'buddy' scheme or befriending system, find out the name of the designated person and, if necessary, prompt the relevant pupil to be conscientious about responsibilities.

- **Establish basic communication links as quickly as possible.** Talk individually to your pupil as often as you can. Teach useful phrases and greetings and make sure your pupil gets daily opportunities to practise. Use other pupils to interpret if possible and repeat the information back to your pupil in English. Speak clearly and slowly. Try to control the noise level in the classroom.

- **Provide visual support as often as possible.** When producing differentiated work, use visual aids such as diagrams, flash cards and illustrated glossaries for reference. You could write key words on display charts with translations that can be provided by English as a Second Language (ESL) teachers or language centres. You can also ask for the provision of bilingual dictionaries.

- **Create an active and participatory role for the pupil.** Don't allow language difficulties to prevent full integration of your pupil into the life of the class. It's quite easy to involve pupils very quickly in the distribution of books and equipment. This will ensure verbal contact with other pupils. Other small tasks can be used to include your pupil.

- **Seek out bilingual texts.** Ask the school librarian what is available. You can also contact school loans services and language centres for loans. The Refugee Council in London and other major cities are also willing to provide material.

- **Provide differentiated materials and devise strategies to aid comprehension.** Reading material can be made more accessible by oral discussion, role-play, illustrations and use of audiotape. If you can record reading material on cassette, a pupil can listen and read simultaneously. Instructions in worksheets should be clear and should always follow the same format. You could also provide individual vocabulary lists in each lesson, or display them on the wall.

■ **Create opportunities for pupils to communicate their experiences.** It might be possible in a lesson where the subject lends itself to discussion of global issues, to incorporate the pupil's own experiences and knowledge into a group discussion. Be careful not to press a reluctant pupil, but it may be beneficial for a pupil to talk about the reasons for their leaving home and country.

■ **Ensure that pupils receive emotional support if necessary.** They will almost certainly have experienced a great many stressful life events. Try to create time to listen. You could also suggest that pupils begin to put together autobiographical scrapbooks or picture books which relate to their past life. Role-play and drama may also help to develop group understanding of complex events and feelings.

■ **Inform pupils of 'safe' places in the school.** English schools are large and noisy places to a refugee pupil. You could provide or direct a pupil to a quiet space which provides a retreat at breaks and lunch times.

9. Identifying pupils who are working at a significantly lower level than their peers

Pupils who are not keeping up with the rest of the class can be disruptive, alienated and difficult to teach. Working out where the problems lie is the first stage in putting together a plan of action to help such pupils to become better integrated and to work towards more realistic personal goals. These suggestions are designed to help you do so:

■ **Watch for an unusual level of dependency.** This may include the need for constant reassurance that work is being done correctly. Pupils may be unable to get started on any task without prompting or encouragement. Pupils may need constant repetition of instructions, and may become tearful or distressed if they think the work is too difficult.

■ **A negative self-image should alert you to possible learning difficulties.** Pupils may take no pride in any work or achievement and may even abuse or destroy their own work. They may seem to have no real friends and prefer to sit and work alone. Attempts to break this pattern may be resisted.

■ **Watch for a poor attention span.** There may be difficulties in listening to the briefest and simplest of instructions. Pupils may even fail to engage in any listening at all. For instance, they may be doodling or making paper darts or picking up materials that are not relevant to your lesson. They may attempt to talk or distract others. They may be frequently off task and often out of their seat.

■ **Anti-social behaviour in the classroom often indicates the existence of learning difficulties.** Pupils may be constantly late to lessons or may leave without asking permission. There is often a marked lack of respect for other pupils' work or property and in extreme cases, stealing may occur. Cheating or copying in tests may indicate difficulties with work.

■ **Reluctance to read aloud or to deal with classroom texts should alert you to problems.** Poor spelling and inadequate knowledge of semantics are further indicators. Pupils may find it difficult to extract information from text or be unable to identify key ideas in the text.

■ **Be aware of inability to express ideas or articulate a response.** Expressive writing may present serious problems for a pupil who is unable to sequence adequately or who hasn't grasped the formal structures of writing, or who lacks the vocabulary to express thoughts and ideas in writing.

■ **Watch out for poor organizational skills.** Pupils may arrive at lessons without appropriate equipment. Often they will have no idea where their next lesson will be. Homework is never written down and is rarely completed. Class work is left on the desk without a name to identify it. Help with organizational strategies may be declined.

■ **Be aware of consistently poor presentation of work.** Handwriting may be poorly formed. There may be confusion over upper and lower case letters. Diagrams, tables, graphs and drawings will frequently be badly planned and executed. Rulers and other aids will not be employed to improve work. Labelling of diagrams and drawings may be illegible and inaccurate.

■ **Watch out for difficulties in number work.** Basic concepts in mathematics are likely to be poorly understood. Facility with tables will be severely limited. Problem solving may also relate to difficulties in reading text and instructions.

■ **Self-marginalization in the classroom is often a cry for help.** Pupils may be reluctant or unable to participate orally and may become distressed or uncooperative if pressed. Alternatively, they may take on the role of class clown to divert attention from their difficulties.

10. Identifying pupils with low self-esteem

Students with low self-esteem often punish themselves and those around them. The causes of low self-esteem are many, and you can't expect to solve them all single-handed. However, here are some ideas you can use to establish which pupils are experiencing problems in this area, which can then help you decide about the steps you can take:

■ **Watch out for pupils who put themselves down.** Self-denigration is a characteristic of such pupils, who will persistently refer to themselves or the group in which they have been placed in a negative manner. This may also extend to indiscriminate criticism of the school or teachers in general and an often expressed wish to change schools.

■ **Look out for quick anger.** Sudden, inexplicable flashes of anger may indicate a pupil lacking in self-esteem. The triggers will almost certainly be trivial. Another pupil may be sitting in what this pupil regards as his or her seat. A mild request to pay attention or sit down may provide a flash point for loss of temper.

■ **Perfectionism can be a danger sign.** Extreme self-criticism may lead to the constant destruction of work that doesn't seem to be absolutely perfect. An entire lesson may be taken up with starting and re-starting a piece of work. Other delaying tactics may include fetching or borrowing mainly unnecessary equipment.

■ **Watch how pupils receive praise.** A disconcerting characteristic is the refusal to accept praise even when it has been well earned. Pupils may respond by criticizing the work, perhaps saying, 'That's rubbish' or by mocking a commendation you may have given for good behaviour. In extreme cases, praise may result in the destruction of a piece of work.

■ **Look out for non-participants.** Refusal to participate in any group or practical activity, even when the other pupils are clearly having fun, is a sign of shaky self-esteem. This pupil may only seem happy in the role of critical spectator. This can lead to unpopularity and isolation, thus confirming a negative self-image.

■ **Be aware of the dangers of sabotage in group situations.** In some cases, such a pupil may be keen to participate in a self-destructive way, acting the part of class clown or deliberately sabotaging the efforts of others in a possible attempt to halt unwelcome or uncomfortable activities.

■ **Fear of failure may be the motivation for negative reactions to anything new or unexpected.** The introduction of a new subject theme or a new mode of working may automatically be met with derision or refusal. For example, the pupil may declare that 'poetry is crap' or 'this is too hard'. A change of teacher may also provoke an uncooperative response.

■ **Dress can give useful clues.** Some pupils may display a negative self-image through their persistent refusal to take off bulky outdoor clothing or to remove caps or anorak hoods. They hide behind their clothes for protection. They may also carry very large loads of personal belongings from which they refuse to be parted.

■ **Watch for power relationships.** Attempts to buy friendship by the indiscriminate or profligate sharing of sweets or equipment, often with pupils who are powerful members of the group, indicate possible problems with self-esteem. Such offerings may also be given as a result of extortion or bullying.

■ **Look out for signs of escapism.** Pupils with low self-esteem may take refuge in an exciting fantasy life which they are more likely to share with less apparently sceptical teachers rather than cynical peers. You may be regaled with exciting accounts of meetings with pop stars who just happen to be relatives. Accounts will be given of admiring and attentive boy or girl friends. Alternatively, this pupil may always be about to move to another town or even country. These fantasies provide comfortable illusions for an unhappy pupil.

11. Strategies to improve low self-esteem in pupils

Once you've established that particular pupils think poorly of themselves, you can then look to ways to help them to help themselves. You're unlikely to see miracles overnight, but even tiny steps forward can make a significant difference to often deeply unhappy young people:

- **Offer praise and encouragement even for the attainment of very small targets.** Make sure that the pupil understands the progress that is being praised. You could point to an increase in output from the previous lesson or you could note an improvement in social behaviour.

- **Use eye contact and appropriate touch when offering praise.** Lightly touch pupils on the hand or shoulder. This helps to tell the pupil that he or she is recognized and valued as an individual. Use pupils' names when addressing them. Other non-verbal contact such as a smile, a thumbs-up sign or a wink can offer reassurance.

- **Encourage pupils to record their achievements.** This record can then be used to boost confidence when they are too self-critical or defeatist. You can provide a tally card or a wall chart to tick targets that have been achieved.

- **Diffuse anger and reduce negative confrontations.** You can do this by trying more positive responses to unacceptable behaviour. For example, rather than saying, 'You're a lazy, rude person' say, 'I'm really disappointed' or, 'I'm very surprised, this just isn't like you.' The behaviour is not condoned but self-esteem is maintained and another chance is implicitly given.

- **Listen effectively and actively to your pupils' verbal and non-verbal messages.** Make your body language say you're listening. Lean forward slightly and make eye contact. Don't be afraid to remain silent for longer than is usually comfortable. Signal that you are still listening by saying, 'Yes' or 'Hmmm!' Nod your head in acknowledgement. These strategies will help the pupil to feel understood. Ask if the pupil would like a further discussion of the problem.

- **Role-play can play a useful part in raising self-esteem.** This can take place within any lesson, not just Drama. If pupils are allowed to not be themselves for a while, they may lose their inhibitions and their fear of failure. Ask the pupil to perform a given task as though he or she is the most able person in the school or to give an opinion as though he or she were the headteacher.

- **Minimize fear of failure.** Pupils who think of themselves as failures will go to great lengths to avoid situations where failure might occur. You can appear to take the risk for the pupil. For instance, you could say, 'This is very difficult, it's my fault for giving you such hard work, but try your best', or you could say, 'Let me try to explain it better.'

- **Help your pupils to see how good self-esteem develops.** Think of all the things that have enhanced your own positive image of yourself. Perhaps you're an acknowledged great cook or mountain climber. Think about how you became good at it, and how you found out you were. Think about ways to help create an environment whereby your pupils can learn a special skill or improve upon skills they already possess and share them with others.

- **Empathize with your pupil's lack of self-esteem.** Perhaps also share with pupils your own experiences of being unsuccessful, such as failing a driving test or giving up learning to touch type, and talk to your pupil about how that felt for you at the time.

- **Create special responsibilities.** Place your pupil in a position of responsibility where success is attainable. Small duties such as collecting the register or acting as book monitor may pass a positive message that the pupil is trusted and needed.

- **Show your pupil how to be a friend.** Offer friendship within the boundaries of a teacher/pupil relationship. Whatever your personal style of friendship, you can be there to offer support and offer a role model of how to be a friend.

12. Establishing successful school contact with parents and carers

Parents and carers of pupils with special needs may be your best allies in helping them to make progress, and certainly should be informed and consulted about developments, worries and specific problems. Building these links is an important part of the special needs teacher's role:

- **Be aware that pupils are cared for in all kinds of different family patterns.** The primary care givers may be birth-parents, step-parents, grandparents or other relatives, foster-parents or foster-home care workers. There may be one, two or more people looking after them. The patterns of care may change from time to time as circumstances change.

- **Be sensitive by not assuming that every pupil has a mum and dad at home.** Pupils are likely to be particularly put out if you make sweeping assumptions about who cares for them. Be aware too that divorced or separated parents may both wish to be consulted about special needs issues, and may not wish to do so in the same room at the same time. Where records provide separate addresses for parents, it may be necessary to send communications about issues of concern or achievements to both addresses.

■ **Remember that parents and carers are already involved in the education of pupils with special needs.** Be aware that parents and carers are significant partners in the education of pupils SEN. Explore ways in which you can establish regular contact. Check the policy of the school and follow procedures carefully. Keep records of all contacts and share these with pastoral staff, who may offer advice about effective parental contact.

■ **Plan your appointments with parents or carers.** If you make a formal appointment in school, find a room where you will not be interrupted or overheard. Ensure you have some time alone with them before the pupil's arrival. Take notice of the interaction between parents/carers and pupil. This may provide you with useful clues as to behaviour or give good indications for potential solutions.

■ **Try to keep appointments informal.** Informal meetings with parents/carers can often be extremely effective, as they are less stressful for them. For pupils whose parents/carers wish to drop in without an appointment, you could establish that you are available for about 15 minutes after school on a named day of the week.

■ **Remember that meeting parents/carers in school may sometimes present difficulties.** Take good care not to compromise your safety or security. If a parent/carer has a history of difficult behaviour ask a senior member of staff, say a head of year, to be present at your meeting. Make any necessary notes after the meeting. Keep calm and listen carefully. Make sure you say what you need to say. Include the parent/carer in potential solutions.

■ **Be ready to meet parents/carers from a wide range of cultural and linguistic backgrounds.** You may need an interpreter. Try to avoid using your pupil in this role. In respect of behavioural problems, explain the requirements of the school and establish a mutually agreed code of conduct in school. Do not imply any criticism of parental lifestyles.

■ **Maintain contact efficiently.** Communication with parents/carers can be time-consuming if you rely solely on written or telephone contact. A useful way of informal contact is by daily notebook carried to lessons by the pupil and shown to parents/carers each night. They may then respond to teachers' comments and send back their own.

■ **Work out how best to respond to truancy.** Responding to truancy is usually the role of the form tutor or other pastoral staff. You may, however, establish a successful daily arrangement whereby you telephone the parent/carer immediately about any unexplained absence.

■ **Help parents and carers to help their pupils.** They may be willing to help in literacy programmes at home but may need some help and advice from you before they can cooperate. Can you provide some books or resources for loan? You might suggest a regular 10 minutes per night, rather than an occasional marathon. Shared newspaper reading can be helpful.

■ **Consider letting parents/carers observe in the classroom.** It may be impractical to enlist the help of parents/carers with work in the classroom but it can be useful in the case of behavioural difficulties if you arrange for them to observe their pupil in class. This may produce a starting point for a cooperative approach to the problem.

■ **Don't base each contact on a problem.** Parents and carers of pupils with SEN are used to visiting the school in response to complaints or anxieties. Perhaps you can involve these parents/carers in more enjoyable activities such as field trips or summer outings. This may be the only opportunity for them to see their pupils in an environment in which they excel.

13. Responding to physical impairment

There may be pupils in your classroom who have a permanent or temporary physical impairment, which may result in mobility problems, difficulties with keeping still or attention problems caused by trying to work while experiencing constant pain. In addition to their educational needs, there may be other needs that you may not have previously encountered. Some of the following ideas may be useful to you:

■ **Relax and be yourself.** Your pupils don't need an over-anxious teacher, so don't fuss around them, causing them to feel self-conscious and drawing attention to the difficulty. Offer the chance of independence wherever possible and scrupulously avoid patronizing such pupils by doing things for them that they are capable of doing themselves.

■ **Ensure that you know of any potential problems.** Read the Statement of Special Educational Needs carefully and make sure that you understand the implications of the information contained within it.

■ **Be prepared for contingencies.** Find out what to do in an emergency or if any medication might be needed, for example with asthmatics and diabetics. Liaise with parents and with any specialists in the school, such as a school nurse. Remember that a little knowledge is a dangerous thing, so don't intervene if you don't know what you're doing. Trust the pupil, since people with physical impairments often know a great deal about their own conditions. If you feel disadvantaged by your own lack of knowledge, take a first-aid course and seek out specialist advice.

■ **Don't be surprised if your pupil is grumpy, distracted or disaffected.** Allow for fatigue and depression and modify your demands accordingly, but watch out too for clever pupils who can manipulate gullible teachers.

■ **Consider the special needs of pupils with mobility problems.** You may need to rearrange the furniture to accommodate a wheelchair. Plan for this in advance, as pupils may be embarrassed by making a disruptive arrival and having to make everyone else move so they can be accommodated.

■ **Welcome and make use of any additional support your pupil may have.** A wheelchair-user may have a carer in the classroom. This person is your best line of communication about the needs of your pupil, so make sure you establish a good working relationship. Extend a warm welcome to your classroom.

■ **Help the pupil with physical impairment to work independently of the carer from time to time.** It can sometimes be hard for an adolescent pupil to accept the presence of a 'minder'. Perhaps you could suggest that the carer works with other pupils or helps with classroom tasks. Everyone may enjoy the break.

■ **Be vigilant to help physically impaired pupils who encounter teasing or bullying.** Obviously you will wish to help but don't over-react. A quiet word to the offender may be all that's required. Persistent bullying, however, should be dealt with by senior school staff.

■ **Check in advance how your pupil wishes you to deal with teasing, if this seems appropriate.** It could be a common occurrence that the pupil may prefer to deal with personally. Some pupils may have developed skills that you don't yet possess. Don't assume that a frail body means a fragile personality, but don't withhold help if you judge that it's needed.

■ **Plan ahead when you know absences will occur.** Frequent absences may impede a pupil's progress. So make plans for known absences and provide work that can be done readily in uncomfortable circumstances such as hospital wards. You might like to consider encouraging your class to practise their English skills by writing letters to their fellow pupil, to help maintain contact through a long absence.

■ **Remember that pupils who can't take part in every aspect of school life may suffer from feelings of isolation.** Explore ways for your pupil to develop compensatory skills and focus on any special talents. If there are no obvious areas of excellence, perhaps you can devise some special responsibilities in the classroom. Make sure your pupil is a fully participating member of the group. Remember this may also include being told off when behaving badly.

14. Devising or modifying homework

An important part of helping pupils with special needs to see themselves as part of the regular class is for them to have regular and challenging homework. However, what's set for the whole class may be totally unsuitable for an individual pupil with special needs. Setting homework that is relevant, stretching and at the right level for the pupil to have a reasonable chance of succeeding is a complex task; these tips are designed to give a few practical pointers on how to achieve this:

■ **Use your time-management skills when setting homework for pupils with special needs.** If the task is to be fully understood, it needs to be explained in a calm and unhurried manner.

You will need a minimum of 10 minutes to do so and, if possible, the work should be given out at the start of the lesson. Write the task clearly on the board. Check that pupils have understood what is required.

- **The purpose of the homework should be made clear to them.** You can explain how it will help them to understand the lesson better or prepare them for the next piece of work. Let pupils know if and when the task is to be tested.

- **Plan ahead for written homework.** Cloze and sequencing tasks are easily devised from the content of the lesson. Make lists of key words for spelling. Vary the length and sophistication of response on standard homework tasks.

- **Pick other people's brains.** It's not necessary to reinvent the wheel. Look at colleagues' resources: the subject matter might not always be appropriate for your purposes, but the methods and strategies may adapt. Book fairs and exhibitions provide masses of ideas and often plenty of free samples if you show interest. Primary school resources may be of use, but be careful that illustrations are not too young for your pupils. Nevertheless, there is a good chance that you will be able to customize or adapt materials for your target pupils.

- **Remember that homework tasks need not require a written response.** Drawing and labelling will improve vocabulary and can be used to contribute to classroom displays. You can set spellings and tables to be tested later. Pupils can report back orally on findings of set tasks such as interviewing a grandparent about the war or recounting an item from the previous night's news.

- **Clarify to pupils that homework doesn't have to be done at home.** Keep pupils informed about any after-school clubs available. Tell pupils if you can offer 10 minutes at lunch times to go over what's required. You might also be able to persuade colleagues to share in a cooperative venture to supervise or support homework. It can take some work off your shoulders and the pupils may enjoy a change of company.

- **Motivate pupils to do homework by showing them that you value it.** Mark and return homework as quickly as possible. Make sure pupils see you recording homework and praise punctual delivery. Spell out your expectations and refuse to settle for less, but make sure your expectations are realistic. Insist on corrections. Keep a regularly changing display of homework on a special board in the classroom. Finally, show your appreciation with suitable awards.

- **Note that projects need guidelines and regular supervision.** It's all too easy for pupils to be daunted by seemingly huge tasks, or conversely to feel that it can all be done at the last minute. Set short deadlines and small structured tasks. Suggest where the relevant information can be found. Check and store each piece of work as it's completed. Make friends with the school librarian and try to give plenty of notice of imminent projects.

■ | **Be aware that homework can aid oral skills too.** You can ask pupils to obtain information that can be delivered orally, as a change from having a written task for everything. For example, asking pupils to learn a few lines of a simple poem or to make up a short dialogue with a partner can be fun and can add variety to what pupils often see as drudgery.

■ | **Remember that reading skills can be developed through homework.** You can have standby reading homework for those occasions when you don't want to set written work. You could suggest that pupils read story books to younger siblings. Find some easy reading texts with more mature storylines. Keep a record of what's been read and encourage pupils to recommend books they've enjoyed to others. Give achievement awards for an agreed number of books read each term.

15. Identifying strengths and weaknesses for multi-sensory teaching strategies

Multi-sensory teaching techniques allow pupils with a range of learning difficulties to access their education in the ways best suited to meet their needs. This means that both their strengths and weaknesses are accounted for. If a pupil has a weakness in one sensory area, then using a strength in another area can help to compensate and encourage the use of strategies to overcome the weakness. Teaching to a weakness through a strength encourages a sense of success and confidence, rather than reinforcing failure:

■ | **When teaching a new concept in your subject, be aware of the pupil's strengths and weaknesses.** Use the strength first to motivate the pupil into success. If you then follow up with a series of exercises that simultaneously input the information through as many senses as possible (seeing, hearing, saying, feeling), then the memory can store this information more effectively and give the weak sense some back-up material to aid recall.

■ | **Use a series of activities for assessing strengths and weaknesses that can prove to be fun for both you and the pupil.** You may want to do this with the pupil on his or her own or make it part of a small-group activity. It will be difficult for you to do these in a large class and be able to note down the results. You will need to have prepared materials in advance and have a sheet prepared for the results.

■ | **Look for ways to expand digit span recall.** This is the amount of information a pupil can handle effectively at any one moment, for example, how many digits in a telephone number can be remembered in order, or how many letters in a word can be learnt in order. An individual's capacity to recall digits varies, but if it's as low as three or four, then that pupil may have difficulty copying from the board or writing from dictation. You can teach them ways to extend their recall, but you need to know whether they have more difficulty with visual recall or auditory recall.

- **Test out auditory and visual digit span.** You can do this by preparing a pack of cards with letters or numbers on. The first cards should start with three digits, then move to cards with four digits and so on, until you have cards with eight, nine or more digits. If you think about it, a telephone number has seven digits, but if you include the code it can have at least four more.

- **For visual digit span, show the cards to the pupil one at a time.** Start with the lowest number of digits, and show it for eight seconds. Don't allow any verbal back-up. After eight seconds turn the card over and ask them to write down what they saw. Repeat this, moving up in numbers of digits. Try to do about three at each level. Make a note of which letters/numbers they recall correctly, which are recalled out of order and which are totally incorrect. Stop when the pupil has reached their limit, for example, when the pupil is unable to recall most of the correct digits.

- **For auditory digit span use a similar set of cards but with different digits.** This time you should read the digits to the pupil in a measured voice, taking care not to group the digits. Afterwards you should ask the pupil to repeat the digits back to you. For a variation you could ask them to write them down. Again you should make a note of the responses and the limit the pupil reached.

- **Test for lateral preference.** There are activities you can carry out with the pupil that will help you to decide whether the pupil has a preference as to which hand, foot, eye or ear they use. So a person can be right dominant, that is, always use right hand, foot, eye and ear or they could have a mixed dominance, where neither right nor left is the sole preference. Similarly they could have a confused dominance: right dominance in all but one area, where the dominance shifts to the left.

- **Evaluate directionality.** This refers to a pupil's understanding of up/down, top/bottom, back/front, over/under, inside/outside, as well as left/right. This can be a problem if they have poor awareness of these concepts and find it hard to apply them to instructions. You may find this displays itself in mirror writing or reversals of the letters 'b' and 'd'. You can help this pupil by identifying this and finding ways of strengthening their auditory or visual sequencing memory.

- **Use a range of activities that help identify these factors.** These could include asking a pupil to write, throw a ball, remove and replace a screw-top lid, hop on one foot, kick a ball, look through a telescope, look through a key hole, listen to a watch, listen at a door and so on. With each activity (at least two for each part of the body) note whether the pupil had a left or right preference. A simple exercise in paper folding (origami) can identify directionality.

- **Use sequencing activities to identify areas of strength or weakness for multi-sensory teaching.** You could ask the pupil to recite the alphabet, forwards and backwards, days of the week and months of the year. Similarly you could get them to count to 20 singly, then go up in twos, and so on and go back in reverse.

16. Multi-sensory teaching strategies for Specific Learning Difficulties

Once you have identified the areas of strength and weakness for a pupil you can begin to devise a series of teaching strategies that may help them with reading, writing, spelling or Specific Learning Difficulty (SpLD). Multi-sensory methods mean the simultaneous use of the ears, eyes, speech, fingers and muscles. For many people this comes naturally, instinctively; pupils with SpLD need to be taught how to use these skills together:

- **Use the 'Look, Say and Write' approach.** A new word to be learnt is shown and the pupil writes over the word at the board, on the paper and repeats the sound at the same time. You can build more activities into this at the blackboard. You will be surprised how much pupils enjoy coming to the board.

- **Facilitate independent learning approaches.** Tape-recorded work alongside visual display, as in the Language Master machines, can help to reinforce this approach without you needing to work one-to-one with a pupil. Try to ensure that the system you use has a self-correcting facility. You may find pupils want to make their own materials: let them, this will motivate them.

- **Make use of packs of cards with letter patterns printed on one side and words containing them on the reverse.** The pupil looks at the letter pattern and it acts as a cue to remind them of words with that pattern. They say the sound of the letter pattern, for example, 'ai' says 'A', then they recall the clue word on the back of the card (train). At this stage they can turn the card over and see if they were correct.

- **Use packs of cards like this repeatedly to strengthen the pupil's visual and auditory memory.** They can also help pupils to respond automatically to visual or auditory prompts in the future. You could help by making this a regular starting exercise in a lesson. You could work on a pack of five cards per week.

- **Use Pelmanism to reinforce learning.** This is a card game that uses the same approach. You might know this game simply as Pairs, where you have to pair up matching cards. You could develop games from this theme, so that the pupil has to find a card with the letter pattern on it that matches the card with the picture of a word spelt with that pattern and so on.

- **Use multi-sensory approaches to bring home the message.** Lesson activities can be planned to ensure that the new work is presented visually on the board, through an experiment/demonstration or video, and then reinforced aurally or orally through written work, a quiz, a tape-recording, or reading exercise. Wherever possible try to help this pupil experience participation in the presentation of the work, for example, coming to the board, being involved in the demonstration, giving a talk about an aspect of it. All of these will help store the information more effectively in the memory.

■ | **Don't overlook kinaesthetic memory.** This is the area of the senses where the pupil remembers through the movement and actions of the body what has been taught. If you can involve the pupil in some area of activity that is kinaesthetic, it will help them all the more. Try to visualize this area of their learning as ' hands-on' experience such as learning to drive a car and knowing which pedal is which without looking.

■ | **Incorporate 'Thinking Skills' lessons.** Some schools have introduced Thinking Skills lessons to help pupils understand which skills they can use across the curriculum and how to maximize on their own strengths. You may have already used the games and activities where you try to extend a pupil's retention of a list as in the 'shopping list' game. Each pupil has to recite the shopping list as far as it has got and then add on one more item. You can have a shopping list the size of a class. Pupils should be taught how to improve their memory by repeating the list in their head, grouping items together, using link ideas and so on.

■ | **Train and encourage development in observation skills.** Again you can play games that teach these skills, such as 'Kim's game,' where you show a tray of items and then remove one; pupils have to spot which item was removed. They can do this visually and orally, or they can write down what they saw as a competition.

■ | **Give feedback to pupils.** However you approach multi-sensory teaching, you should constantly be giving feedback to the pupil and listening to their feedback. If you have tested their digit span recall and they were weak at recalling what they saw, then suggest to them that they say the digits in their head and keep repeating them until they're asked to write them down. They might find it easy to make up words from the sound of the digits in order, or to group the digits into pairs or threes. You probably do this to recall telephone numbers.

17. Looking after your needs as a teacher of pupils with SEN

Teaching is a stressful job, and working with pupils with SEN can be enormously demanding, frustrating and exhausting (as well as being rewarding and satisfying). If you're to be effective in your work, however, you need to ensure that your own needs are catered for, hence the tips in the last part of this section:

■ | **Try to make time to work with pupils who don't have SEN.** This will ensure that you don't lose sight of the norm or lower your expectations of pupils. You could also offer extension work for more able pupils for use in class, at lunch times or after school.

■ | **Try not to lose touch with your subject.** You will very likely have a subject specialism that you pursued before your entry into this field. On a practical level you may have to support pupils taking examinations and you will need to be aware of curriculum developments. You could also explore the possibility of teaching your subject to adults in your spare time. This may also be a means of keeping your sanity.

■ **Watch your stress levels.** If you're fortunate enough to have a say in your timetable, you can reduce a certain amount of stress by ensuring that the most taxing areas of your work are relieved or at least sandwiched between the less demanding parts of the week. Try to spread your contact with pupils evenly and in small periods of time to avoid exhaustion and over-exposure.

■ **Have fun with your pupils whenever you can.** Learn to take pleasure in the smallest of their achievements. You can play on-going games such as the vocabulary game in which you challenge pupils to find words in the dictionary that you can't explain or spell. You will soon become familiar with the likes of xylophone and zenana. Give small rewards when they catch you out. Challenge them to join you in this game.

■ **Ensure that you avoid frustration at your pupil's rate of progress by being realistic about what they can achieve.** Don't necessarily lower your expectations but be prepared for progress measured in small steps. You may have to wait until someone else notices an improvement. Don't underestimate your part in your pupil's progress.

■ **Don't be afraid to seek help.** Ask for help from other colleagues when you have a pupil who fails to respond to your efforts or resists any attempts to establish a relationship. They may have insights to offer as to what works best with this pupil or they may reassure you that they have experienced similar difficulties.

■ **Look beyond the school when necessary.** Seek advice from outside agencies if you encounter problems that fail to respond to tried and trusted strategies. Your pupil may previously have had support from educational psychologists who are in regular contact with the school and who may be prepared to offer advice or information that doesn't breach confidentiality.

■ **Keep yourself fit.** Make time in your private life for stress-relieving activities such as swimming, dancing, sketching or boat-building, where the tensions of working life are not allowed to intrude. Establish an exclusion zone for yourself. It doesn't mean you don't care and it will allow time for you to recover and be of more use to your pupils.

■ **Exercise good time-management of your free time in school.** Assess very carefully how much time you can spare for lunch time or after-school activities. Stick to what you know you can manage. Make it clear when you're not available. You might consider locking the door while you're eating your lunch if you're subject to interruptions.

■ **Keep an eye on your own physical and emotional health.** Take regular, short breaks. Holidays do not have to be expensive to be effective. If you fail to look after yourself, you can't hope to be of use to your pupils.

IMPROVING UNACCEPTABLE BEHAVIOUR

This section contains a variety of tips to help pupils whose behaviour in the classroom is proving unacceptable. All too often pupils with special needs are assumed to have problematic behaviour simply because their needs are different, but this is not automatically the case. However, some forms of special needs tend to be linked with behavioural problems, and this section offers suggestions on how these can best be managed.

18. Devising and evaluating a diagnostic behaviour questionnaire

Sometimes we're so busy as teachers dealing with the day-to-day business of our work that we don't always effectively record information about pupils that can be helpful to our working practices. Instruments that enable teachers to track and monitor behaviour can be useful in helping to recognize and plan to remediate specific problems that arise. The following set of tips provides guidance on how to devise and evaluate such a tool:

- **Identify pupils who need your attention.** You may have a special responsibility for a pupil whose behaviour is giving concern in many areas of the school. First you need to find out by use of a questionnaire if this behaviour is common to every situation.

- **Ensure that your questionnaire is user-friendly.** It should be possible for it to be completed with the minimum of effort. Keep the size to a single A4 page. Word the questions clearly and leave adequate space for replies.

- **Summarize your concern.** Write a short introductory paragraph of no more than six lines explaining that concern has been expressed about the pupil's behaviour in a number of situations. Make it clear that the questionnaire has been designed to give a quick and comprehensive picture of the pupil's overall behaviour.

- **Justify your questionnaire.** Emphasize that the aim of the questionnaire is to gain information that will enable you to work out strategies to help change unacceptable behaviour in lessons where there is a problem.

- **Assure teachers that the information received will be confidential.** Inexperienced teachers may be nervous about admitting to problems in class. Express appreciation for any answers whatever the opinion expressed. Don't leave the questionnaires in pigeon holes. See each teacher individually and give examples of the sorts of information that will be useful. You may gain insights from this conversation too.

■ **Your first question should ask for brief details about what exactly causes concern.** Answers in note form will be quite adequate. So often teachers will make vague and unspecified complaints. You need to know whether the problem is, for example, calling out in class or provoking other pupils. Ask for any details at all of unacceptable behaviour.

■ **Seek out the causes of behaviours.** In order to understand the causes of poor behaviour, it's useful to have some idea of what triggers that behaviour. Your next question could be a consideration of precipitating factors. You could also ask if the teacher is aware of the prevailing conditions when it does *not* occur. This may be just as revealing. For example, it may be the crucial absence of another pupil, the subject, or just the time of day.

■ **Think about the effects on other pupils.** Your pupil may be causing the most concern in classrooms, but there will very probably be significant interactions with other pupils. Ask for the names of other pupils who are likely to be involved. You could also ask what those pupils are likely to gain from that involvement. Ask if patterns of response have been established and if they need to be changed to assist your pupil to improve.

■ **Find out what the pupil seems to gain from bad behaviour.** Is it to receive attention or to conceal learning difficulties? Does the pupil seek to enhance self-esteem by gaining the apparent attention of laughing classmates? You can ask your respondent to give an opinion on the outcome for the pupil of this behaviour.

■ **Probe into what has succeeded and what hasn't.** The final question you can ask before you begin to devise your own strategies for improvement, is about which strategies have worked for this teacher, and equally importantly, which ones have failed. Provide some space for any other relevant information. You can then use the results of your questionnaire to help you plan your own action.

19. Strategies to cope with rude and negative behaviour

Unpleasant behaviour can be difficult to cope with, and even though we know there are often good reasons for pupils' rudeness and negativity, we can all do with a helping hand sometimes. These tips are designed to offer a range of approaches, with some suggestions on how to react in these circumstances:

■ **Refuse to take the blame for rudeness.** Remember, the anger that's directed at you may spring from a variety of problems over which you have no control. Try not to bear grudges, however hurt you are. Start every day afresh with high expectations of pupil behaviour.

■ **Avoid losing your temper, even though you may have been badly provoked.** Remember, you're the adult and you have a responsibility to provide a good role model. Ensure that you don't raise your voice more than is strictly necessary. Noisy and volatile behaviour from you will be mirrored in your pupils' response.

- **Try to use humour to diffuse tension.** If you give an angry pupil the opportunity to back off without losing face, you may prevent an unpleasant incident. For example, if a pupil shouts, 'I hate you', you could perhaps smile and say, 'That's a shame, because I like you.' Be careful, however, not to make the pupil the object of derisory laughter from the rest of the class. The goal is to diffuse tension, not to create it.

- **Mirror the behaviour of the pupil.** If a pupil has been offensive or aggressive, you could say, 'Have I ever been anything but courteous and supportive to you?' This clearly presupposes that this is true. If you can't in all conscience put such a question, then you could ask the pupil which is preferable: a patient teacher who makes polite requests or one who storms and shouts. If the pupil agrees that the first is more desirable, then it makes a good point.

- **Try to establish a minimum set of rules of behaviour.** Make sure that these rules are applied consistently and fairly. Very often bad behaviour is the result of pupils not knowing where boundaries lie. Your pupils must be absolutely clear about which offence will result in which sanction. The probable inconsistencies in their own lives should not be reproduced in the classroom. Firmness and consistency create stability.

- **Make any punishments positive.** When your pupil has accepted that the behaviour must be punished in some way, you could ask the pupil to suggest an appropriate punishment. It may be that the suggestion is too severe and you can settle for something less strict. Another way of punishing is to use a 'symbolic punishment', which can be written on a piece of paper and thrown away if agreed conditions such as clearing up mess or apologizing are met by the end of the lesson.

- **Make use of cooling off procedures (and this includes you).** You may be able to place the pupil in the corridor for a brief period, although many schools now discourage this for obvious reasons. It may be possible for you to ask a nearby colleague to accommodate your pupil for a few minutes. You may judge it sensible to leave the room yourself on some pretext, which gives the pupil time to calm down. However, don't leave pupils in a situation that could prove dangerous.

- **Try to enable your pupil to empathize with your feelings.** When pupils are rude, we often respond with a warning message such as, 'Sit down', 'Shut up' or, 'You're always starting trouble.' The message implies that the pupil is the problem. You could try letting the pupil know how you feel. Explain instead of blaming. For example, you could say, 'If you talk to Malik when I'm reading this story, I get really frustrated and it stops me finishing the story.' This places your distress on the effect of the behaviour, not on the pupil.

- **Find ways of making encouraging statements that the pupil can accept without feeling patronized.** Offer praise for the smallest of advances such as, 'I noticed that you kept your temper when Tara took your rubber without asking. Well done.' You can find other ways of making positive statements such as complimenting a pupil on sporting achievements.

■ | **Agree contracts for improving negative behaviour.** You could suggest target weeks for focusing on one particular problem such as swearing or not shouting at other pupils or the teacher. Perhaps you could enlist the support of parents and ask them to look at the comments on the target sheet. Make sure that improvements are noticed and rewarded.

20. Dealing with pupils whose emotional and behavioural difficulties lead to disaffection and isolation in the classroom

These pupils form a disparate group, ranging from social isolates to school refusers. They're not likely to give much trouble in the classroom, but they're probably giving anxiety elsewhere about their lack of educational and social progress:

■ | **Identify pupils in this category.** Make sure you know as much as possible about them and consult IEPs. Refer any pupils about whom you are concerned to the SENCO or head of year to make sure their special needs are picked up.

■ | **Record and report absences.** Poor attendance is a useful indication of disaffection, but it's easy to lose track without good record keeping. Be welcoming when your pupils do appear and try not to overload pupils with missed work or issue pessimistic predictions about potential failure.

■ | **Place pupils on internal attendance report.** Selective attendance is a familiar feature of this problem, so you need to make sure you have the necessary data to help you spot patterns.

■ | **Seat your disaffected pupil in a sympathetic group.** You can also ensure that regular group activities take place and encourage this pupil to take some part in activities that feel comfortable and non-threatening.

■ | **Check to see if there are any practical reasons for this pupil's isolation.** For example, a pupil may have some unpleasant habits or an unacceptable level of body odour. You can either engage in some diplomatic counselling yourself or you could refer the pupil to the school nurse or to pastoral staff for extra help. You can also contact parents for their support, although you may find that home is the root of the problem.

■ | **Be aware that depressed or disaffected pupils may be victims of sexual abuse.** If you have any anxieties or suspicions, report them to the designated key teacher for sexual abuse in your school. You can also say to the pupil that you've noticed that they're worried and offer to listen or guide them towards a more appropriately qualified colleague.

■ **Check to see if your pupil is being bullied.** Victims of bullying can retreat into silence and suffer alone. If you don't feel you know the best way to deal with this matter yourself, refer the pupil to pastoral staff. If your school has any special anti-bullying strategies, you can refer your pupil to the people responsible for their implementation.

■ **Keep yourself informed about the intervention of any outside agencies by reference to the SENCO or pastoral staff.** It may be that a disaffected pupil is receiving psychiatric help. This can lead to a deterioration in behaviour in the initial stages which, if you know about it, will make it easier to understand and accommodate adverse changes in behaviour. You may also be able to gain information about which classes are likely to be missed because of external appointments.

■ **Try to enthuse bright pupils who are underachieving because of personal problems.** You can provide stimulating work at a challenging level (not just another worksheet!). Perhaps you can involve this pupil in helping less able pupils from time to time. It may also be possible to create occasional groups of high-flyers to meet from other classes at certain times to work on special projects to provide an effective and challenging peer group.

■ **Be aware that you may have a pupil who has been traumatized.** For example, pupils who are refugees may have undergone appalling personal experiences such as war or murder. The pupil may be withdrawn and over-sensitive to noise, arguments or teasing, or on the other hand the reaction may be one of frenetic and anti-social behaviour. Try to place the pupil in a supportive group with pupils who speak the same language, if this is appropriate. Offer your own personal support by lending a sympathetic ear or providing shelter from the boisterous school environment at breaks and lunch times.

21. Assisting the reintegration of excluded pupils

When pupils have been excluded, the process of re-entry can often be a difficult and painful affair. As a special needs teacher, you may have a good relationship with such a pupil and any advice you can offer may prove invaluable. The tips that follow aim to enable you to build bridges and assist reintegration:

■ **Act as a broker to facilitate reintegration.** An ideal way to facilitate the prodigal's return would be to arrange meetings with class teachers in advance to restore working relations and spell out ground rules without the presence of fellow pupils, although in many cases this will not be possible.

■ **Manage the occasion of first reappearance.** One suggestion you could make is that the pupil should arrive at this first crucial lesson in plenty of time, preferably without a cohort of encouraging acolytes and certainly avoiding any display of defiance or disaffection.

■ **Do all you can to make resumption of study a trouble-free process.** It would be helpful if you could arrange to be available to this pupil on a daily basis at the start of the day to provide practical help. Check if the pupil is adequately equipped for lessons and have some pens to lend if necessary. It's also a good opportunity to discuss potential difficulties and to prepare some coping strategies.

■ **Try to make sure that any necessary paperwork is handled with minimum fuss.** Advise your pupil to present any authorization to return or any report card immediately on arrival and without being asked. If the teacher is busy, these can be slipped unobtrusively on the desk.

■ **Advise returning pupils about how to interact with classmates.** Those returning after exclusion should be made aware of the pitfalls which 'best friends' may present to a smooth return. They may be expecting a return of the entertaining behaviour that led to exclusion. Suggest that your pupil prepares some face-saving excuses as to why trouble must be avoided or seating reallocated. An example might be, 'My dad will kill me/ground me.'

■ **Brief your fellow teachers about how to help the returner to reintegrate.** The welcome-back by other teachers may be unfriendly and this could cause further problems, especially if the first words that greet the returner hark back to the original cause of exclusion.

■ **Remind the returner that teachers have bad days too.** Prepare for this eventuality by rehearsing a low-key response for the pupil to use in these circumstances. Help your pupil to realize that a place back in the group will have to be earned.

■ **Help them to find the words they need to get them out of trouble.** If your pupil misses vital working instructions at the start of the lesson, suggest a conciliatory approach such as, 'I have not quite understood all of that, would you mind saying it again, please?'

■ **Find ways to inform fellow teachers of your pupil's good intentions.** Encourage comments from them to you at daily briefings about the returner's progress and devise trouble-free ways for teachers to let you know of improvements or difficulties.

■ **Share this feedback with the pupil, parents and pastoral staff.** Use any available opportunities to engage your pupil in some self-assessment in order to raise awareness of existing problems. The more pupils are able to understand what's going on, the more likely it is that they will become able to take some responsibility for their own actions.

■ **Don't allow a breakdown of the reintegration to dishearten you too much.** If, finally, after all your work, comes the final and perhaps inevitable exclusion, remember that some of your efforts may bear fruit in another place at another time. Education, like politics, is the art of the possible.

22. Supporting pupils who are being bullied

Bullying is widespread and can have really serious long-term outcomes. Teachers have a responsibility to ensure that pupils are kept safe in schools and that this repugnant behaviour is not tolerated. However, this is far from an easy task, and these tips don't pretend to provide foolproof strategies to stamp it out. However, teachers might find some of the suggestions useful in supporting pupils who are experiencing bullying:

- **Discuss the problem with the class.** It's not necessary to be specific about individual cases or names. You can perhaps say that some pupils in the class are being bullied. You could then organize discussions on how to deal with bullying.

- **Establish firm rules for classroom behaviour.** Involve the class in making these rules. Reassure pupils that telling about bullying isn't 'telling tales' or 'grassing'. All pupils have the right to be safe from bullying, and the consequences of ignoring it can be very serious.

- **Recognize and deal with negative group dynamics.** Assign safe places for vulnerable pupils, but make sure that this doesn't lead to isolation. Place bullies next to strong and confident pupils. Break up any groups that threaten the atmosphere of the class. Assist peer-group pressure against bullies and help coerced members of bullying groups to extricate themselves from that situation.

- **Teach your pupils some self-assertiveness strategies to cope with bullying.** Reassure bullied pupils that it's not their fault. Show pupils how to adopt a confident body posture and how to maintain steady eye contact. You can also provide pupils with some ready responses to deal with taunts and insults. They don't have to be brilliantly witty, but victims often say it helps to be prepared. Suggest something like, 'That's what you think', instead of looking hurt and upset.

- **Encourage pupils to seek help against bullying.** A simple and private way of enabling pupils to ask for help is to provide a bully box (to which only you have access) where they can drop notes about their worries and concerns. Follow up all complaints quickly and involve all pupils concerned.

- **Protect and shelter exceptionally vulnerable pupils at certain points in the day.** Involve senior staff in any decisions about leaving classes early. You may be able to provide a listening post at certain times for pupils who are suffering badly. You may perhaps also wish to contact parents/carers to discuss strategies for helping their children cope.

- **Enable pupils to help and protect themselves.** Suggest that pupils tell a friend what's happening and ask him or her for support. Encourage pupils to conceal their distress or anger from the bully. Explain that the bully gets pleasure from such a reaction. Discourage pupils from hitting back by explaining that this may be dangerous or that they may even be blamed for starting the trouble. You could also suggest that one way of taking the wind out of the sails of a bully is to ask for the remark to be repeated. It also gives an element of control to the victim.

■ **Build up the self-esteem of bullied pupils.** Suggest that pupils make a list of all the good things about themselves and urge them to record whenever other people say positive things about them. You could suggest that pupils extend their range of activities that might increase self-confidence, such as classes in self-defence, trampolining or getting a Saturday job.

■ **Every school should have an anti-bullying policy in place.** Check that you know the details of your school's policy. If there doesn't seem to be a written policy perhaps you can request a staff meeting to discuss this omission.

■ **Make use of professional expertise to combat bullying.** Kidscape is a registered charity that provides free booklets for pupils, parents and schools. In addition, it produces a great many resources for use in school as well as providing in-school programmes. It also provides legal advice and helplines for pupils and parents.

23. Helping bullies to change their behaviour

It may seem strange to suggest that bullies have special needs, but if we want to stamp out bullying, we may need to tackle the problem at source, and that means working with the pupils who are bullies. If we can get them to change their behaviour, it will make our lives easier and will help both the bullies and the pupils who are their victims:

■ **Establish the causes and circumstances of bullying.** You can try to find out if pupils have some understanding of why they bully. Sometimes temporary bullying is the result of trauma such as divorce or bereavement. If the pupil can't or won't offer an explanation, check with pastoral staff or special needs staff for any relevant information.

■ **Keep accurate records of incidents.** You can easily devise a standard form that is quickly filled in with details of each incident. Interview bullies and victims and obtain written statements from all parties. Record the penalties and outcome. These notes may be useful as a record of deteriorating or improving behaviour or to help parents/carers accept unpalatable truths about their children.

■ **Raise the self-awareness of the bullying pupils.** Such pupils may offer a variety of false excuses such as, 'It was just a laugh', 'It was an accident', 'He started it by picking on me.' You could try to get pupils to face up to the fact that very few people were laughing or that no one shared the view that it was an accident or provocation.

- **Try to improve bullying pupils' self-esteem.** Reassure pupils that although their behaviour is unacceptable, they are still valued. It's the behaviour that isn't liked, not them. Bullies are often as unhappy as their victims and equally in need of help. Offer assistance to help change behaviour.

- **Set firm guidelines for future behaviour.** You could make it clear what the punishment will be for bullying behaviour. You can also suggest ways in which pupils can make amends to their victims. Prepare them for the possibility that it may take some time for them to be trusted and help them to keep on trying. Give recognition and rewards for improved behaviour. Praise publicly if this seems appropriate.

- **Identify situations that lead to bullying.** Try to find out which lessons or teachers make the pupil misbehave. It might be useful to explore what the bullying pupil is likely to gain from this behaviour, even if it's a negative gain such as being sent out of a lesson and avoiding a difficult task.

- **Devise strategies to help pupils control aggressive behaviour.** You could suggest that pupils set personal goals such as, 'I won't bug Mark today' or, 'I'll try not to wind up Sita when I see her at lunch.' You could try to get pupils to recognize danger signs and have strategies in place to cope. For instance, old tricks such as holding your breath and counting to 10 can be effective.

- **Control your own reactions to bullying behaviour.** Although you will wish to respond firmly and swiftly, avoid showing anger or disgust. Try to keep calm while putting an end to the incident. You could perhaps have a 'time out' seat in the corridor or at the front of your desk where the pupil can sit until calm is restored. It might help you, too. Give praise and encouragement if the pupil can apologize.

- **Enlist the cooperation of parents/carers.** Check first with pastoral staff to see if this will be appropriate. Be prepared for parents/carers to be distressed and possibly disbelieving. Put them fully in the picture with your records of incidents. Try to be reassuring and positive about their child and suggest solutions to which you can all contribute.

- **Recommend the resources of professional organizations to help bullies and their families.** Kidscape produces free leaflets and advice for pupils who wish to stop bullying. There are also counselling services and helplines available for help to both bullies and their victims.

24. Improving the ethos of a problem class

Sometimes it seems as if a whole class has become a problem, and it's often difficult to know how best to tackle the problem without tarring the whole group with the same brush, or setting up for yourself expectations of how they will behave without this becoming a self-fulfilling prophesy. These tips aim to help you get to the centre of the issues by looking at ways to improve the ethos of the class as a whole:

■ **Identify the root of the problem.** Is the class unrelentingly difficult or are some subject areas trouble-free? Find out if the removal of one or two crucial members would benefit the class. Is there an imbalance of gender or ability? Are there more pupils with behavioural difficulties than in similar groups? Have they suffered from changes of staff?

■ **Don't attempt to go it alone.** Seek the support of pastoral staff and colleagues who also teach this class. Try to agree on a whole-school approach to the problem. Stick to what has been agreed and let pupils know this is a concerted effort.

■ **Institute a range of strategies to improve behaviour.** You may need the presence of a senior member of staff to help you get this off to a good start. You could follow simple rules such as getting the pupils to line up quietly outside the room before entering, or to comply with your seating plan without question. There are very many different kinds of strategies you can follow, but the main thing is not to relax your efforts and to be consistent in their application.

■ **Maintain the momentum of a new start.** Don't become complacent when things get better, as they can soon slip back again. Be generous with your recognition of any improvements, however. If you have to point out bad behaviour, show pupils how hurt and disappointed you are and avoid shouting and complaining. Encourage them to try again and express your support for them.

■ **Devise positive sanctions and punishments.** Try not to impose whole-class punishments. There are always some pupils who haven't misbehaved and they may be crucial allies for you in your plan for improvement. You could try perhaps to draw up a rota for tidying up after each lesson. This might avoid the necessity for keeping everyone in to clear up a ravaged classroom. You could apply this to a wide range of tasks.

■ **Reward all improvements consistently.** At first you may only be praising the first 10 minutes of a lesson or the fact that no one started a fight or arrived late to the lesson. Set long-term targets with rewards such as trips out of school at the end of term or a free choice of activity in a lesson. Involve the class in self-assessment if possible.

■ **Bring in reinforcements if necessary.** There will be times when you just can't manage the problem alone. Perhaps the form tutor could be asked to cooperate on the issue of class behaviour during tutorial periods. You could ask the head of year or a senior member of staff to drop in 'unexpectedly' on your lessons. This can work for praise as well as censure.

■ **Be aware of the needs of your well-behaved pupils.** They are bound to be suffering from the disruptive behaviour of their classmates. Assure them of your understanding of the problem and let them know what you're trying to do to solve it. Try not to create divisions in the group by holding up your 'good' pupils as examples to your 'bad' ones. Let their positive behaviour contribute to an unspoken class ethos.

- **Monitor and assess improvement on a regular basis.** Keep detailed running records of behaviour, attendance and punctuality. Make pupils aware of changes and improvements that you or other members of staff have noticed and reward and praise generously. Show the class you're proud of them whenever possible.

- **Be realistic about the rate of improvement.** Try not to get downhearted if the class seems to take one step forwards and six back. You can't change behavioural problems overnight and sometimes you may be too close to see changes that others have begun to appreciate.

25. Dealing with disruption in the classroom

If you are to provide effective help for pupils who are disruptive, it's essential that you win some early battles. At first you may need to enlist additional support, but in the long run it's all up to you. The following suggestions may help you to nip problems in the bud and establish a pleasant and calm environment in your classroom:

- **Make it quite clear that choice of seating is non-negotiable.** Quickly establish that the pupil must sit where directed without argument or pleading. Allowing the disruptive pupil to sit in the middle of a bunch of mates in an area that's difficult for the teacher to monitor is asking for trouble.

- **Deal with late arrivals quickly and with minimal fuss.** Being late for lessons provides great potential for disruption. If you're already speaking to the class, motion the pupil to stand at your desk until you're free. Record lateness and deal with it later.

- **Set out achievable targets for pupils with special needs at every lesson.** One target could be that the pupil enters the room quietly and sits where directed. Another could be that the pupil doesn't call out across the room to others.

- **Ensure that improvements don't go unnoticed.** Give praise for the smallest achievement and devise a simple form to record accumulated points. This well help the pupil to see that even tiny advances are acknowledged.

- **Keep your cool when things start to get out of hand.** Troubled pupils often over-react to normal classroom situations. There will be raised voices and arguments. Don't be tempted to join in. Keep calm at all times. Lower your voice while keeping reassuring eye contact. Provide a positive role model for your pupil.

■ **Reinforce your calm image with your body language.** Try to relax. Don't look worried or cross. Don't wave your arms about or make sudden jerky movements. You may find it difficult to do so when chaos seems to be breaking out, but your tranquillity might be catching.

■ **Find out what you can about the background of your disruptive pupil.** Knowing what's causing your pupil's problems will help you to deal with the consequences. Consult all available records and talk to SENCOs and pastoral staff about how best to help in the classroom.

■ **Keep in touch with parents and carers wherever possible.** Positive contact with home can be a crucial area of support. For some pupils a daily notebook in which you can record brief comments and provide space for parental response is helpful. However, you may judge that this is not as beneficial as referral to a trusted head of year, SENCO or other key teacher.

■ **Make use of other pupils in the classroom to help your pupil to settle back in to work.** Positive peer-group pressure can be used to good effect. However, be aware of the dangers of scapegoating and paying back old scores. Try to enlist the help of pupils you can trust to encourage and befriend your troubled pupil.

■ **Try not to take anger personally.** You will often be the target of a great deal of anger from a pupil with emotional and behavioural problems. It's not really meant for you. Start every day afresh and don't bear grudges. Learn to like your troubled pupils. Remember the pleasant young adult you bump into in five years' time might be the pupil who gave you the most sleepless nights. It can be reassuring then to think that perhaps you were part of the solution after all.

Further reading

Alcott, M (1997) *Introduction to Children with Special Educational Needs,* Hodder and Stoughton, London

Anderson, D, Brown, S and Race, P (1998) *500 Tips for Further and Continuing Education Lecturers,* Kogan Page, London

Anning, A (1991) *The First Years of School,* Open University Press, Buckingham

Battelheim, B and Zelan, K (1982) *On Learning to Read,* Penguin Books, Harmondsworth

Baumann, A S, Broomfield, A and Roughton, L (1997) *Becoming a Secondary School Teacher,* Hodder and Stoughton, London

Beard, R (1987) *Developing Reading 3–13,* Hodder and Stoughton, London

Bennett, R (1997) *Teaching IT (Part of Teaching at Key Stage 1 Series),* Nash Pollock Publishing, Oxford

Beveridge, M and Conti-Ramsden, G (1989) *Language and Communication Difficulties in People with Learning Difficulties*, Routledge, London

Bird, M H (1991) *Mathematics for Young Children,* Routledge, London

Bradley, H (1991) *Staff Development,* School Development and Management of Change Series, Falmer Press, London

Byrne, J (1995) *Easy Access for Windows 95,* QUE, Indianapolis

Cassel, P (1995) *Teach Yourself Access 95,* SAMS, Indianapolis

Caswell, J and Pinner, S (eds) *SENA+T, Special Educational Needs Assistants & Teachers,* Northumberland County Council Education Department

Courter, G and Marquis, A (1997) *MS Office 97 (No Experience Required)*, Sybex, California.

Cullingford, C (1990) *The Nature of Learning,* Cassell, Beckenham

DfEE (1994) *The Code of Practice; on Identification and Assessment of Special Educational Needs*, The Stationery Office, Norwich

DfEE (1997) *Excellence for All Children,* Green Paper, The Stationery Office, Norwich

Donaldson, M (1987) *Children's Minds,* Fontana Press, London

Gertler, N (1997) *Using MS PowerPoint 97,* QUE, Indianapolis

Haines, C (1996) School Improvement – Practical strategies to enhance teaching and learning, Folems, London

Hayes, D (1997) *Success on your Teaching Experience,* Hodder and Stoughton, London

Holt, J (1964) *How Children Fail,* Penguin Books, Harmondsworth

Hopkins, D, Ainscow, M and West, M (1994) *School Development in an Era of Change,* School Development Series, Cassell, London

Horne, H and Brown, S (1997) *500 Tips for School Improvement,* Kogan Page, London

Horne, H and Pierce, A (1996) *A Practical Guide to Staff Development and Appraisal in Schools,* Kogan Page, London

Horne, H (ed) (1998) *The School Management Handbook,* 5th edn, Kogan Page, London

James, F and Kerr, A (1997) *Creative Computing,* Belair Publications, Twickenham

Kennedy, J (1995) *UK Comms Information Superhighway,* BSB, St Albans

Kent, P (1994) *Complete Idiot's Guide to the Internet*, QUE, Indianapolis

Kyriacou, C (1991) *Essential Teaching Skills,* Blackwell, Oxford

Leibeck, P (1984) *How Children Learn Mathematics,* Penguin Books, Harmondsworth

Levine, J *et al* (1997) *The Internet for Dummies,* IDG Books, Foster City, CA

McDowell, S and Race, P (1998) *500 Computing Tips for Trainers,* Kogan Page, London

McGregor, R and Myers, M (1991) *Telling the Whole Story,* Acer, London

Navarro, A and Khan, T (1998) *Effective Web Page Design,* Sybex, CA

Nelson, S (1995) *Field Guide to PCs,* Microsoft Press, Washington, DC

Nias, J (1989) *Primary Teachers Talking,* Routledge, London

OFSTED/DfEE (1996) *Setting Targets to Improve Standards*, The Stationery Office, Norwich

Pollard, A and Tann, S (1987) *Reflective Teaching in the Primary School,* Cassell, London

Perry, G (1997) *Teach Yourself Windows 95 in 24 Hours*, SAMS, Indianapolis

Race, P and McDowell, S (1999) *500 Computing Tips for Teachers and Lecturers,* 2nd edn, Kogan Page, London

Straker, A and Govier, H (1997) *Children Using Computers,* 2nd edn Nash Pollock Publishing, Oxford

Sutton, R (1994) *Assessment; A Framework for Teachers,* Routledge, London

Thornton, S (1995) *Children Solving Problems,* Harvard, MA

Index

In this index, we have used the following abbreviations:

ICT: information and communication technologies
INSET: in-service training
OFSTED: Office for Standards in Education (England and Wales)
SEN: special educational needs